G-Dog and the Homeboys

G-Dog and the Homeboys

Father Greg Boyle and the Gangs of East Los Angeles

UPDATED AND EXPANDED EDITION

Celeste Fremon

FOREWORD BY TOM BROKAW

UNIVERSITY OF NEW MEXICO PRESS
ALBUQUERQUE

Printed in the United States of America

Library of Congress Cataloging-in-Publication Data

Fremon, Celeste.
G-dog and the homeboys : Father Greg Boyle and the gangs of East Los Angeles /
Celeste Fremon ; foreword by Tom Brokaw. — Updated and expanded ed.
    p. cm.
  Includes bibliographical references.
  ISBN 978-0-8263-4485-4 (pbk. : alk. paper)
1. Boyle, Greg.
2. Church work with juvenile delinquents—California—East Los Angeles.
3. Church work with Mexican Americans—California—East Los Angeles.
4. Mexican American gangs—California—East Los Angeles.
5. Church work with juvenile delinquents—Catholic Church.
6. East Los Angeles (Calif.)—Church history.
I. Title.
  BX2347.8.J89F74 2008
  259'.5092—dc22
  [B]
                              2008015834

Design and composition: Melissa Tandysh

First edition published as *Father Greg and the Homeboys: The Extraordinary Journey
of Father Greg Boyle and His Work with the Latino Gangs of East L.A.* (New York:
Hyperion, 1995) ISBN 0-7868-6089-8

Quote on page xii is from *The Angel of History* by Carolyn Forche. Copyright 1994 by
    Carolyn Forche. Reprinted by permission of HarperCollins Publishers, Inc.
Poem on page xii reprinted from *Bertolt Brecht Poems,* 1913–1956 (1976), by permission
    of the publisher, Routledge, New York, and the Brecht Estate.
Quote set apart from text from *Mariette in Ecstasy* by Ron Hansen. Copyright 1991 by
    Ron Hansen. Reprinted by permission of HarperCollins Publishers, Inc.

Many names in this book have been changed.

For the homeboys and homegirls of Pico Aliso,

for my father

who understood,

for my mother

who felt it all

deeply,

for my son

who lived it with me.

Acknowledgments

There are many people who helped to birth this book:

First, from every part of my heart I wish to thank the friends who opened their lives to make the book possible. There are so many more than I can name here, but among those greatly cherished are Gustavo Martinez, Ramon Rodriguez, Carlos de la Torre, Alfonso Infante, Jesse and Vicente Ibarra, Danny Cabral, Fulgencio and Jason Estrada, Grace and Rosa Campos, Javier Villa, Guadalupe Lopez, Erica Parra, Ophelia Duarte, Isabel, George and Gabby Guillen, Arnold and Victor Vasquez, Gus and Victor Mojica, Cesar Quiroga, Andy Gomez, Timothy Record, Angel Muro, Jimmy Higuera, Leo and Evaristo Rubio, Jose Lopez, Arnold Machado, Robert Salcedo, Osmen Sosa, Joseph Tapia, Rosemary Estrada, Saul Garcia, George Olmos, Mario de la Cruz, Patty Mancillas, Albert Lopez, Joel Chapparo, Tony Barragan, Ernie Garcia, Dora Martinez, Richard Muñoz, Sergio Luevano, "Dino" Valencia, Froylan Nunez, and Robert Leon, plus each PMer (now grown-up) . . . and more. Dearest friends, I hope I have done you honor.

Some friends were lost, and they are deeply missed.

I am extremely appreciative of the wisdom and insight of Mary Ridgway, Leonardo Vilchis, Ted Gabrielli, Walter McKinney, and my spiritual sister, Pamela McDuffie. I am also indebted to Sergio Diaz, for expanding my views of law enforcement with unfailing intelligence and kindness.

On the writing side, I want to express gratitude to my agent, Sandy Dijkstra, for her intelligence, ferocity, and grace; and to the University of New Mexico Press, for midwifing this third edition, specifically with help from wonderfully smart editor Maya Allen-Gallegos, divine designer Melissa Tandysh, and marketing goddess Glenda Madden.

I am also indebted to the research and thoughtful work of James Diego Vigil, Malcolm Klein, Cheryl Maxon, Mike Davis, Joan Petersilia, Luis Rodriguez, Connie Rice, and the fabulous Jorja Leap.

Thanks beyond words to my brother, Phil Fremon, and my friend, Mary Ellen Strote, for reading and editing aid way above and beyond the call; and to Susan Brenneman and Carol Trussell, both of you lit the spark; to Stephanie Marston and Janet Orloff for providing ears and shoulders at all hours; to my sweet mother Elizabeth whose compassion was without limit; and my darling, brilliant, open-hearted son, Will Hunter Mason, for being *lo máximo*.

Finally, most of all, I give thanks to Greg Boyle, a zillion times over—*for miracles nonstop*.

Foreword

At a time when the country is looking for those willing to do the hard work of caring for the young in neighborhoods where violence and death are as common as sidewalks and corner lots, the story of Greg Boyle, a parish priest, is a welcome reminder that heroes still walk among us, guided by God, compassion, and justice.

Father Boyle—G-Dog to the gang members of East Los Angeles—is a Jesuit priest raised in the middle-class sensibilities of Southern California at a time when the images of the Golden State were formed by surfers, the Beach Boys, orange groves, and the promise of ever-expanding prosperity for everyone, working class to professional class. It was the promised land in myth and reality.

However, the Watts riots of the mid-sixties and the rise of teenage gangs in the eighties and nineties stripped the veneer from the California travel poster of palm trees, blondes in bikinis, and the Ozzie and Harriet stereotype family in well-ordered suburban neighborhoods.

The world that Father Boyle returned to from his first priestly mission in South America was the barrio of East Los Angeles, a separate universe of Latino working-class families living in small homes or housing projects. It was a landscape of Spanish language, tortillas and *chorizo*, Sunday Mass, and gang warfare.

I first met Father Boyle while reporting on a NBC News documentary on the violent gang scene in Los Angeles. In 1992 more than eight hundred young people died in gang warfare in Southern California, comparable to the U.S. losses in Iraq in the year after the end of so-called major combat.

Operating out of the Dolores Mission Catholic Church in the heart of East L.A., Father Boyle was reciting the funeral Mass for murdered teenagers by day and walking the streets by night, offering solace and guidance to the families of what had become a war zone.

His flock was not confined to the walls of the mission or regular attendance at Sunday services. He was a priest at large to young people called Dreamer, Puppet, and Wicked, to gangs called the Clarence Street Locos and Cuatro Flats. He introduced me to young gang members, some as young as twelve, dressed in the uniform of white T-shirts and black, oversized work pants and also to those who had grown out of the gangs, the older *veteranos*. As we stood on street corners in the 'hood, they'd talk to me in polite, soft-spoken phrases, but their eyes never left the street as they watched for rival gang members or cars that may be involved in drive-by shootings.

G-Dog was their priest, confidante, tough love counselor, advocate and, most of all, their friend, the one they could count on to treat them as people, not as statistics or inmates waiting to happen.

We've stayed in touch, G-Dog and I, and my admiration for his work has only grown. In this book, you'll enter the world of a Catholic parish priest who does honor to his calling and to all of us by ministering to the young and their families in a community where the struggle between the American dream and the realities of abusive or missing fathers, economic deprivation, and criminal exploitation is unending and too often resolved by guns, gangs, and death.

—Tom Brokaw
Summer 2004

When a child is about to be run down by a car

one pulls it on to the pavement.

Not the kindly man does that,

to whom they put up monuments.

Anyone pulls the child away from the car.

But here many have been run down,

and many pass by and do nothing.

—BERTOLT BRECHT

Whoever can cry should come here

—CAROLYN FORCHÉ

Introduction

As of this writing, it has been eighteen years since I first left my nice, safe, middle-class neighborhood and drove to the Pico Aliso housing projects of East Los Angeles to research L.A. street gangs and the work of Father Greg Boyle. In the time between then and now, I've continued to report on gang life from multiple angles. I've looked at the intersection between gangs and law enforcement, examining what works and what doesn't. I've written about the emotional ordeals of some of the wounded but resilient young women who flutter at the gang periphery and researched the relationship between the staggering dropout rates that plague L.A.'s urban high schools and patterns of gang membership. Most recently I've written a series of stories about the grown-up homeboys and homegirls who struggle to find honorable futures for themselves despite odds and expectations to the contrary.

Yet to this day I don't believe that anything in my professional life has had a more profound effect on my thinking than those first four years I spent following Father Greg around during L.A.'s most deadly gang era.

With the publication of this new edition of *G-Dog and the Homeboys*, released twenty years after Greg first began giving jobs to the violence-haunted young men who clustered around his office, I've been given the opportunity to revisit the lives of the homeboys whose actions I chronicled—and in doing so to analyze what we have learned, and not learned, about street gangs in America in those two decades.

First, to place the discussion in context, let me give you a few quick bullet points that illustrate the scope of the problem:

* In the past twenty years more than 25,000 Americans, most of them young men, have died as a result of gang violence.
* Right now there are approximately 750,000 gang members in the United States, according to the most recent Youth Gang Survey.[1]
* According to studies done by the U.S. Department of Veteran Affairs' National Center for Posttraumatic Stress Disorder, 35 percent of the children exposed to the kind of community violence that gangs typically produce exhibit symptoms of posttraumatic stress disorder. In many cases the PTSD is worse than that found in soldiers returning from Iraq and Afghanistan.
* In Los Angeles alone, it is estimated that 300,000 children and adolescents live in chronically violent neighborhoods where simply walking to school potentially puts them at risk.[2]

Gang violence is an epidemic in the public health sense of the word, and one that is largely immune to general declines in crime.[3] Even now, during a period in which violent crime is down throughout most of the nation,[4] in 173 U.S. cities, gang homicides continue to blow unfixable holes in the fabric of families and urban communities.[5]

Matters used to be much worse. During the four-year period that the central narrative of this book covers—from the fall of 1990 to late 1994—gang activity in Los Angeles was at its most lethal. L.A. was then, and still is, the gang capital of the world. But in 1992 homicides hit a record 2,113, the highest in Los Angeles County's history, with 803 of those murders tied to gangs. Throughout those deadly years, the section of Southern California where gang violence was at its most intense was the sixteen square miles of East Los Angeles covered by the Hollenbeck Division of the Los Angeles Police Department. And, according to law enforcement statistics, the piece of real estate within Hollenbeck where gang activity was the most intense of all was the mile-square area of Pico Gardens and Aliso Village. That tiny, lower-income community, smaller in geographic size than most college campuses, is where this book is set.

Journey into the Laboratory

During the first months of my research in Pico Aliso I had no inkling that I'd stumbled into such an ideal laboratory in which to explore the nature and causes of gang violence. I went to the East L.A. housing projects because, for weeks, a TV producer friend named Carol Trussell had been telling me stories about a Jesuit priest who supposedly dodged bullets while trying to transform the lives of the young homeboys whose misdeeds were being reported almost nightly on the evening news. I decided to meet the guy with the idea of possibly writing a magazine article about him if he turned out to be as colorful and heroic as she suggested, which at that time I doubted. I talked my editor at the *Los Angeles Times Magazine* into assigning a profile. She too was cautious. "He's got to have a dark side," she said.

Yet after six months of shadowing the priest, rather than discovering murky, hidden motives, I began to notice that something essential in me was transforming instead. I wrote the article, which won a big magazine award and then was (briefly) developed as a feature film project, but rather than leaving the Pico Aliso projects, as I'd promised myself I would once the story was finished, I began frantically retooling my professional commitments for the next several years to be able to research and write a book about the complex and vivid world that unfolded itself in front of me every time I drove to the Pico Aliso housing projects— and to Greg's office. It seemed to me that in order to make a dent in the gang carnage that was then spreading like prairie fire, it made sense to try to understand the gang members themselves. By then I realized that there was no corner of the planet more perfectly suited for such an investigation than Boyle Heights and Pico Aliso. It was equally clear that Greg was the ideal counterpoint to force me to comprehend the gang universe from a deeper perspective. Then and now, he has a remarkable knack, not so much for seeing the best in the gangsters, as that implies a kind of wishful thinking, but for shining the beam of his compassion on them for long enough that many begin, for the first time, to see something of value in themselves. Thus, being around Father Greg, I was able to observe not just the conditions that produce gang violence, but also many of the elements needed to facilitate a cure.

G-Dog and the Homeboys mainly concerns itself with the Mexican American street gangs of Southern California. That cohort represents only one of the gang subcultures now found in America, each of which has unique characteristics molded by ethnic makeup, group history, and geographic location. African American gangs are historically different from Mexican American gangs in that their cultural history includes the wounds of slavery. And those two groups are different in character from the newer Vietnamese and Cambodian gangs, which draw membership predominately from the offspring of the war-traumatized refugees who flooded out of Southeast Asia in the late 1970s and 1980s.[6] In this same way, the Latin Kings of New York are different from the Latin Kings of Chicago,[7] which are different still from L.A.-based Mara Salvatrucha (MS 13), a gang with its cultural and psychological origins rooted in the bloody civil war in El Salvador. Despite the range of ethnic and regional distinctions, however, the fundamental reasons that a teenager joins a gang and the ingredients that must be present if that young man or woman is to successfully leave the gang world behind are all remarkably alike.

Children as Monsters

For the first ten years after *G-Dog and the Homeboys* was published, although academics (and a few journalists like me) learned much about the underlying causes of gang violence, very little of this knowledge seemed to enter the arena of public policy. "In dealing in a practical way with street gangs, the greatest impediment has been, and remains, the absence of shared information about their nature," wrote Malcolm Klein in 2004.[8] (Klein is professor emeritus at the University of Southern California and one of the country's deans of gang research.) As a result, most state and national funding was funneled to law enforcement and incarceration facilities with little left over for prevention and intervention measures—a policy that, as Father Greg would put it, is about as effective as attempting to cure cancer by giving all the money to the undertakers.

This skewed emphasis started to gain traction in the late 1980s and early 1990s, when overall U.S. crime statistics spiked just as a precipitous rise in gang violence together with some particularly alarming suburban school shootings began hitting the headlines. In an attempt to explain the phenomenon, a small cabal of prestigious criminologists advanced theories describing a new breed of teenage "superpredator" that was inherently more violent, and less . . . well . . . *human* than previous generations of adolescents, thus less receptive to rehabilitation. In January 1996, the Council on Crime in America, an organization of prosecutors and law-enforcement experts, issued a report written by John J. Dilulio Jr. of Princeton University describing violent crime among adolescents as a "ticking time bomb."[9] Almost simultaneously, Dilulio's friend and colleague, James Alan Fox of Northeastern University, forecast that U.S. cities would be deluged by a veritable "blood bath" of juvenile homicides by 2005.[10] Facing apocalyptic pronouncements by conservative academics and pressure from a public made fearful by a hysterical media, state legislators all over the country began passing punitive new laws without regard for whether those laws were just or effective.

When the crime spike dipped again in the mid-1990s (gang statistics along with it), and the superpredator plague failed to arrive, Dilulio and several others recanted their analyses. Nevertheless, the law-and-order fever remained, much of it focused on youth. As the millennium turned, the juvenile justice system that had protected America's children and teenagers for more than a century was being actively dismantled in state after state. All over the United States, a growing number of kids were being tried as adults. At the same time, legislators responding to public pressure began passing draconian sentencing laws, which meant that young men and women received prison time that was double and triple the terms dictated by states' regular sentencing guidelines, even on first offenses—*if* the crime of which they were convicted could be construed as having anything to do with gangs. In short, not only were more kids and young adults being sent to prison, but they were being sent to prison for far longer terms than at any time in American history.

One of the results of this still unabated trend to criminalize a generation of American inner-city youth and young adults—particularly young adult males—is a prison population that surpasses, both in sheer numbers and in numbers per capita, that of any other country in the world. (Of course, it wasn't just gang prosecutions that caused the nation's runaway prison growth; it was the one-two punch of the so-called war on drugs *combined* with the war on gangs.) In the spring of 2008, the Pew Center on the States released figures showing that one in every one hundred Americans is behind bars—a statistic so startling that it made headlines as soon as it was released. When the Pew researchers pulled apart the figures still further and looked at incarceration rates for certain age groups and ethnicities, they found numbers that were far more alarming: among males age 20 to 34 (in other words, the age range most likely to represent gang members convicted over the last fifteen years) for Hispanics the ratio drops to one in twenty-six. For African American young men in the same 20 to 34 age group the figure is *one in nine*.[11]

Throwing away the Key

The cost of keeping so many Americans locked up has put a staggering burden on individual state budgets. In 2007, total state spending on corrections topped $49 billion, up from $12 billion in 1987, when the incarceration fever began. Unfortunately, reported the Pew researchers, all this prison spending has not had a payoff in terms of public safety.[12] Meanwhile, other studies have suggested that the monetary drain is only a portion of the real cost incurred by imprisoning such a big slice of America's population; there is another price paid in human terms when too many young men from a community are carted off to prison. According to Todd Clear, distinguished professor at John Jay College of Criminal Justice and author of *Imprisoning Communities: How Mass Incarceration Makes Disadvantaged Neighborhoods Worse*,[13] when there are a few well-targeted arrests in an area, crime tends to go down. But when the number of arrests reaches a certain critical mass in any given neighborhood, something surprising happens. "When you remove a lot of males from a lot of families," Clear told me, "the whole community becomes less stable. In other words, with arrests, there's a tipping point when, instead of seeing crime going down in a community, it goes up. Precipitously."

Immediately following the publication of Clear's most recent work, a new study by the Justice Policy Institute made news nationwide when it found that gang suppression alone not only failed to lower gang violence, but it helped sustain it. Part of the problem, the Justice Policy people noted, was that African American and Hispanic kids were disproportionately targeted by gang enforcement efforts, and this targeting often created a negative blowback. For instance, in Los Angeles, the district attorney's office found that close to half of the black males between the ages of twenty-one and twenty-four had been entered in the county's gang database even though no one could credibly argue that all of these young men were current gang members.[14] "Aggressive suppression tactics simply make the situation worse by alienating local residents and trapping youth in the criminal justice system," said the report's coauthor Kevin Pranis. Former RAND Criminal Justice Program director, Peter Greenwood, agreed in his 2007 report, *Changing Lives: Delinquency Prevention as Crime-Control Policy.* "We must first recognize that any involvement with the police or juvenile courts carries a heavy stigma for the youth concerned," wrote Greenwood, "along with a proven negative impact on educational attainment, crime, and employment."[15] To put it another way, if you decide a kid is bad, and treat him as such over and over, how long before he decides to prove you right?

I saw this principle demonstrated repeatedly, and often tragically, while I researched the book and in the years that followed. "When we ask law enforcement to be the sole solution to a social problem," civil rights lawyer and L.A. gang expert Connie Rice told me when we discussed the issue, "it's never going to play out well. We now have a society that *creates* violent children out of *nonviolent* children."

Unsuccessful though it has proved to be, for nearly two decades, the lock-'em-up-and-throw-away-the-key model for reducing gang violence was heavily favored by most of law enforcement in Los Angeles and Chicago, two of America's worst gang cities. Now at the very upper levels of L.A. policing, matters have transformed considerably. Chief William Bratton of the Los Angeles Police Department and L.A. County Sheriff Lee Baca are both smart, enlightened men who, along with their command staffs, state publicly that we can't "arrest our way out of the problem," and that a long-term solution to gang violence requires the three-pronged approach that Father Greg Boyle has long advocated: namely prevention and intervention, in addition to suppression.

Despite such changes in thinking among the best of our police brass, too many lawmakers, prosecutors and, it would seem, a large chunk of the U.S. voting public, view more police and stiffer sentences alone as the solution to every blip in the country's juvenile crime problem[16]—as if gang members are some kind of mutant species existing outside the ken of whatever principles govern you, me, and our children. As this book goes to press, the so-called Gang Abatement and Prevention Act of 2007 has been passed by the Senate and is making its way through committee in the U.S. House of Representatives. The bill, which is cosponsored by California senator Dianne Feinstein, is designed to fight gang violence using the same old failed strategies— i.e., by establishing "new crimes and tougher federal penalties" for "gang crimes," plus a brand-new catchall definition of what constitutes a "gang," designed specifically so that prosecutors might apply the new penalties as broadly as possible.

"Us" and "Other"

Father Greg has always maintained that if we believe gang members are monsters, then we will walk down one road in terms of public policy. If we believe that they are human beings, our public policy will reflect that belief. So how to fix this culturewide cognitive disconnect? Knowledge is usually the best place to start.

I'll give you a quick example. The first time a young homeboy I knew and cared about was shot and mortally wounded, he didn't die right away. Hospital machines kept him hovering at life's borderline for several days while his family decided whether they were willing to donate his organs for transplant. Finally his mother broke down and signed the donation papers. Minutes later, a nurse, whom I'll call Elizabeth, wheeled the brain-dead boy into an elevator in order to get him quickly to an operating room on another floor so his organs might be "harvested."

The kid's name was Richie. (I've called him something else in the body of the book as I had to change all the homeboys' names at lawyers' insistence.) He was killed in the fall of 1991 when violence in the projects was hurtling toward its peak. In an awful demonstration of how extreme matters had become, shortly after Richie was brought into White Memorial Hospital's emergency room, a car full of enemy gang members shot up the ER lobby, and it was only blind luck that no one was badly hurt or killed. The drive-by understandably spooked the hospital staff, and word spread quickly that it was this Richie kid in the ICU whose presence had provoked the incident.

It was in that context that nurse Elizabeth wheeled her charge into the elevator. A moment later, a second nurse stepped in after her and inquired absently where Elizabeth was going. When she explained, nurse two glanced at the pale, still boy and grimaced. "Who would want this monster's heart?" she asked.

"He's *not* a monster!" Elizabeth blurted to her colleague, then began to cry. "He's just a kid! He could be my kid. He could be your kid. He's not a *monster!*"

When Elizabeth told me the story a few days later, she said she was stunned at the intensity of her own reaction. She'd been able to remove Richie from the "monster" category in her own mind, she said, because despite his condition, she'd gotten to know him, at least a little, by watching as friends and family gathered in small, grief-stricken groups at his bedside. She saw young homeboys and homegirls talk to the gravely wounded boy, stroke his arm and face, tape photos of Richie at younger, happier moments to the cubicle walls. "Maybe he'd done bad things. I don't know," Elizabeth said. "But I *do* know he wasn't a monster. He was just a kid. Why don't people understand that?"

A similar incident occurred in the summer of 1995 during the flurry of publicity surrounding the original publication of this book. A reporter asked if I'd mind taking her to the projects so she could get a glimpse of the gang world for herself. One sunny weekend afternoon in late July, I escorted her on a walking tour of Pico Aliso. As we made our way around the projects, various homeboys trotted over to say hello to me and to meet the unfamiliar woman I had in tow. I introduced the reporter to a total of maybe a dozen gang members, all of whom chatted with her amiably, if a bit shyly. Later, as we drove back to L.A.'s Westside where the car was parked, I asked her which of the kids she'd met that afternoon she'd be willing to throw away. "Huh?" the reporter replied, clearly taken aback. I repeated the question.

"Well, *none* . . ." she answered. "Why would I want to throw any of those kids away?" Then after a pause, she got it. "Oh," she said. "I feel that way because I've met them, so now they're people to me." At the most basic level, that's what this book is about.

Please don't misunderstand. *G-Dog and the Homeboys* is not meant as some sort of knee-jerk, bleeding-heart liberal plea for leniency for lawbreakers. If kids or young adults commit crimes, by all means, let's prosecute them. We are, after all, a nation of laws, and there must be consequences for acts that do harm to the community or the individuals within it. But for all but the most serious offenses, let those consequences come in the form of programs that have been proven to help the lawbreakers become more whole, thus less likely to reoffend, not more damaged.[17] And if we must incarcerate a kid, let the term be proportionate to the situation.

At present, in the state of California—which, for better or for worse, is usually the trendsetter when it comes to juvenile justice methods—we have an increasing number of cases like the sixteen-year-old first-time offender who was in the car when a gang-related shooting took place in which no one was hurt or hit. The kid was not a gang member himself; he did not fire the gun or actively participate in the incident in any way. He had never been in trouble with the police prior to the incident in question. Still, he was sentenced to thirty-five years to life in a level 4 adult prison. That sentence and those like it are not proportionate by any civilized standard.

Poets of the Street

Admittedly, the act of looking at gang violence through the lens of intelligent, compassionate analysis rather than the lens of condemnation takes more effort. Dismissing gangsters as monsters is easy. Creating the political and public will to address the complex weave of underlying causes of gang violence is much harder.

Yet the latter is also far more rewarding in terms of public safety and in the individual lives of all involved. To illustrate, here's one more story. It takes place on a warm evening in June 2007. The weather was not yet balmy, but the chill of spring was gone when a group of former gang members gathered in the outdoor cafeteria of Utah Street Elementary School in East Los Angeles with the idea of performing poetry in front of an audience. The overhead lighting was harsh and institutional, and the homeboys (and a couple of homegirls) were milling in little security clumps of two and three near a beige Formica table where cookies and soft drinks had been laid out by staffers from one of the organizations that was sponsoring the event.

The performance was set for 6:30 p.m., early for a Saturday night, so the audience was slow to arrive. By 6:20 one of the younger homeboy poets, a tall, skinny kid named Abel, was so undone by the waiting that he walked into the school parking lot, ostensibly for a smoke, and never came back.

The poet/participants were mostly in their late twenties and early thirties, although a couple were in their teens. They'd all spent the past four months going to weekly classes with a novelist named Leslie Schwartz in order to learn to convert their personal experiences into poetic form. The classes were part of a program called the Homeboy Stories Project, sponsored by PEN USA, a national nonprofit concerned with freedom of expression and nurturing literary arts, the California Council for the Humanities, and Father Greg's Homeboy Industries. The idea was that the work produced in the class would be collected into an anthology, which would in turn be presented at two public readings. The event at Utah Elementary was to be the first.

I was involved as the project's codirector. I also teach journalism at two universities, so I can say from experience that as writing workshops go, this one had more than the usual number of challenges. For one thing, class attendance was sometimes disrupted by the fact that several of our writers got beat up, arrested, and, in one case, *shot*.

Yet homeboys and homegirls showed up because, as they grasped the notion that their voices and experiences could actually mean something to someone else, the realization had a near magical effect. Like any other writing students, they still had to confront their fear of the blank page. But once they did, they wrote and wrote and wrote.

Sometimes the writing was halting and grammar-challenged. Other times, it was mostly a diatribe. Yet frequently the work was eloquent. Almost always, it was breathtakingly brave. And the fact that they came back week after week and were willing to make the effort necessary to find their individual voices . . . was a revelation. Most of the class members told Leslie or me at one time or another how much the class meant to them. But it wasn't until the night of the first performance that the significance of the program came into its truest focus.

By 6:45 there was a full house at Utah Elementary and the reading finally got started. Leslie and I traded off introducing the various participants. Father Greg was prominently placed in the audience, and he gave each jittery poet an encouraging nod. Death, childhood abuse, neglect, and multiple forms of violence were repeating themes in the works read, for understandable reasons. One of the female group members had been born in prison because her gangster mother got herself locked up after she got pregnant. Nearly all of the male participants had been shot at and in many cases the shots connected, with life-changing consequences.

Agustine Lazima, nicknamed Tin-Tin, saw his left hand blown to pieces when at twelve years old he was standing at a neighborhood pay phone chatting with a school friend and a speeding car full of gangsters came down the street, firing wildly. When he got up to read his poems, he did so with the microphone held in his right hand, his left stump shoved hard into his pants pocket. Another homeboy poet named Hector Verdugo accompanied him during each trip, then stood quietly beside him holding the manuscript so that Tin-Tin could recite.

> *I didn't see it coming.*
> *I wish every day of my life I would have.*
> *I didn't even hear it coming.*
> *All I felt was fire roaring*
> *through my left skinny hand*
> *and a car swerving on my left*
> *then rolling away through*
> *the dark street.*
> —from "Cold October" by Agustine Lazima[18]

Gerardo Gamez—called Gera, for short—was paralyzed from the waist down by an "enemy's" bullet. When it was his turn to read, Gera rolled slowly and deliberately to the front of the room in his wheelchair, set the brake, then carefully picked up the microphone. There was nothing inherently unusual about his actions. Hundreds of thousands of Americans use wheelchairs every day. Yet the soft-spoken dignity displayed by Gera and the rest of these once-violent men, nearly all of whom had spent time in prison, gave each a kind of luminosity that captivated all who witnessed.

> *Another thing I mentioned before*
> *It's hard being in a wheelchair.*
> *Let me explain why it is hard being in this position.*
> *When I see a lot of stairs*
> *And by me knowing that I won't be able to go up*
> *It gets me mad and hurts me so much that sometimes I wish*
> *that I wouldn't be here.*
> *But I can't think like that anymore.*
> *I know that I'm better than that.*
> *So what I do is that I have to go around*
> —from "Go Around" by Gerardo Gamez[19]

The event went on for over two hours, nearly twice as long as we had anticipated. But at the urging of the crowd, the writers kept returning for encores. The reading's most startling moment happened near the end of the evening. A former homeboy named Joseph Holguin raised his hand and asked if he could read one more poem. Leslie nodded yes, and Holguin strode up and took the cordless microphone. Then he swiveled toward the audience and with his free hand yanked up his long, baggy shorts. "I've got it right here on my leg," he said and pointed to a dark block of handwriting that was tattooed on his left calf, right above the bullet scar he got when he was fifteen and shot by an a rival homeboy with a .38 Special. The audience members craned their necks, a few of them rising entirely out of their seats to stare at the elaborate markings. It wasn't a usual poem, he explained. It was something his son had written to him the last time Joseph was in prison.

Dear dad,
I don't have much to say
but I want you to stop doing
drugs. I don't want you to die at a
young age. I want you to
be there when I have a child.
It was a sad moment when
my mom told me what happened
to you. Well, that's all I wanted
to say.
*   P.S. Please stop.*
Sincerely, your first son.
I love you.

Obviously Holguin's tattooed text was not a product of the writing project, but the class, he said, had allowed him to think of his son's letter not as evidence of his failures, but as a piece of writing—of art even—that commemorated a hard-won personal change.

One of the subtexts humming below the surface throughout the night was the fact that nearly all of the men in the room—Tin-Tin, Gera, Joseph, Hector, and the rest—had belonged to gangs that in several cases had been mortal enemies of the gangs once claimed by the others in the room. Yet now, although they kidded with each other relentlessly, when it came to listening to and supporting each other's writing, only the deepest sort of kindness was evident between them.

By evening's end, several dozen poems had been recited. But among the last and most compelling was an unfinished piece, again by Joseph Holguin. Before he began to read, he told the audience a story about how it came into being.

Late the night before, Joseph said, he had learned that his brother-in-law had been beaten nearly to death in some kind of fight. The brother-in-law was in intensive care, still alive, but his prognosis was uncertain. "This man raised me like a father, so when I heard, a part of me wanted to go out and get revenge." In previous days, he said, that's exactly what he would have done.

"But instead, I took all those feelings . . . and I wrote a poem."

The longtime motto for Father Greg's intervention program is

"Nothing Stops a Bullet Like a Job." On this particular night perhaps the more appropriate maxim was "Nothing Stops a Bullet Like a Poem." A few days later, Greg put it another way. "The difference between what we're doing now and what we were doing ten years ago in terms of gang intervention is that now we're finally meeting complexity with complexity. Gang violence is a complex problem that requires a complex set of solutions." Sometimes the solution might be a job, or a mentor, or some additional education, anger management, some "financial literacy" or "life skills" workshops, drug rehab, or a new form of family-based intervention called multisystemic therapy.

And sometimes it might be the embryonic belief that one's voice is of consequence, and that the wounds of one's body and psyche need no longer be liabilities, but can be transformed into poems and stories capable of healing.

The Power of Complexity

In an earlier version of *G-Dog and the Homeboys*, I described the book as an impassioned plea for wise parenting. "Think about it this way," I wrote, "if your own kid got into trouble, what would you do? If you're a good parent, you'd probably institute firm boundaries and appropriate consequences—the more extreme the behavior, the more aggressive the boundaries and consequences. You'd also do everything in your power to instill the concept of personal accountability. Plus you'd work to build up your son's or daughter's sense of self, and find ways to provide him or her with alternatives to destructive behavior. But most of all, you'd make it clear that you loved your kid, that he or she was of immeasurable value. You would not ever under any circumstances *throw that kid away*. As a community and as a society we need to apply those same common-sense rules of parenting to all our American children, adolescents, and young adults. We must act as if every one of them belongs to us—no exceptions."

Now, several years later, I still believe unreservedly in the parenting model. But I think there's more to it. Homeboys like Gera, Joseph, Tin-Tin, and Hector are not adolescents. They are adults. Yet they are also men who, because of a combination of factors and interventions, have found their individual worth and in so doing have permitted the strength and hope that fled from them during their respective childhoods to return.

The point is this: if we wish solve the illness of gang violence, and in many ways it is an illness, we must look for the *right* diagnosis—not the easy one. "Gang member as monster" is a bad diagnosis that is guaranteed not to bring us closer to a cure. "Let the police handle it," combined with ever-harsher laws, is not a strategy that works. We must meet complexity with complexity.

The most farsighted of our experts have been telling us this for a long time. "The only way to explain the causes of violence, so that we can learn how to prevent it, is to approach violence as a problem in public health and preventative medicine . . . which, like all forms of illness, has an etiology or cause," writes Dr. James Gilligan, director of the Center for the Study of Violence at Harvard Medical School, in his 1996 book, *Violence: Our Deadly Epidemic and Its Causes.* Gilligan is the former director of mental health for the Massachusetts state prison system where, by the way, under his tenure murders, suicides, and riots, once common, were reduced to nearly zero.[20] Gilligan notes that violence, like charity, usually begins at home. Sadly, among industrialized nations, the United States is a leader when it comes to violence in relation to kids. According to the U.S. Department of Health and Human Services, each year 899,000 to a million children are listed on confirmed reports as abused and/or neglected in this country.[21] And each year between 3.3 million and 10 million children witnessed some form of violence in their homes.[22] Experience tells us that, without help plus exposure to healthy alternatives, many of those kids will one day visit violence on someone else.

"We're going to need a different ethos in this country," writes author and poet Luis Rodríguez, himself a former gang member. "One that values and nurtures every child."[23] I've learned over the years that if there's one silver bullet when it comes to solving the gang problem, Rodríguez's "different ethos" is that bullet. The innovative Harlem Children's Zone Project is trying for such a change in ethos with its mission to "improve outcomes" for poor children and families in some of New York's most poverty-devastated communities by attempting to literally transform the ecology in which children grow up in a 100-block area of Central Harlem. A slew of expensive reports commissioned by the Los Angeles City Council, the L.A. mayor's office, and the Los Angeles Sheriff's Department have suggested that a like approach is needed in America's gang capital. But such a solution is labor intensive and requires all hands on deck. Thus far the political and public will to make such a commitment has been conspicuously absent. Of course, the alternative is exactly what we have now—the ongoing tragedy of community violence and a record number of adolescents and young adults incarcerated at an incredible fiscal, moral, social—and, yes, *spiritual*—cost to all of us. It's way past time to change our methods and our perspective.

And so this new edition of *G-Dog and the Homeboys*.

While I can't magically transport you to L.A.'s poorest barrio so you can form your own impressions firsthand, my hope is that this volume you're presently holding is the next best thing. You'll find that in the body of the narrative I offer few prescriptions. The main part of the book is simply an anecdote-filled true story that will allow you to get to know a group of gang members along with one of the most remarkable men you'll ever encounter. Analyses and solutions are saved for the epilogue. So right now, please allow me to respectfully invite you to accompany me on a journey into the world of the homeboys of the Pico Aliso projects—and into the wise, wild, sorrowful, joyful, compassionate, and extremely *human* universe that is the work of Father Greg Boyle.

Notes

1. Arlen Egley Jr. and Christina E. Ritz, *2004 National Youth Gang Survey* (Washington DC: Office of Juvenile Justice and Delinquency Prevention, 2006).

2. Constance L. Rice, *City of Los Angeles Gang Activity Reduction Strategy Phase 1 Report* (Los Angeles: The Advancement Project, 2007).

3. Ibid.

4. *FBI Uniform Crime Report* (Washington DC: Federal Bureau of Investigation, 2007).

5. Egley Jr. and Ritz, *2004 National Youth Gang Survey.*

6. James Diego Vigil, *A Rainbow of Gangs* (Austin: University of Texas Press, 2002).

7. David C. Brotherton and Luis Barrios, *The Almighty Latin King and Queen Nation: Street Politics and the Transformation of a New York City Gang* (New York: Columbia University Press, 2004).

8. Malcolm W. Klein, *Gang Cop* (Walnut Creek, CA: Alta Mira Press, 2004), xv.

9. The Council on Crime in America, *The State of Violent Crime in America* (New York: Manhattan Institute, 1996).

10. James A Fox, *Trends in Juvenile Violence: A Report to the United States Attorney General on Current and Future Rates of Juvenile Offending* (Boston: Northeastern University Press, 1996).

11. The Pew Center on the States, *One in 100: Behind Bars in America 2008* (Washington DC: The Pew Charitable Trusts, 2008).

12. Ibid.

13. Todd Clear, *Imprisoning Communities: How Mass Incarceration Makes Disadvantaged Neighborhoods Worse* (New York: Oxford University Press, 2007).

14. Judith Greene and Kevin Pranis, *Gang Wars: The Failure of Enforcement Tactics and the Need for Effective Public Safety Strategies* (Washington DC: The Justice Policy Institute, 2007).

15. Peter W. Greenwood and Franklin E. Zimring, *Changing Lives: Delinquency Prevention as Crime-Control Policy* (Chicago: University of Chicago Press, 2007).

16. Center on Media, Crime & Justice, *Voter Poll* (New York: John Jay College, December 2007).

17. Greene and Pranis, *Gang Wars.*

18. *The Homeboy Stories Project: An Anthology* (Los Angeles: PEN Center USA, 2007).

19. Ibid.

20. James Gilligan, MD, *Violence: Our Deadly Epidemic and Its Causes* (New York: G. P. Putman's Sons, 1996), 92.

21. Administration for Children & Families, *Child Maltreatment* (Washington DC: U.S. Department of Health & Human Services, 2000, 2001, 2002, 2003, 2004, 2005).

22. Lucille Glicklich-Rosenberg, MD, *Violence and Children: A Public Health Issue* (Irvine, CA: *Psychiatric Times*, March 1996).

23. Luis J. Rodríguez, *Hearts and Hands: Creating Community in Violent Times* (New York: Seven Stories Press, 2001), 322.

Chapter 1

At 6:55 P.M. on an uncommonly warm night in early March 1990, a long line of black-clad figures unspools parade-like from the Aliso Village housing project toward Dolores Mission Church in the Boyle Heights section of East Los Angeles. The figures affect unconcern, but there is an urgency beneath the cool. The two hundred-some mourners, most of them members of the Latino gang, the East L.A. Dukes, are trying to shove themselves into the rows of scarred wooden pews that fill the sanctuary by no later than 7:00 P.M. in order not to have any lag time in front of the church. They've come for the funeral of Antonio Vigil, aka Puppet, a seventeen-year-old who was killed by a single bullet to the head in a drive-by incident that took place two nights before. As the mourners file into the small stucco building, they cast edgy glances toward the street, clearly expecting trouble. The church is less than two blocks away from Dukes' territory, but it falls technically within the boundaries of territory claimed by their mortal enemies, The Mob Crew.

The attire worn this night conforms to the code of dress specific to Mexican American street gangs of the early 1990s. Girl gang members wear their hair long at the bottom and teased high at the crown, their lipstick blood red. The boys sport perfectly pressed white Penny's T-shirts, some with three barely discernible creases ironed in evenly spaced stripes down the front of the shirt symbolizing *trece*, short for 213 area code, a sign that the shirts' wearers are *surenos*, or gang members from southern California. Over the T-shirts are the inevitable black Raiders jackets and black cotton work pants called Dickies, worn four sizes too big and belted, a contemporary interpretation of the old *pachuco* style. About forty boys and girls also wear black sweatshirts emblazoned with iron-on Old English lettering that reads: IN LOVING MEMORY OF OUR HOMIE PUPPET R.I.P.

Outside the church, the police are very much in evidence. A couple of black-and-whites sit just around the corner, motors running. Two beige unmarked cars favored by CRASH, the LAPD's special gang unit, and one plain white sedan used by Housing Police, continuously circle the block.

At first the mood in the church is tense. But when taped synthesizer music throbs from loudspeakers, the sound seems to open an emotional spigot. The shoulders of the mourners start to shake with grief.

Behind the altar, a bearded man in glasses and priest's vestments sits quietly, watching the crying child gangsters. When the music ends, Father Gregory Boyle rises and steps down to stand smack in front of the first row of mourners.

Father Greg stands over six feet and while not exactly athletic, he exudes a physical ease. His face is expressive. His walk is slightly duck-footed. From a distance, with his receding brown hairline and beard going to gray, he looks well into middle age. Up close, he is clearly much younger, not yet even forty.

Greg takes a breath. "I knew Puppet for a long time," he says, his gaze traveling from face to face in the pews. "He used to work here at the church. I knew him as a very loving, great-hearted and kind man." Greg pauses. "We shouldn't ask who killed Puppet, but rather *what* killed him. Puppet died of a disease that is killing *La Raza*, a disease called gang banging." The crowd shifts nervously.

"So how do we honor Puppet's memory?" he asks. "We will honor him best by doing what he would want us to do." Another pause. "He would want us to stop killing each other."

All at once, there is a commotion in the sixth row. A hard-eyed kid of eighteen with the street name Wicked stands bolt upright and makes his way to the center aisle. Slowly, deliberately, he walks down the aisle until he stands in front of Greg, staring him straight in the eye. Then he turns and walks out the side door.

The air in the church is as brittle as glass when Greg begins speaking again. "If we knew Puppet and loved Puppet, then we would stop killing each other."

Four more gangsters stand and walk out. Greg's face reddens and then turns pale as the rest of the mourners wait to see what he will do.

Finally his jaw sets. "I loved Puppet," he says, his eyes starting to tear. "For me he was *carnal*" (flesh of my flesh, closer than brothers). "And I swear on Puppet's dead body that he would want us to stop killing each other."

The words explode in crisp, stunning bursts like so many rounds of live ammunition. Two more gang members get up and leave—but these boys walk with their heads down, their gaits rapid and scuttling. The remaining mourners sit stock-still, transfixed by the ferocity of Greg's gaze. "We honor his memory," he says quietly, "if we do this."

After the mass is over, gang members and girls form a chattering, protective cluster around Greg.

One of two identical twin gangsters, each known on the street simply as "The Twin," shakes his head unhappily. "That was scan'lous!" he says of the walkouts. "Those fools were scan'lous!" A tall, sad-faced homeboy with the incongruous name of Payaso—Clown—puts a hand on Greg's arm. "The rest of us stayed," he says gravely.

A few minutes later, Father Greg has just accompanied some of the gang members out to the church parking lot when an LAPD officer on duty in front of the church strides over to the priest, stands directly in front of him, and proceeds to shout, "I just want to know *why* you glorify gangs by having these funerals? I just want to know, man to man, why you do it! I want to know how you can live with yourself?"

Greg's Irish complexion flushes crimson. "Look," he says, "I ask them in *every* conceivable way to stop the violence. If you've got a better idea, I'm all ears!" With that, the priest turns and walks away, the cop staring after him.

This is the poverty-haunted heart of the barrio, the part of Los Angeles that much of the rest of the city would like to block from its collective consciousness. Here junkies and baseheads pump gas for handouts at the self-service filling stations, and bullet craters in the stucco walls serve as mnemonic devices, reminders of where this kid was killed, that one wounded. Yet surface impressions are not the whole of the matter. In addition to the daily doses of hardship and grief, there is a vibrant interweave of warmth and life here. Whereas much of the rest of suburban L.A. grows ever more impersonal, in the village atmosphere of this barrio, everybody seems to know everybody else. And beyond the insistent images of gang violence, addiction, brutality, and despair, a uniquely redemptive vision exists in the small urban community—a vision that radiates with particular clarity around the person of Father Greg Boyle.

A year and a half year after Puppet's funeral, I sit across from Greg in his tiny rectory office as he slumps exhausted into the wooden desk chair and the conversation turns again to the walkouts at the wake. I ask what he had hoped to accomplish with his speech to the homeboys. In the time since, I say, things seemed to have gotten worse, not better. Wicked, the leader of the walkout, was still a hard case. Three months after the funeral he'd threatened to kill Greg when the priest stood between him and an intended victim. Clown, the gentle kid who had been most chagrined by the "scan'lous" disrespect of Wicked and company, had been shot shortly after the funeral by rival gang members. He was now paralyzed from the waist down.

"You know," Greg says, "I'm not stupid enough to hope that one speech is going to make these kids lay down their guns. But can I say anything less than what I'm saying? Can I do other than to hold out the brightest and highest hope for them? There's no *choice* to be made. There's no other option. To offer your hope for them is the right thing to do, whether it works or not. And in the long run," he says, his face still lit with the optimism of the true believer, "I think this is the only thing that does work."

Father Greg Boyle is the pastor of Dolores Mission Church, which serves a parish that is dominated by Pico Gardens and Aliso Village, which combine to form the largest public housing project west of the Mississippi and the poorest parish in the Catholic Archdiocese of Los Angeles. Within its boundaries—less than a square mile of Boyle Heights east of the Los Angeles River—seven Latino gangs and one African American gang claim neighborhoods. This means that in an area smaller than most university campuses, there are eight separate armies of adolescents equipped with small and large-caliber weapons, each of which may be at war with any of the others at any given moment.

The gangs—the Clarence Street Locos, the East L.A. Dukes, Cuatro Flats, The Mob Crew (TMC for short), Primera Flats, Al Capone, Rascals, and the East Coast Crips (the single black gang)—vary in size from fifty to eighty teenage boys and young men. However large the membership, the 'hood or territory, that each gang claims is miniscule—no more than a square block or two. A member of one gang cannot safely walk the half block from his mother's apartment to the corner store—if that store is in enemy territory—much less walk the five or ten blocks (across as many 'hoods) to reach his assigned junior high or high school.

Most of the Pico Aliso gang members are first-generation Americans born of Spanish-speaking parents who crossed the border from Mexico with or without documentation during the 1970s. In the last hundred years, immigration from Mexico has ebbed and flowed in response to American labor needs. In the 1920s, for example, the growth-boom states of California and Texas attracted half a million Mexican immigrants. The flow dipped sharply during the depression, rose again during World War II, dropped once more after the war, when servicemen came home needing jobs, and rose yet again in the early 1970s. Since many of the immigrants were unskilled, they were regarded as a source of cheap labor by California manufacturers and farmers.

With each immigration wave, the newest, poorest immigrants gravitated to the areas already most densely populated with other Mexican Americans—areas such as the East L.A. housing projects. When the American economy drooped and joblessness rose in the seventies, and again in the eighties, the poverty of East L.A. began to calcify to form a permanent underclass. As some of their parents turned to drug use and alcoholism, the kids of this immigrant underclass fought feelings of exclusion and hopelessness by banding together.

Mexican street gangs have existed in L.A. since at least the 1940s when adolescent *pachucos* of the zoot suit generation used their flamboyant style of dress to stake out identity, as family dislocation and despair invaded the city's barrios during World War II. In the intervening decades, the pachucos morphed into big, multigenerational *cholo* gangs—like White Fence and El Hoyo Maravilla. Yet, except for Primera Flats, which has been around since mid-century, the majority of the gangs of Pico Aliso sprang up in the middle 1980s after the young African American gangsters of South L.A. began to deal in narcotics, and the accompanying new plague of violence began bleeding east.

Since Mexican-American gangs are traditionally territorially based (for cholo gang members, the word "neighborhood" is used to mean both *gang* and *territory*), the sudden proliferation of new gangs created an unprecedented Balkanization effect. In the sixteen-square-mile area of Boyle Heights that is patrolled by the Hollenbeck Division of the LAPD, there are sixty different gangs, into which an estimated 8,000 members are divided. In the early nineties, the highest concentration of gang activity in the city of Los Angeles was occurring in the Hollenbeck area—and the highest concentration of gang activity in Hollenbeck was taking place in the Pico Aliso housing projects, aka Dolores Mission parish. During his six years as parish priest Greg Boyle has buried twenty-eight kids who were shot to death by rival gang members, and two who were shot dead by sheriffs. He himself has been in the line of fire seven times.

I first came to meet Father Greg Boyle in October of 1990. I'd heard about an unusual priest who had worked miracles with Latino gang members, and thought he might make an interesting profile for the *Los Angeles Times Magazine*, to which I am a regular contributor.

The night I made my initial visit, Greg was conducting yet another funeral, this one for a sixteen-year-old homegirl named Smiley who had been shot in the head a few nights before. A friend who knew Greg was to meet me at the funeral and introduce me to the priest. Plans had gone awry, however, and my friend had backed out. It was a bad night for me all around. I had trouble at home. My own child, not then quite five years old, had disappeared for hours with another neighborhood boy. When he was not home by dusk, I feared the worst and called the police. Just as the officers finished their report, my son arrived home, unharmed. He had stolen ten dollars from my purse and he and his buddy, a six-year-old whom I viewed as a juvenile delinquent in the making, had spent the money at a nearby video arcade. Beset by a roil of feelings—relief, fury, dismay at my parental inadequacy, fear for my son's future—I took him, as planned, to his father, my ex-husband, and attended the funeral, alone and unannounced.

As I drove up to Dolores Mission, I was overtaken by the conviction that I was making a horrible mistake. Here I was, a middle-aged, non-Catholic, non-Spanish-speaking white woman in her nice new white Honda Accord marching uninvited into a crowd of angry, bereaved, highly tattooed adolescents who, likely as not, were heavily armed.

I wondered if my car would be stolen.

Arriving late, just as the mourners were filing past the open casket, sobbing and clinging to one another, I saw Greg, already out of his priests' vestments, at the back door of the church comforting the young cholo-dressed men and women who greeted him before spilling out into the church parking lot. Although he had never been described to me, I knew instantly which of the five Jesuits present was Father Greg. He was, without a doubt, the magnetic center of the scene.

Next I wandered through the church parking lot gazing into the faces of the grief-stricken gang members. It was then that all the fear I had initially felt vanished into the night air. I saw in these faces not the scary monsters depicted in the media, but rather a whole lot of hurting kids.

I knew that it was these very kids—and others like them—who were (and still are) shooting and killing each other, and sometimes innocent bystanders, in every large city in America. However, the expressions I saw that night were not deadened but full of feeling. The eyes into which I looked were not eyes from which all humanity had long ago been drained. They were filled with pain and longing, capable of contact. And Greg was clearly the one making the contact.

On the drive home, something changed deep inside me. That night I'd felt ill-equipped to be a mother of a boy child in this increasingly dangerous world. Afterward, although I hadn't exchanged so much as a word with Greg or any of his homeboys, I somehow felt peaceful; as if somewhere in my subconscious I had concluded that if this unprepossessing white guy could reach these supposedly lost kids, then the world was not as unmanageable as it had seemed a few hours before. Watching him had made my own task of parenting seem possible.

I resolved to return to Dolores Mission. First, I talked my editor at the magazine into letting me do the article on Father Greg. I knew that I had stumbled onto an intriguing story. In a world devoid of heroes, here was a man who, by all accounts, was some kind of larger-than-life, gospel-toting champion of the city's most despised and marginalized adolescents. I wanted to know if he was for real. And if he could genuinely make a difference.

But it was more than that: as a parent and as a journalist, I had long felt the strong desire to somehow penetrate the nature and causes of the youth violence that was wreaking such havoc in every urban center in America—and to determine what, if anything, we could do about it. The solutions to date have been to crack down on the offenders. Separate and apart from the questionable moral and fiscal issues raised by the prospect of incarcerating without rehabilitation masses of our nation's children, there remained the simple fact that the crack-down strategy clearly wasn't working.

It seemed to me that the best way to understand the problem was to better understand its origins, which meant understanding the kids themselves—not from our perspective, but from *theirs*. Father Greg Boyle appeared to be able to provide the most accessible doorway into this perspective.

In the months that followed I found myself, at first with Greg and then on my own, plunging into an astonishing world with its own rules and reality—the world of Latino gangs. Although these gangs had become the fastest growing juvenile subculture in the nation, I discovered that virtually nothing had been written about them apart from a few sociological texts. All the media attention had been focused on African American gangs, which had markedly different rituals and raisons d'être. As I entered ever deeper into the multilayered gangs' realms, I also began to unravel the mystery of a man whose talent for loving was unlike any I had ever before encountered.

The article soon turned into a book. And the months I had intended to spend in the barrio turned into years—three years of research and another of writing. In the course of the research, I became increasingly involved in the lives of the subjects I was following. As a result, my own life began to crack open in ways both joyful and frightening.

———

After my first few trips to Dolores Mission parish, I didn't know how to square the double vision I experienced. On the one hand, to my middle-class white woman's eyes, this part of the barrio felt unsafe, threatening, foreign—especially at night. Yet Greg exuded such a dazzling aura of well-being and normalcy. He is quick-witted, humorous, with equal doses of ego and rebelliousness. He makes funny faces for my benefit when he is talking on the phone to wealthy Westside patrons whom he feels are rambling on too long. In his presence, the most recent gang-related shootouts, which he describes with a story-teller's eye to detail, seem tragic but distant, like fantastic tales of the old West. He comes off as too good to be true.

Greg lives simply but in the extreme. Every cold day I see him in the same burgundy zip-front sweatshirt. When the days are sunny, he wears the same rotating selection of five cotton shirts. His sleeping quarters are a half-mile from the church in a two-story 1913 clapboard rectory that he shares with six other Jesuits. While most priests might occasionally covet expensive wine, and finely woven fabrics, Greg has few discernible indulgences save his penchant for movies (his tastes range from Hollywood blockbusters to obscure foreign films) and the ever-present Hall's cough drops, which he pops into his mouth at moments of stress. He admits that when family members or friends try to spruce up his wardrobe with gifts of better shirts or jackets, he responds by giving the garments away to the first homeboy who displays an interest. Once, unbelieving, I bought him a nice new sweatshirt, thinking I was doing him a good turn. A week later, I noticed it gracing the person of one of the undocumented homeless men who sleep at the church.

I am continually amazed at Greg's stamina. He is awake by 5:30 A.M. and either in his office by 7:00 A.M. or making a trip down to Juvenile Court to testify on a gang member's behalf. His days end close to midnight, when he takes one last ride around the projects on his bicycle to make sure no trouble is brewing. On the nights when events go bad, he doesn't get to bed at all. In between gang-related work, along with the two assistants at Dolores Mission, he performs the conventional range of pastoral duties: saying mass, hearing confessions, officiating at weddings and funerals, or simply working in his monastic cell of an office, dealing with parish business. Although he always deals with the parishioners warmly, Greg is clearly happiest in the presence of the homeboys.

When Greg's office door opens, gang members swoop in like baby chicks for a feeding. They come to him to have their hair cut, to ask for a job through his Jobs for a Future program, to sign up to feed the homeless (to comply with court-ordered community service), to ask for admission to Dolores Mission Alternative, the school that he started as a sort of Last Chance U for gang members. The girls come too, but mostly it is the boys. They come to hang out, to talk, to tease and be teased, to laugh. Around Greg the gangsters' defensive "screw you" expressions drop away. Both twelve-year-old wannabe's and twenty-year-old, tough-eyed OG's—original gangsters—jockey to be the favored child who will sit next to Greg in his car on his daily errands. They aren't afraid to cry in his presence. They find any excuse to touch him. The gangsters have even rechristened Greg with his own *placa*, his street name: G-Dog. But most simply call him G.

In an effort to understand Greg at a deeper level, I become his shadow. I follow him on every errand when he will endure my presence. Many times I simply sit in his office observing the antics of gang members and others who drift in and out, looking for warmth, advice, favors. At first the homeboys stare at me suspiciously. After a while, I am tolerated as an extension of Greg, as if I am a pesky aunt whom they must accept because she is accompanying the beloved dad.

While it takes me far longer to penetrate the nature of his "madness"—the deeper reasons behind his commitment to what he calls his "gang ministry"—the follow-him-everywhere approach gradually gives me a grasp of his method.

———

Greg holds up his identification badge to the guard outside the first set of doors at the entrance to Eastlake Juvenile Hall. The badge-flashing is a formality. The guard knows Greg and greets him by name. Greg comes to Eastlake at least once a week. At any given time there are fifteen to twenty-five kids he knows locked up here—too many to visit in one day.

"I do the best I can," Greg explains as he walks the concrete corridor to the next set of gates. These he unlocks himself. "I have a key," he says with a conspiratorial smile. "I don't think they remember they gave it to me."

The key is a great advantage. It means that Greg can roam the facility at will without having to wait for guards to let him in and out of the maze of doors and gates, all of which are locked from both directions all of the time.

Greg's visits with each kid are short, mostly a touching of bases. He gives this one a message from a girlfriend. He asks that one when his court date is and how his case is coming. He brings to a third a bag of personals—shampoo, deodorant, toothpaste.

"I always give priority to the kids who have no one," says Greg. "About half the kids here have no one, no family member who will bring them personals. So I bring them what they need."

Watching him, it becomes obvious why visiting kids in juvenile facilities has long been one of the building blocks of Greg's strategy. When a kid is locked up he is at his most vulnerable, so the priest has a better shot at turning him around. "They always cry when they're locked up," says Greg. He also figured out early on that his unique position of being able to bring gang members news of their friends who were locked up gave him enormous cachet on the street.

If kids are incarcerated in facilities that are too far away to visit regularly, Greg writes to them, sending packets of personals through the mail as needed. He gets an average of forty letters a month and answers every one. The kids guard these letters as treasured objects, quoting passages to each other and back to Greg months later when they are free.

Greg also goes to court or writes letters on kids' behalf when he believes in their cause. All these things—combined with helping them locate jobs, getting them into school, running interference with the bureaucracy if need be, visiting them in the hospital when they've been shot—give him leverage. "Juice," as the kids call it. Influence.

"So when I want to turn the screws a little," says Greg, "or I want someone to hand over a gun, I call in my markers."

The point is illustrated two days after the Juvenile Hall visit when a Clarence Street homie is discovered to have been on a tagging spree. (Tagging—writing one's street name and/or the name of one's gang on building walls with spray paint—is both a declaration of identity and a way of claiming territory. It is also a potentially lethal provocation, especially if written in or near the territory of another gang.) Greg calls the kid into his office. "I'm going to ask you a personal favor," Greg says in tones that suggest something of incalculable import is about to be requested. "I don't want you to ever tag in the projects again."

The kid nods as if accepting a sacred task. "Okay, G," he says.

"What was understood," Greg explains after the kid is gone, "is that I had gone to bat for that kid many, many times. Now I'm cashing in my chits. And it works."

It also helps that Greg has made a point of penetrating the logic of the streets, allowing him to work from within that logic, turning it to his own advantage. "The highest value in gangdom is being down for your neighborhood," he explains. "This commonly means to kill somebody else or to back somebody up in a fight." Greg doubles the term back on itself.

"There's nobody who's more down for your neighborhood than me," he will say to a group of kids. "And I've never killed anybody and I've never fought anybody." What does a real friend do? he will ask them. Does a real friend kill for you? Or does a real friend visit you when you're locked up? Or when you're in the hospital?

"The downest *vato* that ever lived was Jesus Christ," he tells them.

———

At first all the kids surrounding Greg seem to be an interchangeable blur, but gradually I begin to isolate homeboys and question them on my own, tape-recording the remarks. As the months pass I develop a list of gang members whose actions I track, partially through conversations with Greg—either when following along with him or on the phone at the end of each day—and partially through my own contact with the kids. The first kids I get to know are Juan Carlos Lopez and Javier Vidal, aka Spanky and Cisco.

Spanky's father was gone long before he was born. He was raised by his mother who beat him with the plug end of the television cord, a garden hose, a spiked belt—anything she could find. The beatings were so severe that she was jailed several times for child abuse. Some abusive parents are by turns affectionate and rejecting. Not this mother. In all the years of Spanky's upbringing he never received a birthday gift or a Christmas gift or even a card. "Imagine," says Greg, "not one piece of concrete evidence of caring from a parent throughout a whole childhood. One time, at my urging," he continues, "Spanky tried to reconcile with his mother. And this is what she said to the child she brought into this world: '*Tú eres basura.*' You are garbage."

In Cisco's case it was not so much parents but life in the barrio that inflicted the abuse. Cisco's last memory of his alcoholic father was when he was three; his dad knocked his mother off her feet, cuffed Cisco to the floor, and snarled, "What're you lookin' at?" Cisco's mother gathered her kids and fled. The hotel in which she found shelter was so crime-ridden that before he was five, Cisco had witnessed three lurid murders, virtually on his doorstep.

Cisco's mother padlocked her preschool-aged children in a darkened hotel room when she went to work for the day. "She was trying to keep us safe," says Cisco. When asked if his childhood had any happy times, he thinks for a moment. "I remember this one day when my mom took us all to the park and let us run around. It was so great, you know. For once we weren't stuffed up in that little room. And we felt, I don't know, just—free!"

In mid-December, a few evenings after my first conversations with Spanky and Cisco, I find Greg in his office going over several sheets of paper he has just printed out from his computer. On a whim he'd sat down the night before and made a list of all of the gangsters in the vicinity who came to mind. Next to each name he wrote a coded description of the kid's family situation: AB for absent father; A for alcoholic father; AA for alcoholic/abusive; ABU for just plain abusive; S for stepfather; I for intact original family.

"I didn't stack the deck or anything," he explains. "I just wrote down sixty-seven names, sort of stream of consciousness. I found that most fathers were absent. The second biggest categories were alcoholic and alcoholic/abusive." And out of sixty-seven kids, three had intact families with fathers that were not alcoholic or abusive."

So what does a barrio kid do when family and society have failed him? When he turns fourteen or fifteen he joins a gang, a surrogate family, where he finds loyalty, self-definition, discipline, even love.

Although Greg will passionately condemn gang banging, his strategy is not so much to talk a kid out of gang membership, which the kids see as *por vida*, for life. Instead he attempts to cajole them into "maturing out" of the gang into a more hopeful and expanded view of themselves than the confines of gang membership can offer. Sometimes the shift in self perception is set in motion by something as basic as a new batch of clothes.

On a bright Sunday afternoon in January 1991, Father Greg takes Cisco and Spanky shopping. Both are large kids, bulky and muscular, each with a proclivity for fast, funny patter delivered half in English, half in Spanish. They are members of The Mob Crew and the Clarence Street Locos, respectively—traditionally friendly gangs whose neighborhoods are close to the church. Both gangs are enemies of the East L.A. Dukes, the gang Puppet had claimed. Cisco is nineteen and Spanky is twenty, too old to attend Dolores Mission Alternative. As a result they are desperate to find employment. Their shopping destination is Sears. The idea is to get them non-gangster attire to wear for job interviews.

In the men's department, Greg pulls out pants and shirts for them to try on. He is careful to choose light colors. Spanky and Cisco keep edging back in the direction of the gangster look—dark colors and a baggy fit.

"Hey, G, these pants are too tight," wails Cisco. In reality the pants fit perfectly.

"They're fine," Greg counters, and Cisco relents.

"Look," says Greg to Cisco and Spanky as he hands the cashier a Sears credit card, "I'm spending a lot of bank on this today, and the deal is you have to be dressed and in my office every morning at nine A.M. ready to look for work." The two nod obediently, assuring Greg that they will comply.

Both Cisco and Spanky are staying in Casa Miguel Pro, the temporary residence that Dolores Mission maintains for homeless women and children. "I'm trying an experiment in letting them stay there,"

Greg explains. "A lot of folks aren't exactly thrilled that I'm doing this. But right now neither of them has anywhere else they can go."

Back at Casa Pro, Cisco irons his new tan pants and striped blue shirt. Next he takes a bath. Finally he puts on the freshly pressed clothes and looks in a communal mirror.

"That ain't me," he says softly to the mirror. He stands back a little and looks again. "I look like a regular person," he says, his expression so happy it borders on giddiness. "Not like the police say, not like another *gang* member."

Now that Spanky and Cisco are dressed for success, they are ready for their first job interview. They plan to take a bus to the interview site, but Greg ends up driving them several miles to a "safe" bus stop because the nearest bus stop is too dangerous.

"It's in enemy territory," Greg explains. "See now, everybody is always shouting, 'What's wrong with these kids? Why don't they just go out and get jobs?' What few people bother to understand is nothing round here is ever as simple as it would seem."

New wardrobes notwithstanding, after two weeks of looking, neither Cisco nor Spanky get so much as a nibble of encouragement on their daily job search. By week three, a different kind of problem arises. Greg arrives at his office on a Monday morning to find a message on his answering machine. "Hey, G," says a young voice, "tell Spanky I don't have the money for the gun, but I'll have the money soon." Greg stares at the machine, boggle-eyed. It is nearly inconceivable that someone would leave such a message with him.

He goes to Spanky's room and in a kind of false wall in the closet he finds a gun-cleaning kit plus a metal strong box. The box is heavy and the lid is stuck. Greg carts the box down to his office and shuts the door before prying the lid open. Inside there is $178 in cash, a neat list of investors, and a box of large-caliber bullets.

Greg shuts the box, puts it in a desk drawer, and waits for Spanky's inevitable appearance in his office. The confrontation goes as follows:

"Do you have a gun?"

"No, G."

"Are you collecting money for a gun?"

"No, G."

Greg opens the drawer revealing the strong box. "You've really let me down," he says quietly.

Spanky's face turns to stone. "When do you want me to leave?" he asks. Then eyes averted and brimming, he turns and walks out.

Two hours later Spanky is back. "G, I know I let you down! I let you down *gacho!* I let you down big time!"

Greg cannot bring himself to make Spanky leave. "I know tough love is sometimes required," he says. "But I don't know just how tough the love should be."

The problem of what to do with the $178 is much easier to solve. Late that night Greg makes a point of riding his bike over to where the Clarence Street homies are kicking it. "I really want to thank you guys for being so *generous*," says Greg, a look of cheery beatification gracing his face. The homies say nothing. By now they have heard that he has the money. "You guys are *lo máximo!*" continues Greg, ignoring their ill-disguised embarrassment. "We were able to feed 150 homeless men last night with your money! *Mil gracias!*" And away he rides.

"Nothing is simple." Greg repeats the phrase later that night in discussing the incident. Since Spanky is one of the kids with whom Greg has a special bond, I ask him how the gun-fund incident has affected him personally. "Oh, I got discouraged in the moment, I guess," he replies. "One time last year I was really discouraged and I was thinking, 'Does any of this make any sense?' That same day I happened to be talking to one of the probation officers who works around here, John Tucheck. I was just kind of venting with him. And Tucheck told me how he'd been in and out of Juvenile Hall as a kid, but that there was one person who never gave up on him. And that made all the difference.

"The phrase really clicked with me," Greg continues. "It signals on a theological level the God who never gives up on us. And I think if we believe that's who God is—the God who loves us no matter what; the God who never gives up—then it's our personal task to reflect that kind of God in the world." He hesitates, as if afraid of being misunderstood. "It may sound simplistic, but I believe in that strategy with all my heart. A success for me is when it is clear to a kid that there exists at least one person who will love you no matter what. Most of us have tons of people in our lives who have that no-matter-what quality to the relationships. These kids don't. So hang on to your hat because their behavior will reflect that lack. And that's what this whole mess is about."

Spanky

My name is Juan Carlos Lopez. When I was little people used to call me Carlito. Now they call me Spanky. I like that all right.

You could say my mom and me don't really get along. I ran away from my house when I was fifteen. For any reason, she would start hitting me. Most times she didn't need a reason. When I was fifteen, I said, I ain't going to take this shit no more.

When I was little, I was in four or five different foster homes. My mother would beat me up and the neighbors would call the cops and the cops would come and they would take me to a foster home. When you're small you're scared because you think, "What's going on?" Because there's a difference between a spanking and a beating up. She hit me with the hose, extension cord from the iron, the metal wires from the TV. Anything she could find. She had a belt with spikes on it.

When I was small, I used to be scared a lot. I was scared of spiders. The time when I was scaredest—I was thirteen—my mom and my step-dad were goin' at it. She thought he had went with some other girl. But when he came back, she had a gun. She had clicked it back. I guess she was going to shoot him. But she didn't. When she put it down she left it on the bed. And then she went somewhere. So when I went upstairs and saw the gun on the bed, I picked it up and pulled out the clip, got it out, 'cause in case she came back she wouldn't do something crazy. Then I pulled the trigger, just to close it, because it was cocked back. And it was loaded. I didn't know. There was a bullet in the chamber. And I shot my sister. I nearly blew her away. It was so bad. That was the scaredest I was. She was seventeen and I thought I had killed her.

My mom could be cool when she wanted to be cool. When you're in the foster homes, they let you talk to your mom and dad to see if you want to go back to them. That's how they do it in court, they ask you if you want to go back. So when you're small, if your mom tells you, "I'll buy you a bike," maybe you say, "Yeah, I'll go back." And then you go back and that shit starts happening again. The hitting starts happening again.

I think when I was a baby she mighta likeded me better. Like she might have gave me a gift for my birthday. You give babies gifts, right? So she probably did. I don't really know. It lookeded to me like she hated me. I don't know why. She never took drugs. She didn't drink. So I don't know why.

When I think about my mom, sometimes I think she been the way she was with me because when she was raised in Mexico, her dad was, you know, really strict with her. And she's trying to get back at him. So she started beating up on me for stupid reasons.

Once there was some nice people in a foster home. Usually in the foster home the people have their own kids and the kids try to boss you around. They don't like you.

The last time I talked to my mom she found out I was staying at the church. Father Greg had talked to her. I was working as a security guard and I was living with my cousin. He never told my mom where I was staying at, so she didn't really bug me. I was working and going to school and everything. But then my mom found me and started going to the school and looking for me. So I had to stop going to school. I didn't want to see her no more, so I stopped going to school because she could always find me there. She wanted me to go back with her. How am I going to go back when she's going to be doing the same thing every day?

I used to clean the house for her, when I was little. It sounds crazy, but I used to cook for her and wash her clothes. I was trying to make her be happy. I thought that would make her treat me better. It never did.

What I have right now is my homeboys. That's my family. My neighborhood. That's all I have right now. Father Greg wants me to stop banging and all that shit. But you can't change just like that. Not when you've lost five of your homeboys already. When all my homeboys started passing away, it got to me. I said, "I ain't going to change. I'm going to take revenge for my homeboys who've passed away."

Shotgun and Popeye, they were the hardest. Those were the ones who I was really close to. Popeye had got locked up on Friday night for a violation. And they let him out on Sunday for his birthday. He wanted to get out for his birthday. And on Sunday night, at midnight, that's when they killed him. I was at the church when they told me. The homeboys came and said, "Hey, Popeye passed away right now."

And I said, "Nah. He's at his house." But then when Father Greg came and told me, that's when I believed it.

That same night, we had went to East L.A.'s neighborhood to get revenge, an' we seen this man riding around on a bicycle, but we didn't know who it was. Then I saw his glasses shine and I knew it was Father Greg. So we hid the guns. When he saw us he started woofing at us. He said if we really had love for Popeye we wouldn't be doing' what we're doin'. But the day of peace, that's never going to happen. They're the ones who spilled the blood first.

Now, East L.A., that's our worst enemies. They killed two of our homies and if we have a chance to go get 'em, we'll go get 'em. G-Dog gets mad 'cause we go and try to get 'em. But we can't just let that go. If I'm right next to some East L.A.s, then I'm going to go fuck them up. And if I can go kill 'em, I go kill 'em. They killed my homeboys. They're going to get the same medicine they did to us.

You have to have the heart to kill somebody. If I wanted to kill somebody now, I could do it. But I wouldn't just kill any person. It's only somebody from a neighborhood that's my enemy. If you kill somebody you have to do it right—so nobody will know that you did it. There are some guys who will kill somebody and tell everybody just to prove themselves. They tell this homie and that homie. Then pretty soon somebody snitches and they're locked up. When you do something you keep it to yourself. The only person you have to prove it to is to yourself. The thing is with your enemies, if you don't get them first, they'll get you first.

Before, we used to go head up with our enemies. We used to fight man to man—like boxing. But times changed. If our enemies want to play with toys we have to play with toys back. It started to change when this fake-ass movie *Colors* came out. That's when everybody started popping out with guns.

Times have changed on other things too. Like—maybe in past days, people would fall in love. I'm never going to fall in love. These days, you meet a girl and you scam with her. Then you say, "I'll catch you later." And then you go to another. I guess there's some people who stick with one girl. And there's always a first time when you fall in love. But when it don't work out, then you don't want to fall in love again because it ain't going to work out. And why have kids? Why have kids knowing that I could get killed today or tomorrow? Then you just leave the kid without a dad.

I mean, my dad—he left me when I was small. He went with somebody else. I don't know what happened. I never met my dad. That's why I wouldn't have a kid. My homeboy Popeye who passed away, he had a kid. Now that baby doesn't have a dad. And that baby doesn't have a mom either, because Smiley, Popeye's lady, she passed away too. That's not the way it should be.

I'd like to have a lady but I can't imagine it. I would worry that she would start messing up on me. If she goes out with her friends then they start telling her, "Don't be with that guy." Then that's it for the relationship.

If I could get a good job, I would like that, obviously. But I don't want to plan on it. You can't plan on good things happening. 'Cause if it don't happen, then you feel worse than before.

Father Greg's like the family I never had. I know I let him down a lot and that makes me feel fucked up. Like, when he found money I had been collecting for a gun for my neighborhood, I didn't want to go back to the church no more. I felt like I let him down, *gacho*. But what can I do? We have to stand up for ourselves too. We don't want to get killed.

You can't change just because you say, "I'm going to change." And I don't even know if I *can* change. Because right now what I have is pure hate in my heart. So I'm just going to stick with homeboys. And if they say, "Let's go do it!" I'm going to go do it. I can't stop banging. I just can't. I can't stop.

Nobody knows when it's going to stop.

I live at the church now. But this August they're going to close the part of the church where I'm staying, and I'm going to have to move out. And that's going to be it. If you ask me what I would be doing in ten years, I would say, "In ten years I'm going to be in the *pinta* doing twenty-five to life." But I'll tell you, if I'm going to get locked up I'm going to take out at least ten motherfuckers. Something that would be worth getting locked up. I ain't going to get locked up for stealing a car. If you catch them at the right spot, you could kill a bunch of 'em all at once. Kabooom!

I'm not really happy. I'm always kicking it, smoking some bud, getting drunk. I don't get happy. I got too many problems. I don't got the time to be happy. I care for my homeboys. And I know they care for me. Everybody in our neighborhood really cares for each other. Like, my homeboy Wizard let me stay in his house almost for a year. That's the way our neighborhood is. I watch out for my homies. Like, I watch out for Slim—Popeye's brother—'cause I don't want nothing to happen to him.

If I could go back in time, like in *Back To the Future*, I would go to the day that my homeboys passed away and try to prevent it. I would tell them not to kick it where they were kicking it. Or to tell them to be ready. Or I would get in the way and be the one who was killed instead.

Father Greg is the only thing that keeps it from getting crazy in the projects. We know G isn't going to be here forever. If G leaves, the world's going to end. That's just the truth. But I guess that's the chance that we're all going to take.

Chapter 2

It is late January of 1991.
Greg stands on the front steps of Dolores Mission, giving quick hugs of encouragement to the 150 parish women plus a smattering of men who file past him into the church, their expressions nervous and anticipatory. Although tonight's meeting has been announced at all the masses for a week, Greg worried that at the last minute the parishioners would get cold feet. The previous evening he rode his bike around the projects for hours, reminding everyone to be at the church at seven o'clock. The eleventh-hour cheerleading worked. The pews fill up quickly.

Everyone is just settling down when the front doors swing open again and sixty gang members, male and female, file into the sanctuary. As many as can fit squeeze themselves up the stairs and onto the church's balcony. The rest stand at the back, hands folded in front of them, waiting for the meeting to begin.

Officially, Father Greg didn't call the meeting. Officially it has been sponsored by the parish mothers who comprise the Comite Pro Paz en el Barrio—the Committee for Peace in the Barrio—with Greg and Leonardo Vilchis, the church's on-staff community organizer, acting as midwives. However, everybody here knows that this is not just any meeting: Tonight is a showdown.

The relationship between the Pico Aliso community and law enforcement has recently reached a crisis point. At an emergency meeting of the Comite Pro Paz last Monday, every mother in attendance told multiple stories about this kid or that one being beaten up by LAPD officers. Upon Greg's advice, the women first tried peaceful intervention. Whenever word spread that the police had kids "hemmed up"—held with their hands and legs spread-eagled against a wall or on the ground—mothers would materialize from apartment doorways and silently observe what the police were doing. The idea was that the cops would be less likely to beat up kids in front of witnesses. This did not prove to be the case. The strategy only seemed to inflame certain officers, who countered by shouting the mothers back into their apartments, threatening to arrest them if they didn't comply. Then, according to the women, the cops took the kids off to the factories—as the industrial area behind the projects is called—and roughed them up anyway.

The breaking point had come two weeks ago when the police threw a raid, rounding up approximately twenty-five adolescents. "They took anybody who had the *mala suerte* to be wearing a black jacket," says Greg. The police even arrested a black-jacketed Anglo kid from Loyola High school who was doing volunteer work for the church that night.

"The police think we are all criminals," spits Lupe Loera, the president of the Comite Pro Paz, "Just because we live in the projects."

Greg suggested to the mothers that perhaps it was time to give the police a wake-up call.

The meeting has been called for 7 and at 7:15, Captain Bob Medina, the head of the Hollenbeck Division of the LAPD, sweeps through the front door, three officers behind him. Greg reaches a hand out to shake hands with Medina. Medina moves past the priest without acknowledgment.

The police sit with stony expressions as the mothers stand, one by one, and list their grievances and demands:

"We demand that the police stop beating our kids without cause."
"We demand that when the police address us we not be insulted or

spoken to with four-letter words and obscene language." "Please help us to help our children. We pay your salaries."

At the back of the room, Greg's face grows red with pleasure. "Aren't they incredible?" he whispers. "These are the poorest, most marginalized women in Los Angeles, and they have the courage to face the LAPD and say, 'This is our community! You work for us!' "

Greg has always insisted that his work with the homeboys is only one piece of the puzzle, that lasting change requires the mobilization and empowerment of the mothers of the Pico Aliso community. So, the night of forceful action on the women's part—however well or poorly it is received by the police—feels like an enormous victory. Yet, the road to this moment—for both the priest and the mothers—has been a long and bumpy one.

When Greg Boyle initially came to Dolores Mission in early July of 1986 at age thirty-two, the youngest pastor in the L.A. archdiocese, he hardly seemed a likely candidate to become "the gang priest." He had an unportentous childhood as one of eight children of a third-generation dairyman raised in comfortable Windsor Square on the outskirts of the affluent Hancock Park area of Los Angeles. He attended Loyola high school, the Jesuit-run boys' school, from 1968 to 1971—as did most of his friends whose families could afford the tuition. However, Greg happened upon Loyola during a wildly inspiring period. His teachers led peace marches protesting the Vietnam War, and activist Jesuits made news across the country as Liberation Theology—a movement that married social justice to spiritual renewal—came to full flower.

Caught up in idealistic fervor, Greg spent the next thirteen years in religious training, culminating in his 1984 ordination in Los Angeles. Immediately following ordination, he was posted to Bolivia, then the poorest country in the Western Hemisphere, where he became the parish priest of a small rural village. The experience radicalized the young southern California priest. "Bolivia turned me absolutely inside out," Greg says. "After Bolivia, my life was forever changed." He realized he wanted to work with the poor. And few places were poorer than Dolores Mission.

Greg's first year in the parish was tense and difficult. The priest before him had been a venerable *Mexicano*, and the community was slow to warm up to an Anglo, especially one so young. Since few parishioners came to him, he decided to go to them. Every afternoon, without fail, Greg would walk for hours through the neighborhood, particularly through the housing projects where most of his parishioners lived. He talked to people, listened to their complaints, played with their children. Over time he noticed that the majority of the complaints centered upon one issue: gangs.

A decade before, local activists had worked with the at-risk youth of the projects. But by the mid-1980s, as gang violence escalated, most youth programs disappeared. Now, not only were the gangs at war with each other, the community was at war with the gangs.

Greg made an effort to get to know the gangsters. He began by learning their names. At first they brutally rejected the *gavacho* who spoke only passable Spanish. When Greg walked down one side of the street, the gang members gathered on the other side would laugh, obviously at Greg's expense. "It was the kind of experience," Greg says, "that is calculated to make you feel insecure and stupid. I spent a lot of time in those days feeling *very* insecure and stupid."

If the gangsters weren't hassling Greg, they were avoiding him, assuming that any white man in the barrio must be an undercover cop. On one occasion, Greg visited the house of a parishioner who turned out to be the grandmother of a gang member, a Crip. As Greg was chatting with the older woman, an enormous twenty-year-old suddenly loomed at the front door. Although the kid knew who Greg was, he assumed the priest was snitching to the police so, bellowing viciously, barreled straight for him. "With obvious intent to inflict bodily harm," adds Greg. The grandmother leaped between Greg and the gangster, giving Greg just enough time to retreat out the back door.

But bright and early the next morning, Greg went back to the gang member's house. "I knew it was like the proverbial fall from a horse," he explains. "If you don't go back right away, you'll never go back at all. I would tell myself, 'No matter what happens, I'm going to walk out there every day.'"

Despite the early rejections, Greg kept reaching out to the kids. "And you know," he says, "at some point it becomes sort of flattering that the priest knows who you are." Then he started going to Juvenile

Hall to visit when kids got locked up, bringing messages from their homeboys. Or he'd rush to the hospital if they got shot.

He noticed that the kids who got into the most trouble were those who were not in school, and the reasons they were not in school were invariably gang related. Either they had gotten kicked out because they had been fighting with enemy gang members, or the school itself was in enemy territory and thus deemed unsafe. This was also often true for the girls. Even if they didn't claim a neighborhood, if they dated gang members—and nearly all the projects girls wanted to date gang members—they were considered affiliated, and it wasn't long before they, too, were too spooked to attend public school.

So in September of 1988, Greg and his associate pastor, Father Tom Smolich, opened a junior high and high school for gang members only. Dolores Mission Alternative was started on the third floor of Dolores Mission Elementary, the church's grammar school. Through home study and specially-designed classes, the school aimed to get the kids back on an educational track, or at least to help them pass the high school equivalency exam.

Greg also started hiring gang members to work around the church at five dollars an hour. "Before I knew it there was no turning back," he laughs. "I felt like I sort of related to the gang members. They were fun and warm and eternally interesting." They returned the favor by giving the priest unprecedented access to a cultural substrata more enigmatic and impenetrable than even the African American gangs that were then dominating the headlines. By accident he seemed to have stumbled upon a calling for which his own specific gifts were uniquely suited. "So, gradually," he says, "it became a ministry within a ministry."

The rest of the parish, however, didn't find the gangsters quite so "warm" and "interesting." They saw only hair-netted homeboys doing heaven-knows-what in the same building with uniformed parochial schoolchildren. Worse yet, these young "criminal types" were now hanging out at the church as if it was their personal clubhouse.

Greg's strategy was always to ask, *"Que haría Jesús?"* What would Jesus do? "The whole message of the Gospel," he would say, "is that Jesus hangs out with the people that society says we cannot hang out with—the most rejected, the most worthy of condemnation. There he is. And I think if we really live the Gospel, that's what it will look like."

Gospel or no, in the fall of 1989, Greg's most virulent critics circulated a petition asking then-Archbishop Roger M. Mahony to remove him from the parish altogether. With little strong support from either the community or the archdiocese, Greg became more and more discouraged. "It seemed like my work with the gangs was being blamed for everything."

Things came to a head one October night. Greg had called a meeting to clear the air. "I really don't know what you want anymore," he had said when he announced the meeting at all the masses. "I'll leave the second you tell me to leave. Without looking back I will do it. So come to the meeting and say what you have to say."

The elementary school cafeteria was packed with Father Greg supporters and *contras* when, in a movielike turn of events, a community mother unexpectedly led a swarm of the gang members into the room. One by one the homeboys got up and talked: "We're human beings and we need help. And Father Greg is helping us."

That these tough-looking parish troublemakers had actually called out for help, had an electric effect on the adults assembled. Mother after parish mother rose to speak. "Father Greg is right. These gang members are not the enemy. They are our children. And if we don't help them, no one will."

It was the turning point. The parish stopped fighting Greg's ministry of compassion and began adopting it as their own. In short order the Comite Pro Paz en el Barrio was formed. Parish mothers who had never before attended so much as a PTA meeting suddenly became activists on the gangsters' behalf; they had barbecues for the disaffected homeboys, organized a peace march, held a two-day gang conference. "It was an amazing time," says Father Greg pulling out a file of snapshots of his skinnier, younger self, standing arm in arm with community women. Parishioners who had always considered their religion a distant force that spoke to them from on high began to claim their church and its gospel as their own. "And when people start to do that," says Greg, "miracles happen five times a day."

Once Greg and the parishioners began to join hands and work together, there seemed to be no limit to what they could accomplish. When Greg decided to allow homeless, undocumented men to sleep in the church, the community mothers quickly organized a monthly meal schedule for the men, a different cadre of women making and serving dinner every night. At first, ten men were housed and fed in what came to be known as the Guadelupe Homeless Project. Before long, there were 100 men sleeping in the church and being fed by the community. A shelter for homeless women and children was set up in the former convent across the street.

The year after the homeless shelters were established, Greg and the parish women decided to open Dolores Mission Women's Cooperative Day Care Center in the only space available, the stage of the elementary school cafeteria. Two years later, enough money had been raised by Greg, Father Tom—Tom managed to get himself on the game show "Jeopardy!" then donated his winnings to the Day Care Center—and the women of the community to assign a work crew of homeboys to break ground for a permanent day care center adjacent to the church parking lot. Three months after that, another homeboy crew began work on a newer, larger site for Dolores Mission Alternative.

Suddenly—without help from the government or the archdiocese—this one tiny, impoverished East L.A. parish seemed to be achieving the kind of grassroots transformation that every liberal agenda in the country was hoping for, but few accomplished.

But the shooting didn't stop.

Although Father Greg's work seemed to slow gang violence in Pico Aliso, kids still kept killing each other. By the summer of 1989, as Greg and the community evolved into a hothouse of grassroots empowerment, the priest found himself with a new, more virulent antagonist: the Los Angeles Police Department.

The ongoing LAPD anti-gang program is dubbed Operation Hammer. The police describe Hammer as "a strategy in which we keep the pressure on." The general method for "keeping the pressure on" is straightforward. On Friday and Saturday nights, around 1000 officers are deployed all over the city to locations where gang members are most likely to be hanging out. The police will then arrest as many gang members as they can legally justify—regardless of how flimsy the pretext. "Drinking beer in public," says a Hollenbeck officer. "Anything we can." If the crime can be shown to be "gang related" and the arrestee is a "known gang member," i.e., if he is dressed a certain way, the sentence can be "enhanced"—made longer. For all the monetary expenditure, plus the community bad will generated by these mass arrests, thus far Hammer has resulted in few actual prosecutions.

The evening of the showdown between the mothers and the cops, we return to Greg's office, where I ask him what he thinks of Operation Hammer. "Here's the problem," says Greg. "As a society, we don't believe that these kids are human beings. And our policies and strategies with regard to gangs for the last ten years in this city reflect exactly that."

He then describes the way a South Central LAPD precinct was known to respond to gang fights in the recent past: "Apparently, whenever they used to get a call that two gangs were fighting, they would characterize the call by saying, 'We've got an NHI on the corner of One Hundred Twentieth and Crenshaw.' Which meant, 'no human involved.' This meant you had a lighter touch on the gas pedal, you got there just in time to be too late, to mop up, to take names— because, after all, no human involved.

"If we don't believe they are human beings," Greg continues, "then what we have to do is simple: We will continue to build more prisons, have tougher cops, stricter ordinances. We'll lock them up, and we'll be sure to lose the key. But if we think they're human beings then that opens up a whole complex set of solutions. Most of these kids are hard pressed to imagine a future for themselves. And if you can't imagine a future, then you're not going to care a lot about the present. Then anything can happen."

What began as a simple difference in approach between Greg and the Hollenbeck police gradually inflated into open conflict, with an ever-escalating series of skirmishes. At first, Greg solicited meetings with various officers with the idea of fostering cooperation, but somehow the meetings always seemed to end with both sides further apart than when they'd begun. A written report highly critical of Father Greg was circulated at Hollenbeck, and subsequently leaked to him. This resulted in a flurry of angry letters from each quarter. It wasn't long before the argument spilled from a private to a public exchange.

"Father Greg is in a position where he could be extremely helpful, not only to the Hollenbeck area, but to the entire Los Angeles Police Department," Captain Bob Medina complained to an *L.A. Times* reporter. "I just don't think we're getting the type of cooperation we should be getting. He wants to pamper these people and take them by the hand. The way some of these people have been brought up, that would make it easier for them to go out and break the law. These people understand only one thing, and that's force."

During this same period, Greg wrote a series of emotional op-ed pieces, decrying the LAPD's force-only position as exacerbating "the deep antagonism that already exists between law-enforcement officials and residents of the barrio," and pleading with the city to offer gang members "a strategy that confronts their despair."

Finally, Captain Medina went so far as to telephone Paul Belcher, the head of the California Province of the Society of Jesus and Greg's immediate superior, to request that he be transferred out of Los Angeles altogether.

Greg admits that the notion of bucking authority is not new to the Jesuits in general or to him in particular. When he first came to Dolores Mission, the gangs had yet to come to full force, and the controversy of the day was undocumented immigrants. In 1987, Greg followed the example of a sanctuary movement leader, Luis Olivares, and declared Dolores Mission the second official sanctuary in the Los Angeles archdiocese. Video clips from local television news reports of that period show Greg holding impassioned press conferences and leading crowds of demonstrators to chain themselves to the INS office fence.

At that point, Father Greg ran afoul of then-Los Angeles Archbishop Roger Mahony. Angered that the Jesuits were going against the stated policy of the archdiocese, Mahony demanded that Olivares, Greg, and Mike Kennedy—a third Jesuit publicly involved in the sanctuary controversy—cooperate fully with the INS. All three refused. "When laws trample rights, they cannot be obeyed," stated the priests in an op-ed piece. "The Gospel would have us do no other."

Greg's position on street gangs is at least as controversial as his sanctuary stance. However, he is by no means the only person working with gangs who characterizes law enforcement's approach as ineffective.

Mary Ridgway and John Tuchek are the two officers in the L.A. Country Probation Department who deal with arrested juveniles from Pico Gardens and Aliso Village. "There is the illusion," Tuchek tells me, "that we are rehabilitating these kids. And I'm here to tell you that the truth is we aren't even *trying* to rehabilitate them. We used to. But that doesn't happen down here anymore. That's why what Father Greg is doing is so important. He's their only resource."

Ridgway puts it another way. "At best we can only deal with a fraction of the kids for a very short period of time, while he's there for all of them, all of the time. Father Greg and I are, in many ways, coming from a different point of view philosophically. There are kids that I think should be locked up that he is reluctant to give up on, like a kid we both know who fortunately now is in Soledad. He was trouble every minute he was out on the streets. But, see," she smiles, "Father Greg loves everybody. In all my years in probation I've only met maybe two people who have his courage. He's the kind of person we all wish we could be."

———

The more I am around Greg, the more I see that at times his gang strategy brings him into a gray area where the law is concerned. This is particularly well illustrated by the story he tells me of Gustavo Villareal, known on the street as Happy.

Happy is a good-looking, six-foot seventeen-year-old with broad shoulders, a chiseled Aztec profile, and an expression that covers his distress with amusement. Happy and his younger brother Carlos—Little Happy—are both members of TMC. They have been living by their wits since Happy, then sixteen, broke Carlos, then fourteen, out of a foster home.

Both brothers are famous for their breakouts. A couple years ago, Little Happy led a notorious escape from L.A.'s Juvenile Hall in which four inmates managed to decamp through a window.

The escape occurred on Greg's day off. He had returned to his office to pick up some mail when he heard a sotto voce "Hey, G!" Greg looked up to see the four escapees in full Juvenile Hall incarceration regalia waving cheerily at him from outside the back window that faces on the alley behind the church.

Greg talked the kids into turning themselves in, and the police were none the wiser about the priest's involvement. But Happy's escape was a different story.

Happy had been picked up for possession of a gun and, according to him, beaten by the police while handcuffed. After being booked at Hollenbeck, Happy was taken to Eastlake Juvenile Hall. However, when Eastlake officials noticed that the arrestee was injured they refused to admit him, demanding instead that he be taken to USC County General Hospital. At the hospital, Happy was being readied for an X ray when he asked to use the bathroom, from which he quickly escaped through a window, running barefoot across enemy territories, his hospital gown flapping in the breeze.

The police were enraged at the escape and a vendetta was launched. As the story goes, cops began beating up kids from TMC on a systematic basis. According to Greg, the spoken and unspoken message was, "Until Happy turns himself in, this is what you can expect from us every night."

"I had kids come into my office who could barely walk, they'd been beaten up so badly," says Greg. The police reputedly even went over to the East L.A. Dukes, TMC's bitterest enemy, and said, "We'll give you a freebie. If you get Happy you can do anything you want and we'll look the other way."

"Can we kill him?" one kid asked. According to the kid, the cop thought long moment before deciding, "No, you can't kill him."

The police nearly caught their fugitive when they had stopped a car with four gang members in it. An officer recognized one of them as Happy. Happy sprang from the car and ran before the police could grab him. The police arrested the other three. In questioning the arrestees, the police took one of them aside, a diminutive kid named Chava.

"We know Father Greg is protecting Happy," said the officer. "We know that he's living at the church."

Greg says he would not have gone so far as to allow Happy to live at the church. But, Happy *was* calling Greg every day and coming to Greg's office to talk nearly as often.

"Here's the thing," Greg explains after telling me the Happy story. "My job is to try to talk a kid on the run into turning himself in. I would tell Happy, 'Here's your chance to be in control. To be in charge. Otherwise you will lose control and they will catch you.' What my job is *not*," he says emphatically, "is to call up the police and say, 'Here he is. Come and get him.'"

Eventually, the police did get Happy. He was arrested and again beaten, Happy says. Records indicate that he was again taken to the hospital then on to East Lake. This time he did not escape.

Cisco has been job hunting for the four weeks since the wardrobe outing, but now he is sitting in Greg's office, and he looks terrible. His lips and jaw are bruised and swollen. His hands are cut up, and an incisor on the lower left side of his jaw is broken. He has just returned from the dentist. Greg will pay the dental bills, which may be close to a thousand dollars.

It happened two nights ago, Cisco tells me, when he was stopped by two uniformed police officers. He was doing nothing in particular—just hanging out with the homies—when the officers ordered him up against a car with his hand over his head. "Then they pushed me down on my knees," he says. Cisco responded with a four-letter suggestion. At that point, according to Cisco, one of the cops hit him in the mouth with a billy club. Then, he says, the cops made him lie down spread-eagled and stepped on his hands. Finally the police let him go without an arrest.

Greg is infuriated at the incident—particularly in light of the community meeting. "I'm telling you," he says, "if the police keep using this approach with gang members, I say, 'Congratulations! You're going to create so much heat out here that, Welcome to the Watts riots one more time!' And that will happen. Treat kids like human beings and they'll behave like human beings. Befriend the community and you have everything to gain. But pit yourself against the community and hang on! Because it's going to be Mr. Toad's wild ride!"

Two weeks after Cisco's trip to the dentist, video images of LAPD officers beating Rodney King dance repeatedly across TV screens around the world. The resulting firestorm of public opinion accomplishes what the mothers could not: There is a precipitous drop in aggressive behavior on the part of Hollenbeck police officers.

However, simultaneous to the cool-down from law enforcement, the Pico Aliso gangs begin to turn up the heat. "Things have been awful around here," Father Greg says one Monday morning, more depressed than I've previously seen him. It seems that Snowman, a Crip, was killed on Thursday night as a payback for Shy Boy, a Primera Flats kid, who was shot by a Crip over a year ago. "That's how the game works," says Greg grimly. The night after Snowman was killed, two Latinos, one a transient, the other a basehead, were killed. No one is sure if these killings were gang related. Moreover, Crips and Al Capone, gangs that have traditionally gotten along, have had two fights in less than forty-eight hours.

The bad news doesn't stop there. At 8:00 P.M. on Saturday night, a kid from the Clarence Street Locos is headed down Gless to buy a beer when a Cuatro Flats kid approaches him. Words are exchanged. Immediately each boy marches off to find his homies. In seconds, both gangs appear from around corners like magic rabbits and begin mad-dogging and dissing each other. A kid named Toker from Cuatro hits Cowboy from Clarence, and someone yells, "It's on!" War has been declared.

Suddenly, eighty gang members are blocking the intersection. Fists are flying, heads are bashed, ghetto blasters are swinging. All the while voices scream, "It's on! It's on!"

It is then that Father Greg shows up, almost by chance. His has just dropped a kid off at home when he sees traffic backed up, pulls over, and races to investigate. The situation becomes surreal. Into a tangle of eighty brawling gangsters runs Greg, grabbing arms and shrieking every four-letter word he can think of. At his screamed orders, the Clarence group backs up. Gradually, the Cuatro group stops swinging and halts its advance. At the edge of the action, kids on bikes still circle, shotguns bulging underneath their Pendleton shirts.

Finally, Greg is able to herd the Clarence kids back down Gless; Cuatro moves off, dispersing into the neighborhood.

Afterward, Greg is walking alongside Clavo, one of another set of identical twins who have a lot of juice with the Clarence Street Locos. "You *yelled* at us, G," says Clavo, shaking his head in genuine shock. "You used the *'F' word!*"

"In the moment," Greg says later, "I'll do any damn thing that works."

Although the community is unnerved by the massive gang brawl, Greg seems unperturbed, at least on the surface. When I first met him, he was operating from the conviction that eventually he would make peace in the barrio. He seemed sure that if he could create the right combination of unconditional love, plus jobs and decent schooling, then peace could spread in a kind of tonal resonance from gang to gang. "An explosion of peace" was how he phrased it. And yet, for all Boyle's love, for all his commitment, for all his empowerment of the community, aside from a few respites, the peace never quite materialized, and the tide of violence in the city as a whole rose unabated. Looking back, it seems clear that the violent period ushered in by the Crip death and the megabrawl marked a shift in the tenor of Greg's gang ministry that was to ultimately culminate in a crisis of purpose for the priest.

Yet for now, Greg is still convinced that love and jobs are the answer. The only problem is that jobs for gang members are all but impossible to come by.

———

It's raining. Four CSL homies—Dreamer, Spanky, Wizard, and Ghost—are hanging out in Greg's office as he opens mail and does paperwork.

Ghost, a slim, handsome kid with long, fringed eyelashes and a heartbreaker's smile, rubs Greg's forehead with the palm of his hand as Greg unsuccessfully bats him away. "I'm rubbing your bumper for luck, G!" says Ghost, moving in for another rub.

"Hey, G!" interrupts Spanky. "How come you're in such a good mood?" Turning to Wizard, "Have you ever noticed that whenever G is in a good mood it rains?" Spanky pauses, possessed of a new thought. "Hey, you think maybe G is actually Mother Nature in disguise? That means the drought is his fault, right? You think the drought is your fault, G?"

Greg looks up at Spanky. "Here's a letter from a couple who want to adopt a child," he says, deadpan. "What do you think, Spanky? You think it's right for you?"

"Only if the *madre* is *proper*," sniffs Spanky. Meanwhile, the imagined scene of an unsuspecting young couple being introduced to their new "child"—a six-foot, two-hundred-pound tattooed homie named Spanky—throws the rest of the room into spasms of hilarity.

Spanky is discouraged about his job prospects. He has been answering want ads for weeks to no avail. "You go in there and fill out an application. Then they say they'll call you, but you can tell they're looking at your tattoos and they're not gonna, you know." It's like, when you leave, you see your application flying out the window, made into a paper airplane."

Nonetheless, Spanky has heard applications are being taken at the local post office on 1st Street. "C'mon, let's go," he says to Wizard.

Wizard, a normally quick-witted, jovial kid who has performed the feat of finding an entire set of gangster clothes in his favorite color (green), shakes his head. "Nah," he says, "they won't hire us."

"C'mon, homes," Spanky persists. "Let's just try it. Let's go!" He attempts to drag Wizard. "C'mon, homes!" But Wizard remains immovable. Finally, Spanky sits back down with a sigh. No one goes to the post office this day.

After the homies vacate his office, Father Greg stares dolefully at his checkbook. "Right now I have a hundred dollars in the bank. And Friday I have to pay the kids who work for me." He looks up. "But, you know, it's weird. Somehow the money always shows up. It usually happens on Thursday, my day off. They'll be no money in the bank on Wednesday, and then I'll come in on Friday and there'll be a couple of checks on my desk. Checks coming from nowhere when they *had* to come—that's happened at least fifty times since I first came here." Greg pauses. "It's not like I think it comes from God. My spirituality doesn't really take that form. But I do feel that if the work is meant to be done, somehow there'll be a way."

"Now all I have to do is find one hundred and fifty thousand dollars to give kids jobs this summer," he says. "Invariably, the violence in the neighborhood decreases in direct proportion to how many kids are working at any given time."

With the Jobs for a Future program, Greg usually has three or four construction and maintenance crews working on church projects. In addition, he is on the phone daily to local businesses asking them to hire homies. "We will pay their salaries," he tells the potential employers. "All you have to do is give them a place to work." Greg adds, "Of course, it would be great if the employers would pay the salaries." Unfortunately, that rarely happens.

"The myth about gang members and jobs," says Greg, "is how are you gonna keep 'em down on the farm when they're making money hand over fist selling drugs? The implication being that they will never want to accept an honest job. Well, I have kids stop me on the street every single day of the week asking for jobs. And a lot of times I know these kids are slanging, which is the street term for selling crack cocaine. I always say, 'If I get you a job it means no more slanging.' And I've never once said that to a kid who didn't jump at the chance to do an honest day's work instead of selling drugs."

Cisco has his own explanation for this phenomenon: "When you sell drugs, that's easy money," he says. "But when you've done a hard day's work for your money, it's different. You come home and you're tired, and the next day you feel it in your muscles. You know you've *earned* that money. So you feel good about yourself. Easy money doesn't make you feel good about yourself."

Four days later it is Saint Patrick's Day, a generally uneventful Sunday until Spanky approaches Greg, his clothes and hands covered with paint. "Oh, I've been doing some painting at Rascal's house," he says in answer to Greg's questioning look. Then he screws his face into a grimace. "You know, G," he says. "I'm not going to look for a job anymore."

Greg's expression darkens. "Why not?" he asks.

"I'm just not going to," replies Spanky. "No more job hunting."

Greg looks truly distressed by this news. "What are you talking about?" he begins.

"Nope. I'm not looking for a job anymore," is all Spanky will say.

Greg throws up his hands. "What the hell am I supposed to do? Support you for the rest of your life?"

Finally, Spanky's face breaks into a gigantic grin. "I'm not going to look for a job anymore BECAUSE I FOUND A JOB, G!!!!" he shouts. "I'm a painter! I'm painting *stereo speakers!*"

The rest of the day, Greg cannot restrain himself. He repeatedly tells Spanky how proud he is. Spanky tries to stay cool, but his happiness is obvious and irrepressible.

That night, Greg finishes his bicycle rounds through the projects early; things are quiet and he grows contemplative. "You know," he says leaning back in his chair, allowing himself a rare moment of relaxation, "with these kids, all you can do is take one day at a time. A lot of days it's two steps forward and four steps back. Then on days like today, it's like the line in Tennessee Williams' play *A Streetcar Named Desire:* 'Sometimes there's God so quickly.' Then it's joy upon joy, grace upon grace."

Then he lets slip a secret of which only a few of the community women and none of the homeboys are aware: On July 31, 1992—eighteen months from now—Greg is scheduled to leave Dolores Mission.

A Jesuit pastor is normally given six years in one place—no more. The goal is detachment—it should be the *work*, not the *person*, on which redemption depends. Next summer, Father Greg's six years will have elapsed. He is then expected to spend the next twelve months in prayer, study, and renewal before he takes his final vows. (Jesuits wait until a man hits his middle years before final vows are offered.) "After that," Greg says of his sabbatical, "I'll probably be able to come back here in some capacity, maybe as director of the school." But even this is not a sure thing.

When I ask what effect his departure will have on the homeboys, Boyle is quick to be reassuring. "It'll be fine. A lot of the structures are in place now: the school, the Comite Pro Paz, the Jobs for a Future program. I'll have more in place before I leave. I am by no means irreplaceable at Dolores Mission."

Maybe. Maybe not. A look into the faces of the gang members who love Greg as they love no one else in the world suggests that the implications of his eventual exit are more drastic than the priest can presently bear to admit.

Cisco

My name is Javier Vidal and they call me Cisco. I started gang banging when I was eleven, that's when I got jumped in to TMC. When I got jumped in there was seven people hitting me and I was small. I broke two of my homeboys' noses and a couple of their teeth. But they couldn't take me down.

I've been shot six times. I put in my share. Now I've been trying to stay out of it. I had a good talk with my mom and with Father Greg and I decided I ain't gonna mess around no more. I made the decision a few months ago, when they shot one of my friends, Tiger, from my neighborhood. They shot him in the back but he lived an' everything. And the homies said, "We're going to go and do something. You want to go?" And I said, "Nah, I don' wanna do it." They said, "What? Are you scared now?" An' I said, "I don't gang bang no more, man. It ain't for me no more." And one of them said, "Is that right? Well, I'm ordering you." And I said, "If you wanna do it. That's you. I already done my share while you were in prison. So don't tell me nothing." And he looked at me and he said, "All right." And everybody else said, "*Firme.*" And they shook my hand, and that was that.

That's what I like about myself: If I want to do something, and I know it's bad, then I won't do it. Like a lot of times, my friends are going to do something and I know they're going to get in trouble, I just go to the church instead. I help Father Greg. Or I just kick back and watch TV.

I used to get money selling drugs but I don't like that money. When I work for real for the money, I get all happy. It's the same for everybody that works for Father Greg right now. You talk to them, and they'll tell you, "I'm glad I'm not slanging right now." When you're working, you'll be sweating and breaking your back. You'll be tired at the end of the day. All you want to do is have a couple beers and go to sleep. When you're slanging you want to stay up all night, sleep during the day. And all you got is dirty money, so you don't care how you throw it away.

I'm looking for a job right now. That's what I need the most, a good job. The problem is how I look. The shirt and pair of pants that Father Greg got for me is already old. I wore it all out. Now I just got gangster clothes left.

I'll tell you a story. About two weeks ago we were all at a group meeting for TMC, kicking back. And some of the homies said, "Okay. Who's going to pitch in to buy guns?" And I said, "I ain't gang banging no more so I can't do it." And they said, "That's okay. You're cool." And I looked over at the three of my homeboys who were working for G-Dog. And one of them said, "I ain't going to put in money either. This is the money I earned hard. I ain't pitching in. None of us are. We made a promise to somebody." And the rest of the homies said, "All right."

They got $900 from everybody else who was there. And they bought three Uzis together with clips that hold about 250 bullets. When they got them we were all at a party. I got to say, they looked nice, Uzis brand new in the box. People think gang members only buy stolen guns. But you'd be surprised what kind of people sell 'em to us.

Father Greg has that little something that touches everybody. Everybody like falls in love with him. Like if he wasn't a priest, all kind'a ladies'd fall in love with 'im. I always tease 'im. When I'm with my lady and I kiss her I say, "See, you can't do this." And he says, "I betcha I could." I try to pay G back by just helping him out around the church. Last time he tried to pay me I just left the bill in his hand and ran away. I wouldn't take the money.

Right now, I'd like to live somewhere where it was safe. Where there were no gangs. I'd want to take my whole family with me. Then we could have a good life. We had a bad life where we were living when we were growing up. We lived in a dangerous hotel so my mom got a lock on the door on the outside when she went to work. She'd lock us in so then, when people would come around, they'd see the lock on the outside and they'd think nobody was home. So they wouldn't mess with us. We'd have on the TV real low all day and just stay in there by ourselves.

After a while we moved to the projects and they tore down that hotel where we used to live because they had too many murders there. When I was about five, my sister and I witnessed a couple of the murders. We saw this guy run up the stairs after another guy. And then we heard, BOOM! We went up, and the guy had fell. And we heard him making this noise, like "A-a-a-a-a-ahhhh! A-a-a-aaaa-ahhh!" He had all this blood all over him. I thought it was just catsup but my sister told me different. Another time, there was this one guy who hit this other guy with this big machete like they use in the jungle. And he hit him right in the chest. And that man had his heart in his hand. And he ran downstairs to the manager's office. And he fell right there.

I kept seeing that one with the machete afterward in my head. We also seen when the police killed a man who was trying to hold up a store. I think he was on some kind of drugs. We seen when they hit 'em in the head. We seen him flip backward. My sister and I were hanging out the window watching. I started laughing. I said to my sister, "Look, he couldn't flip right." All these things happened when I was five or six. I don't think it was really good for me. I know that affected me. My sister too. I think all that early stuff got to both of our brains.

When I was little I would think, I don't care no more. I've seen a lot of things. If people could do it, I could do it too. It's that easy. I could just stab somebody. And I started walking around with a knife. In those days, they had switchblades. I got some man to buy it for me from a store, 'cause they wouldn't sell it to me.

I would walk up to other kids and act like I was going to stab 'em. But I knew I wouldn't stab 'em. I knew I didn't have the heart. I was just trying to look all bad.

The last time I seen my dad, he hit my mom and she fell and hit her head on a table. He hit her because he wanted to go to a bar and get drunk and she didn't want him to go an' she was crying. He used to drink all the time and hit her all the time. I seen her on the floor, fainted. So I looked at my dad, like mad-dogging him, looking at him all bad. And he looked at me and said, "What'cho looking at?!" And . . . BAM! He hit me. And I ran to my mom and put her head on my lap and started crying. And when my mom woke up we moved out that same day. We only moved about two blocks away 'cause that's where we could find a place. That's another reason my mom never used to let us out, 'cause she was afraid my dad would be walking around and would see us and know where we were. And then finally we moved over here to the projects. Now my mom has my stepdad. He's a good man.

A while ago, my little brother was starting to want to gang bang. And I took him in my room and I socked him and I said, "If you want to gang bang, I'll shoot you myself."

My mom wanted to put him in jail. And I said, "Nah. Don't do that." Because that's what really messed me up. When I was on probation, my mom kept putting me in Juvenile Hall over and over again. That would just make me madder, and I would mess up more. I told my mom, "Let me talk to him." Then I took him to eat at McDonald's and I said, "Lookit, you want to be like me? You want to get shot six times? You want to be in the hospital for a week without eating? You want to be in and out of jail like me?" He said, "No." I said, "Are you sure? Don't make the same mistake as I did. What I did was stupidness." He said, "So you're stupid?" I said, "Yeah. But don't take advantage of it by calling me names. I'm still bigger than you." And he said, "All right." And he hugged me and gave me a little kiss on my cheek. I had tears in my eyes after that.

I don't want nothing bad ever to happen to my brother. The saddest thing in my life is that so many of my friends have passed away.

The hardest one was Shotgun, rest-in-peace. He got killed on a Friday night and Sunday night I went to jail for trying to get revenge for him, so I couldn't go to see him get buried. That was hard. I was real close to him. Me, him, Smoky rest-in-peace, Popeye rest-in-peace, Smiley rest-in-peace—we all used to be together a lot. We used to go cruising everywhere. Now I'm the only one of 'em that's still alive. All the rest of 'em are dead.

With Shotgun, they said it was a set-up. Everybody was in the alley where CSL kicks it. Shotgun was from Clarence. Then about ten at night some girls came in and set him up. They pretended like they wanted to be with him. But then these guys came and shot him from the hill above by the freeway. They had a .38 and a shotgun. We couldn't shoot back, 'cause Shotgun was the only one who knew where he had put the guns, so we couldn't get them. Finally Toker said he knew where he put them. By that time Shotgun was already hit. I went over to Shotgun, and I was going to pick him up. I leaned over. I didn't feel no air or nothing coming out of his mouth. I looked and I went. "Nah. He ain't dead!"

Right then the cops came, so I ran. But then I came back to see where everybody was, and I saw they had put a sheet over him. So I knew he was dead. The cops handcuffed me and some other of the homies. And took me in for questioning. I said, "You don't need to handcuff me just to question me." And they said, "We'll do whatever we want." And that made me mad so I started cussing them out. They started hitting me and slamming me around in the little questioning room. It happens all the time. They treat us like we're nothing.

When we had a car wash for Shotgun's mom we made about $800. Some guys from another gang came down and gave us another $300, 'cause they said they were sorry that our homeboy had passed away. We always used to be friends with that gang, but now we don't get along. I don't know why.

Popeye got shot when we were all just going to go cruising. We stopped off at a gas station and got into a big fight with some East L.A.s. One of them got the keys to his car and opened the trunk and got a gun out and shot Popeye. We thought he just got knocked out an' we took him straight to the hospital. When the doctor said he was dead, I started running from the hospital. My friends said for me to get in the car but I wouldn't. I just started running even though the hospital was in enemy territory. Some of them started shooting at me and I didn't bother. My mind just flipped. I wasn't the same person. I couldn't take it.

My homeboy, Smoky, died when I was holding him. When he got shot, I ran over and picked him up. He was bleeding from his nose. And I said, "What's up, Smoky?" And he just looked at me and said, "Later on." And he died right when I was holding him.

That night I couldn't go to sleep or nothing. I went to sleep for half an hour and I kept dreaming how it happened all over again. I couldn't sleep the next night either so I tried to sleep during the day. And it was the same thing—that dream over and over.

My homegirl Smiley was with me the first time I got shot. It was right in front of the church. I went down, and she thought I was dead. When I woke up the first thing I heard was Smiley saying," Oh, no! Not another one!" Because Smoky had been killed about four days before.

Two nights before Smiley passed away, she had a dream of a dove. In that dream, she walked into the church and she saw a baby's coffin. But she couldn't see the baby's face. Then she walked closer and the box opened up and a dove flew out. It flew around the church then it landed on her. She told me and Father Greg about the dream. And Father Greg asked her, "How did you feel?" She said, "Real peaceful." Father Greg said it was the sign of peace. But I thought, "Nah. This means something else."

Then two nights later, in the night, I woke up at about four in the morning, all scared. I couldn't go to sleep the rest of the night. And then when I came out in the morning, I heard they shot Smiley in the head. My heart just went down into my stomach. And I started going crazy. I hit the van in front of the house with my fist, and I broke the window.

I knew they took her to Martin Luther King Hospital, so I went there. Father Greg was there when I got there. I looked at her in the hospital, and the person had her body but not her face. She had a really nice face. It was like a baby face. The face was all swollen and black and blue. But then I looked at the chart and I saw it was her. Father Greg held on to my hand, and I had to squeeze it real hard 'cause tears were coming into my eyes.

The nurse told us that Smiley couldn't see us or talk to us but she could hear us. I went down to her real close and I said, "Rosie, this is Cisco. I love you no matter what. You're still in my heart." And when I said that, her hand moved a little bit. I was holding her hand and it felt like she was trying to squeeze my hand but she couldn't. And then I got up again, and I had to squeeze Father Greg's hand real hard again.

Later me and some other of the homies went to the cafeteria in the hospital where her mom and her aunt were. And they started telling us, "This happened because she was hanging around you bums." And I felt like saying, "You know what? You guys were never there for her." They were never there for Smiley. We were the only family she had. The mom was into drugs and never paid any attention to her.

At the wake they wouldn't let us put anything in the coffin. See what we do is put, like, gold chains and crosses into the box. And I had these two gold chains that Smiley had always wanted. And I wanted to put them in with her. But they wouldn't let me. And they wouldn't let us take pictures at the wake.

I told Father Greg I didn't like how they were handling the wake. He said he didn't either. Her family was really disrespectful of her friends who really loved her too.

We got her two big ol' wreaths of flowers with a ribbon on them that said, "To Rosie from your homegirls and homeboys." The day of the burial, Father Greg opened up the church early and let me take pictures. I look at them about every other day. I dream about them all. Shotgun, Popeye, Smoky, and Smiley. I mostly dream that we're all together. When I dream about them I get all happy.

It ain't the same without them. They used to make me laugh. I go every weekend to the cemetery and talk to them. I ask them how they're feeling. What's happening up there. I tell them what's going on in the projects. And I tell them we love them. That they're never going to leave us. That they're still with us. Sometimes I feel better, because I feel like they hear me.

People don't know what it's like to be us down here. We're not like people think. We got feelings. We got love. If I could say one thing to people, it would be, "Give us a chance. Don't turn your backs on us. People make us sound real bad. But we ain't as bad as we sound. We're humans too, just like you. Just give us a chance. We won't let you down."

Chapter 3

Although Spanky and Cisco were windows into the family background that makes a young man gravitate toward the gangs, I had yet to see close up the sequence of events that leads a kid to violence—until I met Dreamer.

Dreamer is one of the regulars in and around Father Greg's office. He is sixteen, has the huge, dark eyes of a yearling deer and a smile that unfolds fast, wide, and bright. His hair is cut Marine short, shaved by Greg with the No. 4 attachment of the church's Sears-bought clippers. A hint of brown velvet sprouts on his upper lip. When he is happy, Dreamer's face is transformed into that of a deliciously mischievous child. In repose, his expression suggests someone waiting patiently for punishment. At all times, his shoulders slump more than is natural.

Dreamer is a Clarence Street Loco. But he is a "new booty," just courted in around six months ago. So far his gang-banging has been confined to compulsive tagging. Walk in any direction from Dolores Mission and you soon see the spray-painted message "CSL *soy* Dreamer."

Tonight Dreamer sits in one of the worn chairs in Greg's office with his head in his hands. "Why can't I live here?" he asks, his voice high and teary. "Why can't I just live here, G?"

This is the predictable third act of a drama that gets played out with increasing frequency between Greg and Dreamer. The drama usually starts around 10:00 P.M. Greg drives Dreamer home to the small, perpetually darkened house where he lives with his mother, his father, and four younger brothers and sisters. Before driving away, Greg always watches Dreamer go up the walk, knock on the door, and be let in. On some nights, that's the end of the story. Greg goes back to the office to finish up work at his desk. Then, after making one last round of the projects, he heads home at midnight. Often the phone is already ringing before Greg can finish unlocking his office door. It's Dreamer calling from a phone booth. His father has thrown him out of the house again.

On these nights, Greg fetches Dreamer from whatever street corner he is on and brings him back to be bedded down for the night on the floor of the church office.

"His father hates him," says Greg. "He says that to him fairly regularly, along with 'Why don't you just never come back.'" Greg says the mom is *blandita*. Passive. Other than much hand-wringing, she stands by and lets the abuse continue.

"With a lot of these kids, not going home is the most appropriate action to take," says Greg. "To go home would be self-destructive. If they had decent families it would be easier to say, 'Please stay off the street. Please do what your mom says. Please be home by nine.' That's why this mess is so complex. As bad a solution as joining a gang is, for a lot of these kids it's an attempt to cope, an attempt to save themselves."

Since last summer, Dreamer has been pestering Greg for a job. Finally, the priest has talked a local self-storage company into hiring two homies, salaries courtesy of Dolores Mission. Dreamer and Silent, a kid from TMC, get the call.

The timing is fortuitous. Dreamer's father has just gone to visit family in Mexico. With the weight of his dad's anger briefly lifted, Dreamer is a new person. Instead of partying with the homies until all hours, he has started asking Greg to drive him home every afternoon before dark. He has all but stopped tagging, and has started showing up at Dolores Mission School every day. Since Dreamer has a history of tagging and truancy, these are hopeful signs.

The day before Dreamer and Silent are to start work, Greg drives them to meet their new boss, the manager of the storage company, a matter-of-fact woman named Yolanda. The boys listen politely while she explains their duties—gofering and general cleanup. Afterward Greg takes the two kids to McDonald's to celebrate.

"We won't let you down, G," says Dreamer.

One week later, events derail Dreamer's promise. On the first Sunday in April, Greg is driving toward the church from East L.A. Dukes territory. He sees a group of five Clarence kids, Spanky and Dreamer among them, running in Pecan Park near the baseball diamond. It is not a playful run. Dreamer has a long stick under his jacket as if he's packing a shotgun. On instinct, Greg turns to look behind him and sees a group of East L.A. Dukes near home plate, also running. The Dukes are sworn enemies of the Clarence Street Locos.

Greg swerves his car to a halt on the wrong side of the street and yells to the Clarence kids to get the blankety-blank out of there. Amazingly, they do. As he raises his hand to open his door, there is a terrifying BOOM-BOOM-BOOM-BOOM-BOOM. Just behind Greg's head, the car's rear window on the driver's side shatters. When the shooting stops, Greg gets out to confront the Dukes. They disappear fast as lightning.

Back at the church, together with a keyed-up crowd of onlookers, Greg surveys the damage to his car. Glass shards are spread like icicles across the front and back car seats. There is a bullet lodged at the very edge of the far right side of the metal frame between the front and rear driver's side windows. Greg gazes wordlessly at the bullet.

"*Mira! Mira!*" shouts one of the smaller of the boys who crowd around the car, craning their necks to see. "Look how close it is!" It is very close indeed. Had the shot been an inch further to the right, the bullet would have entered Greg's head right about the base of his brain.

Later he drives the car back into Dukes territory. This time he finds them. At his arrival they blink and wince. "Did you want to fucking kill me! Is that what the idea was?" he yells, hoping to shock them into a new state of consciousness. "I prayed you would hit me so then maybe it would end! I'd be willing to die to end this!" The kids stare at Greg, then at the missing car window and the bullet holes. They murmur frantic, ineffectual apologies. Then one boy looks up just in time to see two gangsters on the hill above them—East Coast Crips. An instant later the noise comes again: BOOM-BOOM-BOOM-BOOM-BOOM-BOOM. Everyone dives under Greg's car as the sky rains bullets. Miraculously, no one is hit. Instead, a bullet punctures the car's right rear tire, just missing the gas tank, finally coming to rest inside the trunk.

The next day, Greg wakes up with no obvious ill effects from the near misses except for a piercing headache. The pain is localized just behind his ear, where his neck meets his skull, about where the door-frame bullet would have hit if it had taken a slightly different course.

As usual, violence begets violence. On Monday morning, when Father Greg arrives at the church, he gets a call from Yolanda, the manager of the storage facility where Dreamer and Silent are working. She is going to have to fire Dreamer, she says. It seems that Friday, he not only crashed the facility's motorized cart but, when he was supposed to remove graffiti from a wall, he replaced it with new inscriptions: CSL *soy* Dreamer.

It does not strike Greg as entirely coincidental that Dreamer's father returned from Mexico a few hours before Dreamer began this orgy of acting out. Nor does it help matters that the mood of the Clarence homies in general is restless. Two Clarence Street homeboys have been killed by Dukes in the past two years, and Clarence has not as yet retaliated. After yesterday's shooting they will probably begin to feel intolerably pressed. And the most pressure is likely to fall on the *little heads*, the younger gang members like Dreamer who have yet to prove themselves.

Greg takes Dreamer to lunch to break the bad news about the job. First he gives him a stern lecture about responsibility and consequences. Then he turns good cop and assures Dreamer that losing the job is not the end of the world. "You know I'll never give up on you," says Greg, followed by a string of other words of encouragement and caring. "*Te quiero mucho,*" he says finally. "*Como si fueras mi hijo,*" I love you as if you were my son. At this Dreamer starts to cry. Once started, he cries for a long while.

At the end of the day Dreamer's actions are swinging farther out of control; he gets into a fight with one of his own homies. When Greg sees him again, he is covered in blood. "It's nothin'," he mumbles.

Then the next afternoon, Father Tom sees Dreamer deep in Dukes territory with a can of spray paint; he is crossing out the Dukes graffiti and replacing it with his own. It is a dangerously provocative act, considering the events of the last two days. Father Tom demands that Dreamer hand over the spray can. Dreamer dances rebelliously away.

Almost simultaneously, Greg is driving down Third Street when he sees a black kid, an East Coast Crip, loitering near the alley. "That kid isn't where he should be," Greg remarks uneasily.

Two hours later, Dreamer is back in Clarence territory, on the pay phone, talking with his girlfriend, Monica. He sees L'il Diablo, sixteen, another new booty from Clarence, walking north toward First Street. Sensing something is up, he follows. All at once Dreamer sees what is up: L'il Diablo has a gun, a .22—recently acquired from the loitering Crip—and there is a group of Dukes gathered across the park. L'il Diablo raises the gun and fires one shot into the air. The Dukes scatter, running for Aliso Village. L'il Diablo drops his weapon and runs in the other direction.

At first Dreamer follows him. But then, on an impulse he cannot later adequately explain, Dreamer turns back and picks up the gun. He points it in the direction of the by now faraway Dukes and empties it. Most of the bullets fall harmlessly to the pavement. One bullet strays into an Aliso Village apartment where a six-year-old girl named Angelina is watching television with her mother. Angelina kicks up her small foot just in time for it to meet the bullet. Blood spurts, and her mother begins to scream.

Holding the empty gun, Dreamer stands on the sidewalk still as a statue for a long moment. Finally, he runs.

In short order the neighborhood is alive with rumor, and word of what has happened quickly reaches Greg. It is hours before he finds Dreamer, milling nervously with some other homies, a block from the church. Wordlessly, Dreamer climbs into Greg's car.

"I know what happened," Greg states flatly. "Did you do it?"

There is a silence. "Yeah," Dreamer says without meeting his gaze.

Greg informs him that he has hit a little girl. Dreamer is horrified. "A lot of people say," Greg tells him, "that in order to be a man you have to shoot a gun. But I'm telling you that isn't true. The truth is, in order to be a man you need to take responsibility for your actions. That means you need to turn yourself in."

Dreamer starts to protest. Then he is quiet. "Let's go, G," he says finally.

Inside Hollenbeck Police Station, two CRASH officers order Dreamer to spread his legs. As the officers briskly frisk him, he stands with his lips pursed, trying not to cry.

———

Greg sits at his desk, looking with irritation at the sheet of paper that was delivered by a marshal early this morning. He has been subpoenaed to testify against Dreamer.

It seems that after Greg left Dreamer at Hollenbeck, he was put in a room and left there. No one took his statement. No one questioned him. After waiting alone the whole night, defiance set in. And perhaps fear. By sun-up Dreamer no longer wanted to tell the police anything. After hours of belated pressure, Dreamer eventually did confess. But it is questionable if all the rules of Miranda were followed, so now his public defender is trying to get the confession thrown out as a Miranda violation.

"Of course nobody is read their rights out here," says Greg, tossing the summons on the desk. "Kids rarely even bother to complain about it."

The D.A.'s office needs something that will corroborate the now-tainted confession—hence the subpoena. This situation puts Greg in a unique bind. Since Greg drove Dreamer to turn himself in, the police know that odds are Dreamer first confessed to Greg. Of course, if Dreamer is willing to confess on the stand it will all be a moot point.

Yesterday Greg visited Dreamer at Juvenile Hall, hoping to bolster the kid's resolve. Greg told Dreamer how proud he was of him for doing the adult, responsible thing; that even the Dukes were impressed by the fact that he had turned himself in. TMC, Clarence, and the Dukes had been unusually vocal in their admiration for Dreamer's action. "That's *firme!*" they said.

Dreamer's mother and father also visited him yesterday at Eastlake. "We could have gotten you to Mexico," his dad told him, his voice scathing. "Can't you do anything right?"

Dreamer was withdrawn and confused by the time Greg got to him. "My father is always right," he said. "I've been trying to prove him wrong for so long. But I guess he's right."

"This is so discouraging," Greg says later. "It's so rare that a kid would have the guts to do something like this. And then to have the police blow it, and every adult tell him he's been a fool . . . And my experience with attorneys is that the issue for them has very little to do with right or wrong. The only goal is getting somebody off."

———

As the day for Dreamer's hearing approaches, Greg has another close call. Late at night, he is walking a young kid back to where his brother and friends had gathered at the southwest end of Aliso Village. He and the kid are just talking when the kid suddenly whispers, "Look out!" Greg turns around in time to see gangsters, guns ready, creeping along the bushes that fringe the Santa Ana freeway at the east edge of Aliso Village, headed toward a group of TMC homies. This time, seeing Greg, no one shoots.

"It was very similar to the day the Dukes shot," Greg says, "but that time I arrived a split second too late and the action had already been put into motion. This time I think I arrived just early enough to stop it." Yet the new shooting unsettles him.

"As I walked home I felt so weird," he says. "I kept saying to myself, 'I really think this is where my life will end. I'm going to die in this barrio.'"

He pauses, his eyes searching some interior distance. "But, you know, what should I do differently? Would I not have intervened that day between Clarence and East L.A. and just kept driving instead? I don't think that would be possible. So, what should I do differently?"

The other Jesuits at Dolores Mission, however fond they are of the gang members, keep an emotional distance from a situation that can be overwhelming and tragic on a daily basis. For Greg there is no distance, no film of protection. He cares for the gang members as if they were literally his own children. Certainly it is Greg's offer of unconditional love that is the source of his magic. But what happens if you give your heart to ten dozen kids, many of whom will die violently and young, the rest of whom are dying slow deaths of the spirit?

"Burnout is the cost, I think," Greg says quietly. "Because I'm so invested in each kid, tragedies and potential tragedies kind of get into my gut in a way that probably doesn't get into other folks." He laughs nervously. "A lot of it is the classical ministerial occupational hazard of co-dependency where you get too invested. Only it's kind of writ larger here, I think. And it's also parental. It's like, 'Oh my god, my kid hasn't come home yet and it's already midnight'—times a hundred."

The analogy of Greg-as-parent can lead to even riskier territory. If you ask most parents what they would die for, they reply, "My children." Greg grows uncharacteristically quiet when the question is posed to him. "I would die for these kids," he says finally. "I don't know how that would play itself out. But I don't think there would be any question. It's not a choice, you know," he says. "It just is."

"Sometimes my *confreres* tell me that I should relax, not worry so much," he continues. "But I think if I were to shut myself off in that way it would be at my own peril." He expels a long breath. "I'm in too deep. I care like crazy what happens to these kids. So, I struggle with perspective. And I hope for the best, you know? I sort of pray that there's not another death. Or if deaths are inevitable that there's some, I don't know, lead time. Because the deaths get more painful rather than less. You get more vulnerable and fragile, rather than less."

———

There have been sporadic shootings on the part of various gangs. Droopy, one of Greg's workers, was walking his girlfriend to school when a car full of gangsters drove by and shot at him. A bullet skimmed the top of his skull, parting his hair in a grotesque parody of Groucho Marx.

Droopy is from Cuatro and the shooters were possibly from Capone. Greg is also worried about a growing tension between Clarence and TMC. "It's like I see freight trains coming from opposite directions down a track," he says, "and I'm frantically trying to find the switch that will head off a collision."

Greg decides he needs to hire another TMC. "I'm going to get some key TMC kid who can work full time," he says, thinking aloud. He already has Green Eyes, a high-profile TMC. "But I need another." The idea is that when the crucial moment comes he can call in markers, pull the switch to keep the trains from crashing.

––––

Accounts of Father Greg's various close calls are being discussed throughout the community. The community mothers have held a meeting to discuss whether they should try to get Greg's Provincial to remove him for his own safety. Greg laughs at this, attempting to flick their worries away. "It's no more dangerous for me than for any other member of the community," he says to the mothers. But it isn't true and both the mothers and Greg know it.

"You'd have to be an idiot not to be scared," says probation officer Mary Ridgway of Greg's cavalier denials. "Look. After a certain time of night even I never turn off the ignition." Two months ago, she says, she was taking a late-night drive through the projects with another P.O. when she saw a gangster carrying a shotgun. She pulled the car to a stop, then became alarmed when the gangster swung the gun upward, raising it in a stalking motion. Still, she assumed he'd try to slip by the car unrecognized. He did not. He turned and shoved the gun in her face and growled, "East L.A. Dukes!"

"He said it in a real guttural voice," explains Ridgway, "which is exactly what they do before they blast you." Ridgway reached her hand out and pushed the kid's gun down. "Don't," she said.

The kid deliberated for a beat, then stalked off into the night.

"I'm required to have a gun and required to know how to shoot it," Ridgway says. "But I'm not allowed to carry one when I'm on duty. Just when I'm off duty." She shrugs. "It just shows you how stupid our department is. We get death threats all the time."

––––

On Sunday there is a respite from the tension as the church holds its semi-annual *kermesse* across the street in the school parking lot. The kermesse is an old-style Mexican village carnival complete with flimsily erected ring-toss and win-a-fish booths. The bingo game is a popular attraction, as are the multiple food concessions where parish women sell home-cooked *tacos de carne asada* and *aguas frescas*. Nearly everybody in the projects, Catholic or not, makes at least an appearance at the kermesse.

The highlight of the day is the greased pole event. Cash and prizes are strapped to the top of a fifteen-foot-high pole slathered in Crisco. The first person who makes it to the top of the pole claims the loot. Midway through the pole machinations, a mystery contestant shows up. It is Greg dressed in elaborate cholo regalia. He has borrowed a pair of Spanky's largest Dickie pants which he wears belted comically high with a rag hanging out of his pocket, and the darkest, meanest sunglasses he can find wrapping his eyes. Greg struggles elaborately with the pole, pratfalling clownlike over and over, as the crowd laughs and cheers with abandon.

It is often said that you can leave the projects but the projects will never leave you. The kermesse is an illustration of why this is so. Life may be dangerous and tragic in Pico Aliso, but it is also rich with myriad small-town revelries and the kind of intricately braided relationships between residents that makes day-to-day modern living less lonely. Neighbors know each other's business, and gossip is everpresent. Yet community members also care for and support each other here, pulling together when trouble arrives. Life in the other, more "desirable" areas of the city seems cold and isolating by comparison.

———

It is nine in the morning on the day of Dreamer's scheduled hearing at the Eastlake Juvenile Court Building. The benches outside the courtrooms are filled with parents and friends of kids who are up on charges, their voices ricocheting shrilly off the building's flat gray walls and ceilings. As Greg walks through the crowded hallway, he is hailed every ten feet or so by someone who knows him. Most of the people waiting are Latino and African American, and most appear to be working class or poorer. Virtually the only Anglos in evidence are attorneys or cops.

Dreamer is charged with a violation of California Penal Code Number 245, assault with a deadly weapon. If he is convicted he will likely face nine years in California Youth Authority, reemerging when he is twenty-five years old.

Although the shooting must have been seen by a dozen neighbors, only one eyewitness has come forward, a sixteen-year-old named David who is a cousin to the little girl Dreamer hit and was upstairs in the apartment at the time of the shooting. David is also a former member of the East L.A. Dukes, the gang for which Dreamer's bullet was intended. Although Greg says David is not actively gang-involved, it is an easy bet that Dreamer's attorney will use the gang connection to try to make him a less credible witness in the judge's eyes.

When David talked to Greg the day after the shooting, he said he hoped that Dreamer would not be arrested. "I think because he wanted to do him dirt himself," says Greg. But the combination of the fact that Dreamer turned himself in plus the simple passage of time has ameliorated David's position. Earlier this morning David stopped Greg outside the courtroom to spill out his misgivings. "I just don't want to see Dreamer do a lot of time," David said.

Other than David, the D.A.'s strongest prosecutorial card is Greg. But if Greg is asked to reveal anything Dreamer said to him about the shooting, he plans to invoke what is called "ministerial privilege."

The assistant district attorney who is handling the case is tall and intense, with a rumpled physical appearance. He fidgets as he tells Greg what he plans to ask him on the stand. At the very least, he says, he needs to get on record that Greg drove Dreamer to the police station. He is looking for a circumstantial way of suggesting that a confession took place.

Greg looks at the D.A. and lets a few beats pass before he replies. "You need to know," he says evenly, "that I'm not going to say anything that might help convict this kid."

After the D.A. leaves, Jorge Gonzales, a juvenile defense attorney friend of Greg's, is in the building for another case and wanders over to talk. Gonzales has looked up the statutes on ministerial privilege and tells Greg that his refusal to testify falls into a legal gray area that may or may not be covered. "I gotta tell you," Gonzales says, genially clapping Greg on the shoulder, "if you wanna push this, you may end up needing legal counsel of your own."

"Well, they can lock my ass up, but I'm not going to say a damn thing."

Gonzales tolls his eyes at Greg, who shrugs. "Three squares a day and time to read a novel," he says. "Doesn't sound too bad at all."

"I really want Dreamer to take responsibility for this," Greg tells me when Gonzales has moved on, "but I could never testify against him—or any other kid, for that matter. It would be a complete betrayal of trust. I always tell myself that the exception would be if I actually *saw* a kid shoot somebody. But sometimes I'm not even sure I would do it then.

"With Dreamer," he continues, "it's so infuriating because the police dropped the ball. For a kid to turn himself in is the hardest thing imaginable. Dreamer turned himself in. And the police blew it. Now they want me to jeopardize all my work to do their job, and I won't do it. There's a huge distinction between getting a kid to take responsibility for his actions, and me standing up there and saying, 'Yeah. He's the one who did it.' I don't do suppression. I do prevention and intervention. My goal is to get a kid to be responsible for his life, not to get one more kid off the street. And if they don't like my attitude, I don't particularly care."

Dreamer's public defender, a nattily dressed fellow named Brady Sullivan, makes his way over. Sullivan, who has yet to actually meet Dreamer, reels off a list of defense strategies. He has already succeeded in getting the assigned judge "recused," legal language meaning dumped from the case. Sullivan's logic is that this judge has read the tainted confession and thus cannot rule fairly even if the confession is thrown out. Sullivan is now working on getting the next judge recused for reasons that are unclear past the fact that Sullivan doesn't like him. "Nobody wants to present to that guy," explains Sullivan. "I'm papering him right now, even as we speak"—"papering" being more lawyer slang for filing a petition of prejudice.

"Why'd this kid do a stupid thing like turn himself in and confess anyway?" asks Sullivan after a pause in his recitation.

"Because," Greg replies, "it was the right thing to do."

Across the hallway, Angelina, the six-year-old girl whom Dreamer shot, has just returned from the ladies' room, accompanied by her mother. The two sit down alongside David and a neighbor woman who has come along for moral support. Angelina is dressed entirely in pink and clutches a stuffed bunny, also pink, which she alternately hugs, tosses in the air, then dangles along the floor by its ears. Her eyes are big and dark, her hair short-cropped and wavy, her disposition much sunnier than the circumstances would seem to warrant. Her left foot is in a cast, with a plastic apparatus strapped over the cast for purposes of walking. Her right foot sports a new white Reebok tennis shoe.

Angelina talks about her recent experiences in a practical little girl's voice. She says she wasn't scared when she went to the doctor. When asked if the shooting was scary, Angelina nods her head vigorously. "I was lucky I was sitting down," she says chirpily. "Because if I'd 'a stood up I'd be dead."

"I feel terrible about her," says Greg when he has moved back to his own side of the hallway. "But people have this thing where everything cancels everything else out. My heart goes out to this little girl and her mother. And my heart goes out to Dreamer. To me this is obvious. I don't get why people don't get it. One doesn't cancel out the other. It's not like you have a divided heart."

By 11:00 A.M. Public Defender Sullivan's "papering" of the second judge has been successful. The hearing is postponed until tomorrow, when it can be heard by a third judge. Everyone must go home.

On the way out of Eastlake Juvenile Court, Greg is stopped by a kid from a non-Pico Aliso gang. The kid is looking for a job and pleads for help in finding one, assuring Greg he's not banging any more, that he's tired of having to watch his back. Without warning the kid's expression changes. He looks Greg straight in the face. "We're all gonna die," he says.

"What?" asks Greg, not sure he had heard right.

"We're all gonna die, G," says the kid. "I just know it."

———

The hearing has been moved from Eastlake to a juvenile courtroom in Pasadena. All the witnesses are present, including two Hollenbeck police officers who are to take the stand for the D.A. Greg returns from getting coffee and sits two benches away from the cops, Officer del Rosario and Detective Castro. The cops give Greg a laser stare.

"What I don't understand is why he won't even preach against guns in the church," says del Rosario. Then, with disgust, "I can't stand that guy."

As the hearing gets under way, Dreamer's mother and father arrive and take seats in the back of the courtroom. The father is handsome and hard-faced. The mother is delicate, with an eager-to-please smile, nervous eyes and hair falling past her shoulders. Her long legs taper to doelike ankles that look like they might snap in a high wind. She wears high-heeled, strappy sandals to show off the ankles and a cotton dress that is chosen with the knowledge that she is a very pretty woman.

Dreamer sits in the chair to the left of Sullivan wearing the orange uniform that indicates he is in one of the high security sections of Eastlake Juvenile Hall, sections normally reserved for the most dangerous juvenile offenders. His hair is shaved so short it approaches cueball status.

David is first up for the prosecution. He says he saw Dreamer shoot four times. In the redirect, David says he didn't tell del Rosario, the first cop on the scene, the shooter's name because he was afraid of retaliation by the Clarence Street Locos. David also testifies that he knew Dreamer had been arrested, "because Father Greg told me."

This last admission is potentially troublesome for Greg. In getting on record that Greg told David that Dreamer had turned himself in, the D.A. is attempting to shoot holes in the priest's upcoming claim that his interactions with Dreamer the day of the shooting are protected by the sanctity of confession.

At the recess David is sober and shaken. "Dreamer looks so scared," he says. "In these things, nobody wins."

After lunch, a little purple tennis shoe, prominently pierced by a bullet hole, is admitted as Exhibit A. Angelina, the tennis shoe's owner, is belatedly excused as a witness. After the day-and-a-half spent pointlessly in court hallways, she is allowed to go home.

Finally Greg is called to the stand and sworn in. The prosecutor asks him if he had a conversation with the defendant, Eduardo Castro, on April ninth. Greg says he "won't answer any question with regard to this minor on that date."

The judge, who had seemed cordially bored by the proceedings up until now, jerks awake.

"Is that based on church doctrine?" he asks. "Or the advice of counsel?"

"I don't need counsel to tell me what I'm willing to say in this court," replies Greg.

The judge narrows his eyes slightly, his interest turning to irritation. He curtly informs Greg that a conversation not held in the confessional does not fall within the parameters of ministerial privilege. "I'm going to order you to answer counselor's questions," the judge says.

Greg goes flint-eyed. "I'm not going to—" he begins. At this juncture, Sullivan springs up and asks for a five-minute recess.

"Maybe I should have brought my toothbrush," Greg jokes glumly outside the courtroom. Sullivan emerges from the courtroom and tries to talk Greg into at least saying he was with Dreamer.

"Nope. I'm not going to do it."

"Then I think you're going to need counsel," says Sullivan, and returns to court.

Facing the actual possibility that he will be locked up, Greg's manner turns rebellious. "I want Dreamer to confess, for God's sake," he says in an adrenalized whisper, "but I feel no compunction to defend the fact that I won't do it for him! And if they want to find me in contempt . . ."

He is interrupted by the court translator, a short Latino in his mid-fifties, who shyly approaches. "I know who you are," says the translator as he grabs Greg's hand and pumps it up and down several times. "Thank you for standing up for my people."

Just then the door to the court opens again and Sullivan reemerges. "You're off the hook," he says. "I asked the prosecutor if he really wanted to be written up in the *L.A. Times* as the one who got L.A.'s best-known priest put in jail. He decided he didn't."

Greg thanks Sullivan for his intervention. "Now what I have to do," grins Sullivan with a nod in David's direction, "is deal with that scumbag witness."

Greg's jaw muscles twitch. "I think you should know that David is a terrific kid who's doing a very courageous thing by being here," he says, but Sullivan's attention has already wandered.

"That's 'No human involved' played out on a more sophisticated level," Greg says after Sullivan has again exited.

The afternoon wears on. David is recalled. Sullivan is aggressive in his cross-examination, his foot wiggling under the counsel's table as he rapid-fires questions at the witness. Sullivan easily establishes David's gang membership, then probes the inconsistencies between David's testimony and that of the police officers. Increasingly confused, David attempts to explain. Sullivan interrupts him. "There's no question being asked," Sullivan says curtly. This two-beat interaction is repeated five or six times until David wilts in confusion. When David steps down, he looks shell-shocked.

Sullivan makes sure Dreamer is never put on the stand. By the time the hearing has ended, it's clear that the smart money is on an acquittal.

Dreamer doesn't move for the first few seconds after the judge announces his decision, unsure if the judge has just found him innocent or guilty. Finally Sullivan turns to Dreamer with an ersatz big brotherly expression and says, "Well, you really got lucky this time, fella." Only then does Dreamer look around, startled, his expression not one of happiness, but more that of a rabbit who has unexpectedly escaped being eaten by a fox. He stands uncertainly and is led away.

Outside the courtroom a solitary figure remains on the hallway bench. It is Greg. He sits in quiet repose with knees together, overhead lights reflecting off his glasses, hands folded in his lap. Unaware he is being observed he looks unexpectedly lonely. When the double doors to the court swing open Greg looks up, mouth slightly parted in surprise.

"The judge kicked it, didn't he?" he asks, the adrenaline of the morning gone. "Should we be happy about this or sad?"

Sullivan expels himself from the courtrooms, beaming and swaggering. "This," he says with a flourish, "is the highlight of my Juvenile Court career."

Late in the afternoon, Greg is the one to tell David and the rest of Angelina's family that Dreamer got off. "You did the right thing," Greg assures David. "You did the brave thing. You told the truth."

Angelina's family doesn't understand. If David told the truth, then why wasn't the shooter convicted?

Greg's own reactions are still mixed. The good news, he says, is that a sensitive kid with no prior record won't spend five to eight in a California Youth Authority lockup. The bad news is that two rare attempts to be responsible and honorable have come to nothing.

"Dreamer is a wonderful, wonderful kid," Greg says, as the light of the day fades. "And he shot a little girl. A lot of people can't hold those two thoughts together. But the task of a true human being is to do precisely that."

Still later, Greg is again standing talking with David and one of his friends. Mid-conversation, David says to Greg, "I wish you were my father." Greg has become accustomed to such wishes. He brushes a hand against each boy's shoulder. "If you were my sons I'd be the proudest man alive," he says softly. All at once, David directs Greg's attention behind him. Greg turns quickly but, seeing no approaching danger, turns back to David. He then apprehends the reason for the misdirection: David is sobbing.

Dreamer

My name is Dreamer. I don't know why I got my name. I guess 'cause I think about things. Some people look like what they're called. Slim is all skinny. And Spanky's name fits with him. That's not true for me. If it wasn't for Solo, who's from my neighborhood, I would've been called Solo instead. Because a lot of times when I'll be with the homies, I always disappear 'cause I like to be alone. I just kick back and look around.

Like in Juvenile Hall, they had me in lockdown almost all the time I was in there. In lockdown, they wake you up at six in the morning to go out to wash up. Then they lock you back in your room. They just bring you out for breakfast and lunch and dinner, or for a shower, or when you need to go to the toilet. Sometimes if they're having school in the unit, you have school for maybe an hour. The rest of the time, you're just in your room. You're not allowed to have books or anything personal. The whole day, the most you would come out would be two-and-a-half hours.

I loved it. I got bored sometimes. But I liked being alone.

It was hard to go and turn myself in. Nobody wants to go and turn themselves in if they didn't catch you. I know Father Greg wanted me to, you know, take responsibility for my actions. He kept on saying it was the right thing. It was the right thing. But it's *hard* to do. I don't know, I just felt sorry for the little girl.

My public defender never talked to me. To tell you the truth I didn't like him. He never came to see me. He never asked me any questions. He acted like I wasn't even there. Like I didn't count.

Ridgway asked me about why I did it. "Was it that the older guys were putting pressure on you, or what?" But to me, nobody makes me do anything. Everything I do is because I decided. Not 'cause they tell me. Not even the older guys can make me do something. See, like before, the older guys would say, "When are you going to go do missions in this neighborhood or that neighborhood?" They would say that a lot. And I wouldn't do it. I didn't want them to tell me what to do. And I would tell them, "You'll see when."

To tell you the truth, the only shooting I've heard of that Clarence has done for the whole year is that time when I done it. It's not really scary when you're shooting a gun. But then they told me I hit the little girl. I felt messed up. When you're doing that you don't mean to hit little girls or ladies. I felt messed up. Messed up.

I thought about it when I was locked up. I thought that probably the only way they could stop the shooting is if they didn't have gun stores. See, 'cause people rob the gun stores. Then they take the guns and they go sell them. And also, they smuggle them in from another country, and they get on the street. But the only way to stop the shooting is if we couldn't get the guns.

I would rather jump out and beat up an enemy. To me that's fun. I don't want to shoot 'em. Shooting, that's not fun because you're gonna kill 'em. You can't keep killing 'em and killing 'em. What is that about? But if you fight 'em, then maybe beat 'em up. Then maybe the next time they beat you up. That's okay. I don't like hurting nobody.

But see, it's like a game. That's the way the game is played. And you have to play the way your enemies play or you ain't gonna survive. If you don't play it the way they play it, you're going to die and they're going to laugh.

One thing about gang banging. You can't have a priest telling you, "Don't do it." It's a hard situation, because you want to listen to him, but then you don't. See 'cause if you keep on listening to him, sooner or later your enemies are going to realize that you're not doing nothing.

Then that gang ain't going to exist no more. I know that's what Father Greg is trying to do. But then you disappear. You're nothing no more.

Say you'd be walking down the street, and say some guys from East L.A. come by. And they know you. And they hit you up. And you say, "I don't gang bang no more." And they say, "But you used to be from Clarence." And you say, "Yeah. But not no more." They'll still beat you up. Even if you're like a lot littler than they are. Sometimes when I would be a twelve- or thirteen-year-old, and I would be walking back from school, these guys from Evergreen would pop out and beat me up. And they were way bigger than me.

It used to be that I would see guys who are littler than me, and I would never do anything. And then one day I saw this little guy from Evergreen. I wasn't going to beat him because he was littler than me. But then I remembered all the times when they'd beat me. And I said, "No. I'm gonna do it." So I beat him up. That's the way the game is played.

Right now my mom's trying to keep me away from the projects. And Father Greg's trying to keep me away from the projects. But I know for a fact that sooner or later I'm going to go down there. I can't walk out on my homies. I can't do it.

When you're just kicking back with the homies, having a good time, that's the best part of being in a gang. See like before I was in a gang, I wouldn't really depend on nobody. Now I know that I could depend on my homies. We're always together. Everybody has their own little group. On Friday and Saturday nights, everybody gets together and kicks it. And then there are girls that'll come and get together with us.

If you ask me what is the happiest time in my life, I wouldn't really know what to say. I can't think of nothing. I can't remember when I got so, *so* happy. The day I got out of Eastlake I was happy.

I guess the saddest time was when my great-grandma died. I was a little kid when she died but I used to like her a lot. I don't have any so happy times with my mom. Ever since I was a little kid I wouldn't stay in my house. I didn't want to be with my dad and my mom.

My dad gets mad a lot. But I don't really care no more. If I try to think what is the best thing about my dad, I can't think of nothing. I don't see nothing best in him. I know he cares. But see, he don't do me anything bad and he don't do me anything good, neither. He don't do me nothing at all. It seems like as if I'm not even there. Probably when I was little he told me he loved me. I don't know. Not since I grew up.

By the time I turn eighteen, probably I won't be gang banging. I don't really know what I want to be doing. I would like to start a family. Get a job. I don't want to live in the projects. Ever since I was a little kid, I had a dream about playing baseball for a major league. I haven't played for a long time. I remember when I used to be good. Anything I used to throw I used to hit. Not anymore.

I have a lot of respect for Father Greg. He's told me he loves me like a son. And I ask myself, "Should I believe him?" Sometimes I think it's true. And sometimes I don't. He's nice with me and everything. I don't know him for the longest like the other guys. I've only known him for a half a year. But even, like, if it's true that he loves me and everything, I might still do a lot of the same things he doesn't want me to do. But I'd try for him not to find out.

My dad was mad that I turned myself in. He said, "You do the thing you do, then you go to the cops and turn yourself in? Isn't it the other way around? Aren't you supposed to get away from them?" He says one day I'm going to wind up locked up for a long time. I don't know. Everything he tells me about myself, one way or the other it winds up to be true.

When I turned myself in, my mom didn't do nothing. She never does nothing. You can tell when she's mad because she makes faces. My mom, she's a nice person. My girlfriend, Monica, when she first seen my mom and my dad at the church, she said, "Your mom looks nice but your dad, he looks scary. Like he might do something."

My girlfriend won't come to my house because she's afraid of my dad. I don't want to talk shit about my dad. But if I could have a magic wand, I'd make him turn, you know, nice.

My dad works in the night. If I'm ever at home, I try to come home after he's gone to work already. When he was gone in Mexico it was better because I could bring friends over to my house. And they could even sleep over. Nobody will go to my house when my dad's there.

People join a gang for a lot of reasons. One is that you live in that neighborhood. Another is that you want them to protect you because you've been, you know, getting beaten up all the time. Another reason is you want to be in it because you feel something for them. And you want to be there with them. Like, in other words, you have love for the 'hood. And that's a good feeling to have.

See that Gulf War was like the same thing. It's like a war between two gangs. The only difference is you're fighting neighborhoods, not countries. And you're fighting people right next to you. Like for example, when the guys from Clarence were little, I know for a fact they used to play with the guys from East L.A. They used to go to their houses and everything. But then you grow up and you start with gangs and everybody splits up and gets into a different neighborhood. Now you got to go shoot your ex-friend. It's a little crazy.

Another thing I noticed—when you kick back with your homies, you're kicking back like little kids. But when you go to a party with other gangs, you try to be serious. You don't act like a little kid. You got to be real serious. You got to look tough.

You've got to show them you're not afraid of them. Like the other day I was on a bike and there was five of them—East L.A.'s—and I just stood looking at them. I didn't turn away. They started calling me all kinds of names. But I just wasn't afraid of 'em. I didn't run or nothing. I just stood there. Even when this guy, Danny Boy, pulled a gun. I said, "Give the gun to your homeboy and let's go head up just you and me." And he said, "Nah. I'm going to just shoot you, right now." But he just stood there. He didn't do nothing. It was already dark. And no one was around but them. But he didn't do it. See if you act like you're not afraid then they think, "Hey, maybe he's got a pistol."

I was courted in just about half a year ago. They didn't hit me very hard because there was only three guys. The only big guy was Clavo. You know *his* hits are gonna hurt. The other two guys were little. When there's more guys, they can mess you up worse.

I coulda got into White Fence instead of Clarence. See White Fence is one of the biggest gangs, and I live right there where they kick it. But I never felt nothing for them. I didn't care about 'em. But when I met the guys from Clarence, even though I don't live around them, I went, "Yeah! I feel something for them!" I like hanging around with them. I'd do anything for them.

I worry that I'm going to die. Especially because I live in White Fence's neighborhood. And they know where I live. I feel safer in the projects. Even though East L.A. is right there, I know I'm safer in the projects than I am in my house. See, White Fence killed my homeboy Smoky, rest-in-peace. That's why I'm hardly ever at my house.

It's also hard to be at home with my dad. He gets to me a lot. I'm at the house doing nothing. He won't let me go to school at Dolores Mission. So I'm just at home doing nothing. And he starts telling me that I'm just home and not at school. And I say, "You're the one who wouldn't let me go to school. He says, "Well, that don't matter." When he gets really mad, I just walk away from him. It would be all right if I could live at home and go outside. Then I would stay home. I wouldn't mind. But I can't go walking around right there. It's too dangerous. In the projects, I feel safer. I go to the church. Kick it there, and try not to go home. I just knock on the homeboys' doors and ask if I can stay. See, like, it's all right to stay at their house for one or two nights. But I can't be living at their house. I don't feel comfortable. I feel like I'm bothering them.

That same day I shot at the East L.A.'s, I had already heard that East L.A. wanted to get me. And that gave me an idea. So then when I saw L'il Diablo had the gun, I said why wait for them to come to me? Why not do it right now? See they wanted to get me, because I'm the main one who is always crossing them out. It used to be Cowboy crossing them out. But then I got in the neighborhood, and now I'm the one crossing them out all the time. No one else was doing it, so I might as well.

I like myself okay. I don't think of myself as a good person. The thing I like best about myself is, for one thing. I don't do what somebody else tells me to do. I do it 'cause I wanted to do it.

If I had a son, I'd try to be a good father, not hassling my kid all the time. Not like my dad. I'd treat my son nice. I guess if I could change anything about my life, I just would want a dad that I could get along with. I don't care how he would be, as long I could get along with him. See, like, I know my dad. He don't talk shit to me 'cause I'm in a gang. It's that he's always been like that. He's always talked shit to me no matter what. If I would not be in a gang and do good, he would still be the same. It wouldn't really matter. He would probably tell you the reason he don't like me is because of this or because of that. But I know it's not true. It's been like that since I been little.

Lately I haven't been writing or crossing out. It's been two weeks. To me that's long. To me three days without writing that's long. I like writing on the walls. I don't know why.

Before I got into Clarence, I used to be a tagger. I used to write all over the buses, the walls. You have to choose a name. It's more fun to be a tagger than being a gangster. Because, look: Taggers have tagging crews. Instead of fighting, they call it battling. Instead of shooting, they get their spray cans and write on the wall. Like they might say, "Okay. Let's battle for a month." And in that month, the crew that you see their writing the most, they win.

Or it could be just like two guys who battle, just writing their names. An' then it's like, "If I win you have to change your name to something else." That's the deal. Or it could be, "If I win, you have to give me twenty spray cans." Or you could do it another way. You could do the battle in one day with what they call "pieces"— murals. You do it in one day and whoever does the best one wins. It's exciting.

Sometimes you'd go fight. But it was never, "I'm going to go shoot you." It was fun. You get on that bus and you go far. I used to go way over there to San Fernando, as far as the RTD bus pass would go in L.A. County It used to be boring sitting on the bus for two hours. But to a tagger it's worth it. I would always write my name in different styles. It would be like a adventure.

Then you get into a gang it's different. You get killed or go kill someone. I wouldn't mind tagging again. I still like writing. It's like a habit I have. I be writing all over wherever I am. In my house I write with hairspray. You have to look real good to see it, but it's there.

If I was locked up, it might not be a bad thing. But not for more than six months or a year. If I would do more than a year, knowing me, I would wind up AWOL.

If I could have one wish in the world, I'd probably say, "Get me a good life." Like having an all right job, like away from trouble, where you ain't going to have no problems. Maybe a job in a warehouse. Six dollars an hour. That would be okay. Also the world could use some improvement. I'd send food and money to all the poor people. I'd make the whole world to be in good shape, with nobody to be starving. And I'd get rid of the guns.

Sometimes I think to myself, "I don't get nothing from being in my gang." I tell myself that a lot sometimes, but still that don't convince me. I guess I could stop kicking it with them and like make other friends. But then I think to myself, it will take a long time to make friends so why not just stick with these friends?

If I get killed, it don't really matter to me. I don't know why. It's just a feeling I have. Like I don't really care. I don't really know what happens when you die. It's kind of hard to think about. A lot of people say you go to heaven or you go to hell. I don't think so. I can't say I'm going to go to heaven, because I haven't been a nice boy, or nothing like that. But I don't know if I'm going to go to hell either. I'll probably go somewhere else.

Last week I had a dream that they killed me in front of my lady. If I got killed, my mom would probably cry for a while. My dad, for him it'd probably be no big thing. Father Greg, he'd say mass, and that'd be it. I don't think if I'm alive or not really makes a difference. There's a lot of people in the world already.

Chapter 4

In the simplest of terms, Greg's work with the homeboys can be described as lighting a pilot light. For most of these kids, the pilot light of hope burns very low or has gone out altogether. With love, jobs, schooling, and sometimes a place to live, Greg relights the pilot light. Inevitably it goes out. So he lights it again. Again it goes out. Again he lights it. And so goes the cycle. Then one day—if everyone is lucky—the light stays on of its own accord.

Dreamer's pilot light has just gone from low to out. The Dreamer who was released from Juvenile Hall is different from the Dreamer who went in. Something in his spirit has cracked. Maybe it's as he said, that he had spent a lifetime trying to prove his father wrong, and now that's no longer necessary. In his eyes, his father has just been proved irrevocably right—he's doomed to failure and always has been. Consequently the new, nothing-to-lose Dreamer doesn't wait for catastrophe to come and find him. He is running pell-mell into its embrace.

As of today, Dreamer hasn't been home for three days. He is once again ditching school. And he's tagging like there's no tomorrow. This morning, when Father Greg made the rounds, the walls of the projects were bleeding Day-Glo bougainvillea spray paint in the shape of

Dreamer's name. Dreamer is not only tagging, he is "crossing out"—putting big "X's" through other gang insignias, especially those of East L.A. This act is equivalent to a personal invitation to war.

"It's suicidal," says Greg.

Other than tagging, Dreamer's only regular activity is walking his girlfriend Monica home each afternoon. Monica, the girlfriend, lives in Aliso Village, dangerously close to Dukeville. It concerns Greg that Dreamer's daily walking route has taken a predictable pattern which ELA is bound to notice.

"So many people are looking for him," says Greg, meaning enemies. Post-Juvenile Hall, Dreamer's status has changed from anonymous new booty to known shooter, complete with a whole new set of mortal enemies, some of whom are calling his mother's house to issue threats of retaliation against her son.

Greg is somewhat unsure which way to move with Dreamer. "I don't want him to feel boxed in," he says. "Because then he might feel like the only thing to do is to go out in a blaze of glory or be locked up." Greg grimaces. "I've seen it happen too many times. If you're dead or locked up, at least it's someplace to go."

In addition to the ongoing Dreamer drama, there has been a string of mishaps involving Greg's day care center construction crew. First Green Eyes was shot. Two .38 caliber bullets passed through his left shoulder and out again. A third passed through his chest, a little below the heart. Community mother Pam McDuffie drove him to White Memorial Hospital for treatment. An hour later he was released and back on the street, bare-chested and cocky, his bullet wounds minimally covered by bandages, his left arm dangling loose and stringy by his side.

The following Sunday, Droopy of the bullet-parted hair was picked up by the police. Someone, not Droopy, had trashed a basehead's car in Pico Gardens. When the police swooped down, everyone ran, so the police snatched up the only gang member on the street they could find—Droopy.

Greg goes to see him at Juvenile Hall and finds him defeated. "I'm trying so hard, G," he says. "I've got my job and my lady. I just wanted to take my lady to the prom. I've never been to a prom, G." Droopy breaks down in tears at this last statement, as if even the word "prom" is a magic talisman, a golden ring of normalcy that swings perpetually out of his grasp.

With Droopy locked up, the other three day care workers—Green Eyes included—are acting out. They are showing up late and leaving early. One day it was reported that they were throwing dirt at each other and passing cars with all the maturity of seven-year-olds. Greg suspends them for a few days as a disciplinary action.

"I want to make it clear to them that it's not that they're lost causes. It's not that they can't be helped. But they have to take ownership for their actions."

In Droopy's place, Greg hires Cisco. "I think all Cisco needs is a job and somebody to sit on him about his drinking problem," Greg says hopefully. "Drinking killed his father."

———

Every year in mid-May, the community throws Father Greg a surprise birthday party, and every year he pretends to be surprised. The big surprise planned for this birthday was supposed to have been a peace treaty between Clarence, the Dukes, TMC, and Cuatro. But other than Greg himself, there is no one who can quite pull such a miracle off. As second best, the homies from TMS, Cuatro, and Clarence all get together—sans ELA—to sign a gigantic birthday card for Greg to be presented at the party.

At the party, a lively group of mariachis encourages the crowd to dance. Greg salsa dances good-naturedly with a limitless lineup of local women. After the mariachis pack up, the card is presented, and the party breaks up by ten without incident. A tired Greg makes his way to bed by midnight.

It is nearing 3:00 A.M. when Pepé from Clarence decides to wake Greg. There is a riot, he shouts breathlessly into the phone receiver. What he means is there are sixty kids massed on Gless Street, a potentially explosive mix of Cuatro, TMC, and Clarence—the three neighborhoods who had written messages of peace on Greg's card only a few hours before.

Bottles have been thrown. Warning shots have been fired in the air. A wounding or a death seems imminent. Pepé had already run to his nearby house and dialed the police. "We're closed for the night," the desk sergeant at Hollenbeck supposedly told him. In any case, the police never came.

When Greg arrives, furious and bleary-eyed, the riot breaks into pieces. Girls begin crying. "We're so sorry, G."

"I love you guys so much," Greg yells to anyone within earshot, as he threatens/cajoles an extremely drunk Cisco into his car, "but I *hate* your neighborhoods. I *hate your fucking neighborhoods!*"

The morning after the riot, Dreamer and Turtle, a bright-eyed TMC homie of similar age and build to Dreamer, find themselves in a near disaster. Dreamer and Turtle have recently joined up as tagging partners. They are on a tagging mission in ELA territory when they are spotted by armed and angry Dukes, the Twins prominently among them. A hair-raising Keystone Cops chase ensues, with Dreamer and Turtle dodging between apartment buildings all through Aliso Village. Finally the twosome is able to duck into the house of a friend's sister, where they hole up and send word to Clarence homies for help.

Clarence immediately prepares to launch an armed rescue mission, with Spanky leading the charge. By luck, Greg gets a phone call from a panicked Aliso mother who alerts him to the impending mission. He flies out of his office just in time to catch Spanky as he is headed down Gless, his car loaded with homies.

Spanky is belligerent at first, but soon backs down in the face of Greg's fury. "G finds out everything," he mutters, supposedly in disgust, but mostly in relief. Greg then spirits the wayward twosome out of Aliso to safety.

———

The What-to-Do-About-Dreamer discussion is now a nightly event for Greg. Dreamer's living status has deteriorated. He is now sleeping in the cars of friends and on the street, going back to his mother's occasionally only to shower or change clothes. Dreamer's own latest solution to his housing problem is that he should live at the church—or, more accurately, across the street at the homeless shelter, where Spanky presently resides. Greg frowns at the prospect, fearing that letting Dreamer into the homeless shelter would set an unworkable precedent.

"See, Spanky's different," he says. "He literally has no place else to go. But if I open the door and let in all the people who hate it at home, I could fill the homeless shelter and the Hilton Hotel.

"Besides," says Greg, running his hands through his hair in frustration, "my confreres here will freak out. They only barely put up with me in terms of Spanky being in Cas Pro, which is really supposed to be just a shelter for women and children. They also roll their eyes because I've taken in a bunch of undocumented kids from court who always stay longer than the court-mandated three months. So if I took in one more homie . . ." Greg grimaces.

"Part of the thing is . . . I know too many kids who live with too many awful parental configurations. They say, 'I can't live there.' And I say, 'As a matter of fact you physically *can*. You just dance around that fool. And you get affection and support somewhere else. So you have a jerk who shares the same roof with you. *Y qué?*' You know? Wizard's a perfect example. His father's drunk all the time. But I've watched him learn to dance around his father. You learn to survive."

———

It's the Sunday night of Memorial Day weekend and Greg's mother's birthday. There is a party at his parents' house where almost all his siblings and their families have gathered. Greg is the last to arrive at the large two-story colonial house, and the first to make his way back out the door. The family collectively groans when he leaves. "Workaholic," they good-naturedly call after him.

His family's mild, even affectionate disapproval sets Greg to fretting. "Are they right? Am I a workaholic?" he asks. Then he quickly answers his own question. "No! I wasn't leaving to return to my work as a lawyer would return to his, you know, legal briefs. The truth is, I felt like I had left my wife and kids at home. And I wanted to get back." He is getting worked up now. "Dolores Mission isn't just my work. It's my *life*. And there's a great difference. If my brother or sisters had been there without their spouses they would have been the first to leave."

Greg's own words seem to relieve him. "That's exactly it," he says, as much to himself as to anyone else. "Emotionally, this isn't my work, this is my wife and kids."

At 1:00 A.M., the same night, Greg is awakened by gunshots. Since no one calls or pounds on the door, he turns over and drifts back into a fitful sleep.

Spanky comes to the Jesuit residence at 6:30 A.M. Dreamer has been shot, he says. He was with a group of TMC and Clarence homies near Fourth and Gless. Someone drove by and opened fire. It is unclear if Dreamer was the intended victim. The bullet grazed his head just above his left ear.

"He's so lucky he's not dead." Says Greg, after he has seen Dreamer's wound. "When stuff gets that close to the head or to the heart . . ." His voice trails off.

By 8:00 A.M., Greg has already figured out who shot Dreamer. "Cars are very important. I know it was a truck that shot at him and I know who owns the truck." The truck belongs to a kid from ELA whom Greg knows well. The kid lost an eye last year after a shooting by TMC. "And he's still very angry and embittered."

Dreamer tells his mother that the shots were random. Privately he confides he thinks they were meant for him. Every night, he adds, just before he makes the mad run from his girlfriend's house back to the church, Monica always says the same thing: "Call me if you get shot." The words are like a charm. "Only last night she forgot to say it," he says.

Greg hopes that the shooting will slow Dreamer down. Instead Dreamer walks an ever riskier tightrope, tagging daily deeper and deeper in Duke's territory.

Mid-morning on the second day after the shooting, Greg capitulates on the housing issue. "You can stay here in my office," he tells Dreamer. He sets down three conditions for residence: No tagging, no banging, in the house by 10:00 P.M. every night.

Dreamer is ecstatic at the offer. "Really, G?! Really?!" he keeps saying as he hops around the office. For an hour or so, Dreamer wears the mile-wide smile of the old Dreamer.

In the afternoon, Greg takes Dreamer shopping to buy a toothbrush, deodorant, and other such necessities, plus a couple of sets of clothes purchased at low cost from a local swap meet. Dreamer says his mother has tossed out all his clothes in a fit of rage. That night Greg breaks the news about the new tenant to his fellow

Jesuits. They are not at all happy with the arrangement and make their feelings known.

"I didn't know what else to do," Greg says when he is by himself again. "I guess it's okay. I *hope* it's okay."

———

Greg has not talked about an overall peace in the barrio for a long time, especially not since his near misses.

"I don't know what victory or success is any more," he says when questioned. "For me it's now, 'Is it right and good and true and what we should be doing?' On that level I have no doubt about my strategy, or about the strategy of Dolores Mission community."

In reality he has had a string of success that are measurable by a conventional yardstick: Although the Clarence Street Locos have lost four homies in the last year, with the exception of Dreamer's shooting foray, they have thus far refrained from retaliating. This previously unheard-of restraint can be laid directly at Greg's feet.

There are also individual successes: Some kids, once they acquire the magic combination of a lady, a baby, and a job, have been helped by Father Greg to "mature out" of the gang existence. Then in early April, as Greg was on the eve of burying yet another kid, he got a call from Rebel, the most influential and flamboyant of TMC's "big heads." Rebel asked urgently to talk to him.

"I want to stop this," Rebel blurted when Greg arrived for the talk. "I want to stop now. I've got my baby daughter and I want her to grow up with a father. I need you to help me. I want to stop today." Rebel kept repeating it: "I need your help."

Greg was thrilled. "Of course," he said. "Of course." Since that night the famous Rebel has kept his word. No more banging.

Ghost and his best friend Wizard have likewise moved into the no-banging category. Both are CSL homies who test in the gifted range, and although both come from troubled families, they have a friendship with each other which is rare in its warmth and depth. The two have responded to Greg's influence by taking pains to avoid violence. They have also developed an aptitude for defusing violent situations when they cannot be avoided.

There is a story about the night of Ghost's little sister's birthday party. He had gone into the alley in back of his mother's house to empty the garbage when some enemy gang members drove up, placed the business end of a very large gun barrel against Ghost's chest, and threatened to shoot him. When Wizard appeared, unarmed, to help his friend, more guns were pulled. Both boys, while frightened, talked calmly. "Look, we don't want nothing with you guys," they said. "Kick back." By the end of the encounter the enemy gang members found themselves saying, "We don't want anything with your neighborhood, neither." As a result, for a while, at least, the two gangs stopped shooting at each other.

"The way Wizard and Ghost handled the situation shows a high degree of self-care," says Greg. "That's the main thing you hope for."

Today is Ghost's birthday. When Greg sees Ghost across the church parking lot, he races to give him a hug and shoves a hastily scrawled card into his hands. Although Greg can barely recite his own mother's phone number, he remembers each one of the homies' birthdays. Those dates he doesn't know by heart, he has recorded on the pages of his Day-Timer calendar. Every December Greg spends an afternoon transferring several hundred birthdates from last year's calendar to that of the year upcoming.

Ghost goes off by himself to read the card, then returns a little later, shutting Greg's office door for privacy.

"Thanks a lot, G," he says, suddenly shy. "Nobody in my family remembered it was my birthday."

Greg shakes his head after Ghost has gone. "How can a mother not remember her son's birthday?" he mutters. "Especially a kid who's that terrific!"

Dreamer has been on his best behavior since moving into Father Greg's office. He has stopped tagging, at least for now, and is careful to respect the ten o'clock curfew. He and Greg have already established a silly nightly ritual. "G'night, G," says Dreamer in a singsong voice as he snuggles down into the makeshift bed on the floor—a kid on a camp out. "G'night, D," replies the priest in the same voice.

"I feel like I'm in the middle of a weird version of 'The Waltons,'" says Greg.

There have been some small snags. The church's secretarial staff isn't exactly overjoyed by the fact that each day Dreamer has taken nearly an hour with his morning toilette, tying up the rectory's only bathroom. When Greg suggests he might speed up the process, Dreamer looks at the priest aghast. "Don't you know that you can't rush excellence?"

———

It is early on an overcast morning and Greg is already in his car driving—trying to wake up. He is scheduled to be the speaker at a 7:30 A.M. breakfast at L.A.'s exclusive Jonathan Club. Despite the fact that he was at the hospital until two in the morning attending to a gunshot thirteen-year-old from the ELA Tiny Dukes, he shows up at the breakfast hoping for a healthy honorarium which will enable him to make this week's homeboy payroll. At the end of his speech there is much applause but no money. Greg's mood is not helped when, as he is about to leave, an expensively dressed woman attorney comes up and hands him a twenty-dollar bill folded with another piece of paper. He stuffs both into his pocket as he exits the building. When he gets back to the office, Greg absently pulls out the twenty and unfolds the accompanying paper. It is a neatly written check for two thousand dollars—just exactly enough to cover the next salaries.

"A *milagro!*" he grins. "That's how it always happens!"

Although the check is a shot of good fortune, the rest of the day turns troublesome. Early in the afternoon Greg catches Dreamer and Turtle on First Street right across from ELA territory. The two are back to tagging. Presently they alternate between lounging on the grass in full view of any Duke who might happen past, and running across the street to the phone booth on the ELA side, to make calls to girls—never mind that there is a safer phone on the TMC side just up the street. Greg wheels up to them, yelling furiously. "Why don't you just wear fucking signs that say 'Shoot me'?" he screams.

Dreamer hangs his head. Beside himself, Greg continues to shout. "I ask three small things of you! You don't bang! You don't tag! And you be in by ten! If you've got a better deal than here, then take it."

Nothing from Dreamer. Greg loses it. "Can't you control yourself?" he yells, his tone harsh and sarcastic. "Can't you *stop tagging?*"

Dreamer's arms fall energyless at his sides. "I can't," he says flatly, talking in the direction of the ground. "If you make me stop writing, then you leave me with nothing."

An hour later, Greg is in his office. Romie, his office manager, buzzes him to say that a counselor at Roosevelt High School is on the line. The counselor informs Greg that Ghost refuses to attend graduation ceremonies. Can't Greg do something about it? The counselor wants to know.

It is 9:00 P.M. by the time Greg gets Ghost on the phone to give him a pep talk about the merits of graduating publicly. Ghost is completely unwilling. "What's the point?" he asks.

Although Wizard has quit school, Ghost has done well. Although he had dropped out of Roosevelt his sophomore year, after attending Dolores Mission Alternative he had returned to Roosevelt to get all A's and B's his senior year. Greg reminds Ghost of all this now.

"I want you to be as proud of yourself as I am of you," says Greg. "If you won't get up there for yourself, do it for me." Unconvinced, Ghost says he will think about it.

It is nearly midnight when Greg makes his last round of the projects. He is too exhausted to ride his bike, so he takes the car instead. ELA territory is deserted. At the back of Aliso he finds a group of TMC's just kicking it and talking. Drifter, an intelligent, emotionally articulate seventeen-year-old from TMC who rarely dresses gangster-style, motions to Greg.

"I need a minute, G."

"Step into my office," Greg replies, leaning over to swing open the passenger door of the car.

Drifter confides the usual problems and Greg dispenses the usual fatherly advice.

They are still talking when the hill above Greg's car explodes in light and sound as four large guns open fire. In the first instant of deafening brightness, Drifter grabs Greg's head and pushes down to the car seat, simultaneously flinging himself across him as a mother might to protect her child. Greg is too stunned to stop him. The shooting goes on for two full minutes, fast and constant, like too many fireworks on the Fourth of July.

"Get out of here, G!" Drifter keeps screaming. The other homies start to scream it too. Greg won't move the car, fearful of exposing the homies who've dived under and behind the car for protection from the gunfire.

"It was like something out of 'The Untouchables,'" says Greg. "None of us thought we'd live through it."

Finally Drifter reaches down and presses his hand on Greg's gas pedal. The car jolts forward. Homies hop back and scurry crablike to the shelter of other nearby parked cars. Seeing little choice, Greg straightens up, takes the car's wheel, speeds out of the line of fire and around the corner.

A beat later, a black-and-white squad car and two Housing cars screech past Greg. After several beats, Greg hears that the gunfire has finally stopped.

Greg drives cautiously back to the scene, bracing himself for what he will find. Miraculously, no one has been seriously hurt. One TMC has been shot in the foot. The rest are being searched by LAPD—legs spread, hands against an apartment wall, as if the cops are unsure whom they should be arresting.

Dizzy with relief that there are no deaths, Greg and Drifter start to giggle. One officer glances back with disdain as Drifter hugs Greg and won't let go.

The next day, his day off, Greg sleeps later than he has in months. He only rouses himself when Ghost and another CSL homie, Toro, pound on the back door of the Jesuit residence. Ghost informs Greg that he's decided to go to the graduation ceremony after all. Greg is ecstatic. He claps Ghost on the back, assuring him that he will pay the thirty-seven-dollar cap and gown fee.

In the afternoon Greg is vested and standing at the church altar ready to begin mass for the Dolores Mission Elementary School eighth grade graduation. Greg picks up a mike and moves it to center stage. Without warning, five sharp popping noises blast through the church's

P.A. system. Two women in the back scream in fright. No one laughs. Greg stands stock-still, white-faced and silent, unable to move.

Eventually the spell cracks and he gathers his wits enough to begin the mass. But his rhythm is off. Mid-mass, Greg looks up to see Dreamer standing in the light of the side door.

When their eyes meet, Dreamer flashes Greg his most beautiful smile.

For the rest of the day Greg is gripped by an icy fatigue. When he talks again about the previous night's near-miss his voice is blanched by shock. "They wouldn't stop shooting," he says several times as if trying to grasp something just beyond his perception. "They wouldn't stop. This shootout was worse than anything."

At 10:30 P.M. Greg decides to lock up his office and go home early. He is discouraged when he finds no sign of Dreamer. Tired to the bone, he drives up and down the streets of the projects to find the missing house guest. He finds only Cisco, who is drunk to the point of staggering.

Cisco solves the mystery: Dreamer was just stopped by the police with a loaded .38 in his possession. Turtle was with him. Both were arrested.

Greg takes Cisco home, then heads home himself. He forgoes praying and falls quickly into a deep sleep.

"It was so weird," he muses the next morning. "I wondered why I didn't have that usual anxious feeling. And then I realized it was because Dreamer was locked up. I felt free. Because finally, at least, I know where he is."

Greg pauses. "I've sometimes seen this same thing with mothers after their sons are killed. There's this peculiar aura of relief because finally they don't have to worry any more. Finally they don't have to wait up any more nights, or have their hearts drop to the floor anymore listening for shots and sirens. Finally they know where their sons are."

———

The feeling of freedom disappears quickly. The Crips have gone crazy with shooting, spraying even a Housing police car with bullets. The unrelenting strain on Father Greg is starting to manifest itself in physical ways. He snaps at his fellow Jesuits, and starts feeling nauseated at unexpected moments.

"Everything seems so out of control," he says. "People are not stopping for anything."

To maintain balance, Greg clings to the bright spots and the brightest spot of the moment is Ghost. The woman from the Jonathan Club calls with a great six-week summer job in a downtown law office, and Greg offers it to Ghost. He responds with delight, telling Greg he has just received A+ in his senior-level computer course.

"You think they'd give me a chance to learn any, like, new computer stuff at this law firm?" Ghost asks excitedly. Greg assures him he will find out. He is to start work the Monday after graduation.

It is mildly problematic that Ghost is required to dress up for this job, as his present wardrobe consists mainly of grossly oversized jeans and white Fruit of the Loom T-shirts. Greg schedules a clothes-buying spree for Saturday morning. It's obvious that the priest is looking forward to the outing as much as Ghost.

Friday is payday and Greg wheels around to the various neighborhoods delivering checks. When he arrives in Aliso Village to pay his ELA workers, he is told of an incident that has just occurred earlier in the day at Roosevelt High. "Some guy from Clarence shanked a guy from White Fence," says one of the Hang Out girls, the girl gang that is loosely affiliated with the Dukes. White Fence is an out-of-projects gang. "I think it was that guy Bashful." The injury is rumored to be critical.

Back at the church, Greg finds Bashful helping some community mothers serve dinner to the homeless men, a task he is doing to fulfill court-mandated community service hours. Greg calls Bashful into his office.

"Your name's come up with this stabbing today, homes," he says. "You know anything about it?"

With a look of panic, Bashful confesses all. He was headed to his locker at lunch, he says, when he heard that four White Fence gang members were gathered near his locker. Since White Fence and Clarence "don't get along," this likely meant trouble. Bashful flagged down a friend and asked him to accompany him to the locker as backup. Bashful will not identify the friend to Greg except to say that he has known him since junior high. He vaguely suggests that this "friend" lives in South Central and claims no neighborhood.

Bashful then proceeded to his locker with the "friend" standing by and, as expected, there was immediate tension. A teacher whose classroom was nearby saw the impending explosion. According to Bashful, she told all six guys to vacate the premises but did not wait to see if they did so. Instead, she closed her door.

Bashful says the White Fence guys then made a menacing gesture, indicating one of them had a pistol in his pants pocket and that it was pointed at Bashful. "Why you tripping, man?" Bashful's friend asked repeatedly, using the ritual jargon to defuse the rising tension.

"Fuck Clarence!" purportedly was the only reply.

"Then fuck *welfare!*" Bashful says he spat back, "welfare" being the pejorative term for White Fence.

Then, according to Bashful, the four from White Fence proceeded to jump him and his friend. There was much punching and kicking. Bashful pulled a knife from his pocket. He was about to swing it. But the "friend" grabbed it from him and took a broad swipe at the White Fence guys. Lots of blood. Both Bashful and the friend ran. End of story.

"If what you're telling me is true," Greg tells Bashful, "you have nothing to fear by going to the police. Besides," Greg cautions, "if your name has reached my ears, it won't be long before the police hear it too."

Bashful agrees to turn himself in. With Bashful still in his office, Greg calls the detectives at Hollenbeck. Incredibly, they say they are too busy to see Bashful right now. An appointment is scheduled for Monday, June 17.

On Saturday, Greg takes Ghost to the May Company for the promised shopping spree. Ghost picks out two pairs of pants, three shirts, two ties, five pairs of socks, and a pair of dress shoes. The total comes to $220. Cashless, Greg puts it on plastic. On the way back to the projects Greg asks Ghost why he didn't want to graduate.

"I didn't feel like I deserved it," he answers.

In the afternoon, Greg drives to Juvenile Hall to visit Turtle and Dreamer. Turtle cries profusely the whole time Greg is with him. He explains the "extenuating circumstances" of his and Dreamer's misadventures. He tells Greg that some Dukes had been driving around the church yelling provocatively.

"So what was your hope in getting the gun?" Greg replies. "Who did you think you would protect?"

Turtle starts crying again. "This gang life is not for me," he says. "I'm not like the others."

With Dreamer there are no tears. He is calm, almost placid. Greg prepares him for the fact that he will most certainly do a year in detention camp. Dreamer nods. Greg looks at Dreamer, who listens but does not look at him, gazing instead out the window to the flat blue of the sky beyond.

"This was what you wanted, wasn't it? To be locked up."

"No," says Dreamer. But his voice lacks all conviction.

———

At two-thirty in the morning, Father Greg's bedside phone rings. He startles sharply awake, staring at the clock as he grabs for the phone. Calls at this hour rarely have cheery outcomes. It is Silent, calling from the hospital emergency room. "Spanky was shot," he says, then hastily adds, "he walked to the car and he's not dead. We took him to White Memorial. They say he's gonna be okay. I'm sorry to call in the middle of the night," says Silent, "but, you know, since you have custody of Spanky and everything. . . ."

After Greg hangs up the phone, he lies in his bed angrily refusing to get up. "Nobody has custody of Spanky," he mutters to himself. "Not even Spanky." At 3:30 A.M., Greg is still awake, so he calls the hospital. A nurse assures him that Spanky is stable and about to enter surgery. She says that the doctors have been unable to find a bullet. This means that the wound was probably a "through-and-through."

Greg waits until seven to go to the hospital. By that time Spanky is out of surgery and asleep in a room of his own, Teenage Ninja Turtles playing above his head on the hospital TV.

Greg says Spanky's name softly. Spanky opens his eyes and reflexively reaches out a hand to grab Greg's. "Oh, G!" he says in the keening whine of a frightened toddler. "I was asking for you all night long! It hurt so much, G!"

Any anger Greg may have felt is banished by Spanky's vulnerability. He comforts and reassures the large homie.

"Will you visit me more times today?" Spanky asks. Greg assures him that he will.

The nakedness of Spanky's vulnerability startles Greg. "I've never seen Spanky like this," he says. "When the homies get shot they always ask for their moms and often revert to this kind of childlike state." But "Mom" is not a name Spanky would evoke, no matter what his state. "I guess calling for me was the next best thing," Greg says. "It's like suddenly I got a window into the childhood this kid never got to have."

At 10:00 A.M. the same day, Greg takes Bashful to Hollenbeck where he is questioned by Detective Jack Forsman, a smart, no-nonsense cop with a Clint Eastwood demeanor. To the homeboy's surprise, Forsman releases him.

In the afternoon, the story of Spanky's shooting spills out in bits and pieces. Spanky was hanging out on Gless with other Clarence and TMC homies. He crossed the street, intending to go to Slim's house. (Slim is a soft-spoken Clarence homie whose older brother, Popeye, was killed by Dukes the year before.) Just as he reached the other side of the road, a car came out of nowhere and opened fire. Silent and Spanky both swear they don't know who the shooters were. The first and most obvious guess would be ELA. But there is the wild card of White Fence because of the Roosevelt incident. White Fence has been on a rampage since the shanking.

The day lightens when Ghost and some other Clarence homies show up in Greg's office. In the midst of the usual kidding and rowdiness Ghost disappears to his car, then reappears in a few seconds, holding out a bag to Greg.

"Happy late Father's Day." He says. Inside the bag is a turquoise Garfield T-shirt with "MR. G." emblazoned in large letters across the chest.

Touched, Greg thanks him, his forehead flushing bright red.

Near the end of the day, Greg goes back to see Spanky. By now the room is awash with flowers, balloons, and other tokens of homie affection brought by Clarence guys and girls to whom Spanky has been holding court. Even Spanky's bed sheets have been autographed to resemble cholo murals.

There was one thing the nurse found curious. Spanky had firmly instructed the nurse not to let his mother in if she showed. And, indeed, the mother showed up in the afternoon. Feeling uncomfortable barring a mother from the room of her nineteen-year-old kid, the nurse let her in anyway. During the whole time she was there, the nurse said, Spanky had pretended to be asleep, refusing to answer when the mother called his name. Finally the woman gave up and left.

Just before dark, Turtle calls. He is back at home. His case was a D.A. reject, he says. This means that the district attorney could not find enough evidence to file. Dreamer is still detained.

———

Tonight is the Roosevelt High School graduation. Father Greg is bringing two doe-eyed fifth-graders named Fernie and Jaime with him to the Shrine Auditorium where all the pomp and circumstance is being held. Both boys are members of a group of ten- and eleven-year-olds who hang around the church after school, driving the secretaries crazy. The kids refer to themselves as the *Pandilla Mugrosa*, which translates literally as "filthy gang." More often than not they live up to their appellation. A cluster of the PM'ers—as they are known for short—have taken to draping themselves on Greg, marsupial-like, at any and all opportunities, with Fernie and Jaime among the prime drapers.

Greg and the two boys stop for pizza beforehand. Fernie looks at Greg, smiling sagely as he munches. "We know why you're bringing us tonight," he says. "You want us to stay in school so that we'll graduate some day." Greg swears to them that no matter where he is in the world, he will come back to see them graduate.

On the drive to the Shrine, a car pulls up alongside Greg's. It's Ghost and Toro. Ghost rolls down the passenger window. "I need to talk to you," he yells to Greg. Greg waves and nods "Yes."

Greg and the PM'ers are seated so high up in the bleachers at the Shrine that the figures who walk to stage to accept their diplomas are much too far away to be recognizable. Nonetheless, the priest and the two boys cheer enthusiastically at every familiar name they hear. When Ghost's name is called, Greg stomps and claps as if for a son of his own blood.

The after-graduation scene is a madhouse. There are huge crowds pressing forward to greet the graduates, so Greg catches a glimpse of Ghost and Toro only from a distance. Finally he gives up and ferries the now-restless PM'ers back home.

It is near midnight when Ghost drives into the church parking lot to find Greg still at this desk. Greg stands to embrace Ghost and to shower him with verbal expressions of pride.

"Did your parents come?" Greg asks.

Ghost shrugs. "I dunno," he says. A pause. "Hey G, I got a problem about the job tomorrow. Mr. Ramirez needs to see me." Ghost says this casually, but his underlying tone is anything but casual. Ramirez is one of the deans of Roosevelt High School. Puzzled, Greg at first says nothing. Then all at once he sees the inevitable coming straight at him with the force of a runaway freight. He takes a breath.

"Do you know something about the shanking?" he asks.

"You might say that," Ghost replies.

"Did you see it?"

A breath. "You might say that."

The next question comes out of the darkest, weariest corner of Greg's psyche.

"Are you the one who stabbed him?" Ghost says nothing. Instead he and Greg just sit there in silence, bonded by the tragedy of the moment.

After a while Ghost spills out the story. His version is identical to Bashful's except that he is the unknown "friend."

Greg is devastated. For a few illogical moments he considers telling Ghost to go to his new job—Ramirez be damned—and that he, Greg, will think of something to tell the dean.

Naturally, Greg does not say this, would never say this. Instead, he tells Ghost what he already knows, that he will have to face this bad, sad music like a man. Greg will tell the new boss that Ghost will not be in tomorrow. Or perhaps ever.

Ghost

I'm known as Ghost. I got my name when the homies were bagging on me. Saying "Look! You got such white skin, you look like that cartoon about the friendly ghost." A lot of the names come just like that, from bagging.

I just live with my mom. My dad died when I was five or six. He drowned. He was drunk and he went swimming. The seaweed and the current dragged him down. I remember walking in the house and seeing, like, bloodstains on someone. And then they kicked me out. My uncle and his friends were with him. Once in a while I dream about him, and it'll all come back. When I dream about him, I see him, like, driving in a car. And he stops at a red light. In the dream I'm not young. I'm my age now.

And I wave at him and like yell, "C'mere! C'mere!" And he doesn't stop. He just skies up. Leaves. And I'm just like, "Fuck you, then, fool!" And then I wake up.

I miss having a role model. I was the oldest one, so I had to take care of my four sisters. All I have is pure sisters. So if I have a problem I would talk to Wizard about it. I look at him like my brother. He's only a couple of months older than I am but I look at him like an older brother. We've been friends since the second grade. I used to tell him all of my problems and he'd tell me his. We've had a couple of tears here and there, but that's about it.

My mother's supportive, in a way. She wants me to have faith in her and tell her everything. She got married again to a fool who was from the Air Force. He got shot up in Vietnam. He was like, loony in the head. He just stayed with her a while, then skied up.

Wizard is always there for me. When I'm down he picks me up. When I barely got here to L.A., when we first moved, I didn't know nobody. And right away Wizard and me got hooked up and he became my friend. I walked into class and he became my friend then and there. He was the best part of growing up.

I can't remember any other happy times when I was growing up except for when I was really small and my mother used to read me stories. My favorite was, what do you call the flying horse? Pegasus. When I was small I would think about the story a lot and how they kidnapped the horse. The horse was flying around and then he landed to drink some water. All of a sudden you'd see a rope coming out of nowhere and getting the horse. To me it was like taking the horse's freedom away. He couldn't do what he wanted to do anymore. I hated that.

I've been shot at a lot of times. I've been lucky, though. I was with Wizard when he got shot. He was shot in the leg. It was about a year ago. We went to buy some beer. And all of a sudden: BOOM! And I looked and I said "Come on. Hurry up!" And he said, "I can't walk. I can't walk." That scared me a little bit, but not a lot. 'Cause I knew he was okay.

When I got into the 'hood, Wizard had been in already a couple of months. One of the homies caught me and started hitting me, and we went at it. Then he said, "You're from the 'hood now." And I said, "No, I'm not." "Yeah," he said. "You're from the 'hood now."

But I know I had a choice. It felt right.

There are good things and bad things about being in a gang. One good thing is the adventure. Exciting and dangerous things happen. It's a little like being in a movie, only it's real life. Also, more people know you. You'll be walking down the street and a girl will say, "Hey, you're Ghost?" And I say, "Yeah. I'm Ghost.

Being in the neighborhood gave me a way not to put up with anybody's shit. I used to be real quiet. Kind of timid, really. Now I ain't going to let anybody cuss me out, no matter what he could be. He could be the president. I'd cuss him out right back. The president's just a person. Now when I get mad, I only have to use the anger one time. Usually people back off after that. I didn't know how to do that before.

The best thing about being in a gang is it's another family. Like when I was in the eighth grade, I ran away from home 'cause I got in a big argument with my mom. And one of the homies told me, "Hey. You can come and stay at my house." At that same time, the homies would say to me, "Hey, you hungry?" 'Cause they knew I wasn't at home and didn't have no money. So they'd give me some of their food. That's love.

The down side of being in a gang is that you get burned. You can't do nothing. You can't walk any place. Like before I used to walk all over. Now I can't show my face. I'm known. Your life is in danger all the time.

I've shot at people before. I started shooting when everything went crazy. We would tell people, "We don't want nothing with you." But they wouldn't listen. When some of my homies got shot, I started shooting back.

When I was going out on a mission, I would dress all in black. Everything black. Black pants. Black sweater. Black shoes. Black rag. Black beanie. It got so when my little sister would see me all dressed in black she would start crying. She didn't know where I was going but she knew I was up to something, and she would get scared. That made me feel bad. I've stopped banging now. I wanted to get my mom's faith back. Stop hurting my family.

I never hit anyone when I shot. I'm glad I didn't. Every time I hear G say, "I buried so many people this year," I think, I don't want to be the next one. He's already going through a lot. If I died, or if I hurt somebody, it would be like putting him down.

I don't know how you could get the violence to stop. The way the homies think about it is this way: "If we give our enemies a chance, then we'll be open targets. So let's not give 'em a chance." If everybody has that attitude, then nobody's gonna take a risk. If somebody does take a risk, they could get back-stabbed. So nobody's gonna take a risk.

In terms of goals, I'd like to see the world. I also want to get my education. I want to study computers. Then I want to get a house and a wife. In ten years I'd like to have a little house . . . a thousand kids . . . and be the Partridge Family.

I guess if I could have one wish . . . I'd like to have my dad still alive. If I had him here—right here, right now—I'd ask him why he left my mom. Why he died. If I could spend one day with him, I wouldn't care what we did together, as long as we just could talk.

The night that he died, he was supposed to pick up my mom. They were supposed to go dancing. And he didn't go. He went with his friends instead. Every year on that same day—the day that my dad passed away—she has a dream about him. It's the same thing, over and over. She says, "Let's go. Let's go!" And he says, "No, I got to take care of some business first." Then he skies up. And he never comes back. She doesn't have it written down, the date he died, but she always knows. And she has the dream.

I have weird dreams too. One time I had this dream about me and Wizard. We were walking down the street and there was a car passing by. And we just kept on walking. And then we looked at the car and it just started letting out: DA! DA! DA! DA! DA! DA! DA! I got

Wizard and kind of threw him down on the ground. And when I threw myself down on the ground, I got shot in my leg. I went, "Oh fuck! I got shot!" Then I went, "Hey, Wizard. Wizard, I got shot!" And was just, like, shaking him. And I looked. And he just passed away. Croaked. And when I woke up I felt . . . scand'lous! Scared. I woke up sweating. Sweating.

This other dream I had, I was walking by my house. And all of a sudden I hear, "Ghost!" And I looked and I see somebody and I didn't know who it was. "C'mere!" they say and they keep on getting close and yelling "Ghost." And then they say, "Where're you from?" And I say, "Nowhere, homes. I don't bang no more."

"Where're you from?"

"Nowhere."

And then I hear, "Ghost! I thought I knew you, fool!"

And then shoot. BAM! And I could see my body on the floor. And then they come over and say, "See I told you, I fuckin' told you! Stupid! See I told you, *fuckin' told you, fuckin'* . . ." BAM!

Wizard

My name's Jorge Fuentes, but they call me Wizard. I have one brother and three sisters. I'm the youngest one in the family. My dad's my real dad. He's an alcoholic. The doctors say he's going to die from the drinking, but he won't stop.

When I was growing up, I was in my own little world. I was a wild kid. I was always talking back to teachers.

When I got older, they kept on putting me in the gifted classes. I liked that. But when they have you in those classes they expect you to do a lot of homework. There was no place to do it at my house. I used to always blame it on my dad. He's kind of violent. He used to beat up my mom. He'd say things to me—things like I wasn't his son and stuff. And call me all kinds of names. I used to leave and just kick it outside; take a deep breath before I got mad and try to hit him.

When I grew up, I'd leave when he started drinking. But then I'd come home and find out what he'd done, and I'd get mad. I always wanted to fight him. I wanted to take out my anger, once and for all. I never did. Some nights I used to break out in tears because I wanted to hit him so badly and I couldn't, because my mom would come out and say not to step onto his level because he was an alcoholic; that I should understand, and this and that. He'd find any little excuse to go drink. Then he used to blame it on me. Say it was my fault. It was not my fault. He was an alcoholic.

Then I started drinking too.

My mom stayed with him because she's from Mexico, and in Mexico they're not as into women's rights. In Mexico you stick by the man and that's how it has to be. No matter what the man says or does. She's a good mother. Very understanding. No matter what I've said or done, she's always stood by me.

Ghost's my best friend. We understand each other. When something happens, I try to tell him not to think about it the hard way, but to think about it in a way that's good for him. And when I get upset or all flared up, he tells me not to think about it.

I got courted into the neighborhood five years ago, at fourteen. I was going to get into another gang—Cuatro Flats. They used to be called Pico Stoners. They said to me, "We're going to court you in." I said, "If you jump me in, you're going to be mugging me. You're not going to be courting me in." But then CSL said they'd have somebody fight me, one on one. So I said, "Okay. Bring 'em on."

Sometimes at night I think, "Why did I get in?" I got in because I thought it was fun. But it was very disappointing. I wish I could go back to school and not be in a gang. There ain't nothing good in it. I wish I had an education. But if I wasn't in a gang, I'm pretty sure I would have been getting jumped all the time. So things would have gone wrong either way—in a gang or not in a gang, I would've gotten into trouble either way.

A lot of guys don't have the guts to say, "I'm going to stop banging." They got no will power. They're like little toys being controlled. I try to make some of the younger guys, on both sides, understand. But they don't listen. They think they're just having fun. They're just going through what I was going through. I thought I was having fun too.

I'd like to give all these gang members one more last chance. The chance would be to take away all the things you regret that you did—whatever that is—and see what happens. I'd do it for everybody in all the neighborhoods. See what they do with the chance. Also, if I had a fairy godmother I'd want her to take away the guns. You know when the guns got introduced to us? It was when that movie, *Colors,* came out. The movie didn't make it happen. But the movie introduced a whole new concept. When the Mexican gangs saw all the fighting happening between the Crips and the Bloods, we said, "Damn! We ain't going to stay without a gun 'cause we could die!" In about a week, everybody had guns and deaths were happening.

I've blasted. I don't hide it. And I've hit somebody more than once. They all lived. I don't know if any one of 'em knew it was me. The thing that leads up to it is anger. Your friends dying. Your friends getting shot or stabbed. Then—damn!—you're so mad you want to get revenge. The first one to die from our neighborhood was Toker's twin brother, Armando. We were so young. We were in the park kicking it when some guys popped out with guns. We all ran, but he slipped. And when he got up again, they shot 'im. BAM. Everybody was crying.

The second one was Shotgun. He was cool, always joking around to make you laugh. That's why it really hurt. He used to shoot a lot. That was during the time when I used to hold the guns. You can't be unpredictable and take care of the guns. I guess they wanted me to do it because I was very trustable.

I'll tell you how you hide a gun. You should hide it in the most obvious place because people are too dumb to look there. Like in the dashboard of a car. Or inside the speaker box. There's a really powerful magnet inside a car stereo speaker box. You can just put the gun in and it'll stick easily because of the magnet. It won't rattle or nothing. Or you can put it in the front of the car right near the radiator—there's a little space. Make sure the wires are on top, so the gun won't jump out. It's really easy. Even now, if I want a gun, I just dial seven numbers and it'll come.

I knew I needed to stop banging for a long time. I knew it in my heart, but I still needed to let the doors open, and let it come into my head. I stopped banging for my two kids. I adore kids. The homies got mad at me one time, because they said I wasn't going to the 'hood often enough. I said, "You gonna take care of my kid at night or what?" Pretty soon we had fists flying all over the place.

You could say that technically I *haven't* stopped banging. I don't blast, but I still go to see what the homies are doing—just to kick it with 'em. At one time, when I was a lot younger, right when I very first got in, we were so violent, we were so *low*, we were so desperate for fights, that we used to go around jumping people. I feel embarrassed even to say this. I mean we'd jump *men*. And sometimes we'd steal their money. I look back on that now and I feel really bad. I mean, they'd worked hard for their money. And for some hoodlum just to come, and jump 'em, and take their money away, when they were just going to the market to buy stuff for their wife and family and kids—that's low. That's terrible. When I think about that, I get mad at myself. But what am I going to do? Sock myself? I wish I could go back and make up for that. But I can't.

There was a time when I had a gun. G heard about it and he got mad. He tried to get me to give it to him. He kept saying that a real man would give it up. When I wouldn't give it up, he was very disappointed. I said, "I'll become a man, G. It'll just take a little while."

One thing about me, I may have an attitude, but I'm not a hypocrite. I don't lie. Lying just makes you look dumb. I told G what I'd done, one time. I said, "I shot this many people," and I told him a number. He just looked at me and smiled. He didn't believe me. And I thought, "Oh well, at least I got it off my chest."

G calms everybody. He always tells me what it takes to be a man. He tells you the same thing so many times, it starts going in, little by little. We don't mind him cussing at us. We understand. He's like a father—to me—to a lot of people. He does everything a parent is supposed to do. He lectures you. He loves you. He tries to help you.

G was the person who told me that I was an alcoholic. "You drink to get drunk," he said. "I bet you pass out." My eyes started getting all watery. I was realizing when he was saying it, that there was no way I could say it wasn't true.

The saddest thing in my life is when I'm drunk. Drinking calms me down. But when I look at myself, I'm scared to become like my dad.

In ten years I want to be living somewhere far from where I live now. I want to have a nice job and live with my kids and stuff. And then I want to come back to the projects for a visit and see what everyone is doing. I want to talk to the people who hated me once, who wanted to kill me once. I want to see my friends. I'd love to talk to everybody and say, "Hey! What's up?" To see who's still playing that stupid game. And who understood, and stopped.

I'm planning to move to El Paso soon with my lady and kids because if I stay around here I'm afraid I'd get into blasting again, like I did when I was young. I don't want to do that again. But I don't trust myself.

In terms of a job, I could do anything. You tell me how to do it one time, I can do it, no matter what it is. I'd be happy with any kind of job. I'm not really picky.

I hope I have a happy life. Whenever there's two ways to walk— if one way is the long, safe way, and the other way is pure fences—I always have to go through the fences. But I guess I'm lucky. 'Cause I'm still right here living.

Chapter 5

During the summer months, events flash from hopeful to apocalyptic, then back to hopeful with unnerving speed. Greg holds his breath for the week following Ghost's talk with the high school dean. Surprisingly—as with Bashful—no charges are ever brought, and Ghost is belatedly able to don his new clothes and show up for the job at the attorney's office. To some observers, Greg's obvious elation at Ghost's escape from legal retribution for a serious stabbing might seem to be a questionable ethical stance. Actions must have consequences. Yet it is difficult to see the virtue in demanding an eye for every eye in a barrio where so many eyes have already been lost.

Greg had also feared that the heat of the summer would bring on a drastic jump in violence all over East L.A. In the projects, at least, the violence never materializes. This is partly because in June, Greg managed to hire or find jobs for a record number of kids.

The downturn in violence makes the joys in the community stand out in sharper relief, as when weeds are removed from a garden and flowers become more visible. In June and July there are several *Quinceañeras,* the wedding-like coming-out parties that represent a

Mexican American girl's passage into womanhood. While Greg performs few weddings at Dolores Mission, every fifteen-year-old girl whose family can save, scrape together, beg, or borrow the money necessary, wants a *Quinceañera*. These are fantastic events at which the girl being "presented" wears a frothy white tulle, satin, and lace creation. At the reception following the presentation mass, she, her attendants and their male escorts, are required to dance a formal waltz. Thus, several times this season, the church parking lot has been the scene of remedial waltz lessons given to lumbering, reluctant homies by earnest community women.

As the community enjoys a period of comparative stability, the fortunes of specific kids continue to whipsaw. Now that Dreamer is locked up in probation camp, Turtle is starting to tag along after Green Eyes. It is easy to see Green Eyes' appeal for a kid like Turtle. Where Turtle is impulsive and prone to bouts of adolescent insecurity, nineteen-year-old Green Eyes is the epitome of cool. He is tall, lanky, and charismatic. Although his cheeks are dented with acne scars, his face borders on handsome. He wears two real diamonds in his left ear and his T-shirt and Dickies are always perfectly pressed. When Green Eyes lies, even when you are liable to catch him, he lies smoothly without a belying trace of guile. As one of TMC's main shooters, he is on every enemy's most wanted list.

In late August, Turtle is returning from the local swap meet when some kids from State Street open fire. Turtle is shot in the back. Although the bullet is lodged too close to his spine to be safely removed, the doctors tell Turtle he should be fine unless the bullet begins to travel.

Precisely a month later, Turtle and Green Eyes are crossing out Dukes graffiti and replacing it with their own when another drive-by occurs. One bullet comes so close to Turtle it knocks him to the pavement, shredding the back of his cloth belt. The second shooting incident so fast on the heels of the first has a sobering effect on him. The very next night he agrees to allow Greg to put him on a bus to San Jose, where the priest has found him a job as an apprentice baker learning how to put sugar icing roses on wedding cakes.

"Turtle's gonna have a life now," Jesús, Turtle's ten-year-old nephew, announces in a soft, hopeful voice, the day after Turtle's departure. "I hope he gets a good life. Don't you? He deserves a good life!"

Although Greg has twenty kids still working, as summer turns to fall the seasonal jobs dry up, the Santa Ana winds move in off the desert, and the mood of the projects begins to darken. Matters are made worse by two new players who have entered the delicate ecology of the Pico Aliso gangs. The first is Sergio Castaneda, aka Oso, a physically large twenty-year-old, just out of the state penitentiary. The second is Happy, the escape artist from TMC, who is released from long-term camp the day he turns eighteen.

It is a rule of thumb that the activity level of any given gang is greatly affected by who is locked up and who is out on the street. This rule proves to be true in the case of Happy and Oso.

Immediately upon his release, Oso reestablished himself as the primary shot-caller for Cuatro Flats. Most Hispanic gangs are organized as leaderless armies controlled by the democratic will of the collective. Yet, although gang members deny the existence of a hierarchy within their ranks, every neighborhood has its shot-callers—kids whose natural leadership abilities move them to a position of influence. Greg always makes a point of identifying and cultivating the shot-callers, a strategy that pays off when he needs localized pressure points in order to exert control when the inevitable emergency arises.

Oso, however, does not have in mind being anybody's pressure point. He is as sweet as sugar on his good days, with an ebullient personality that makes him popular with community mothers and the ten-year-old wannabes who trail him around Pico Gardens like a kite string. But on his bad days—read on his drunken days—Oso is dangerously unpredictable.

And he won't listen to Greg.

Greg thinks some of Oso's volatility is due to the fact that he was locked up when his best friend Night Owl was shot to death in the projects by L.A. county sheriffs in an incident that community onlookers still insist was a wrongful use of deadly force.

"If a kid doesn't get to attend the funeral and go through the grieving process," explains Greg, "it leads to trouble. He's had no outlet for his anger and grief, so the minute he's out it explodes."

Since July, Oso has exploded on a regular basis. He starts trouble with Clarence Street and TMC every time Greg's back is turned. Only in the face of a direct confrontation with the priest will Oso back off, grumbling loudly that he doesn't trust anybody.

Interestingly, Oso keeps asking Greg to hire him. Greg repeatedly tells Oso he can't have a job until he stops wreaking havoc. This battle of wills goes on for two months. By September Greg's had it. "Oso's so impossible," he sighs, "although I never could do it, part of me wants to write him off."

Instead he goes to Oso with an offer. "No one's going to hire you," he says. "You're an ex-con and a gang member. And you've done a lot of damage in this community. If you will undo the damage—get the big heads of Cuatro to mend relationships with Clarence and TMC— then and only then will I give you a job."

Oso says he will try. Nothing comes of it.

Greg's relationship with the TMC shot-callers is as good as his relationship with Oso is diccy. TMC is a neighborhood filled with strong personalities, the two strongest of whom are Rebel and Green Eyes. Rebel has long been devoted to Greg and, since his I-need-your-help conversation last March, he has held down a good job as a construction worker and kept his pledge to forswear banging.

Green Eyes, however, is not in good shape. In June he blew his position on the day care crew. Since then, he has been loaded with guilt and anxious not to do anything to further alienate Greg, trying sometimes to win points by intervening between his homies and trouble. Rumor has it that Green Eyes is shooting again, but only out of the projects where he hopes the news will not get back to the priest.

Now that Happy has returned to Pico Aliso, the TMC twosome has become a troika. Like Rebel and Green Eyes, Happy considers Greg to be his "real father." However, also like Rebel and Green Eyes, Happy is considered to be the downest of the down with nerves of ice and a talent for making those around him feel invincible. Because Happy has a crazy streak, he tends to run his own show more than he leads. Nonetheless, with Happy back on the street, a restive cockiness seeps into the attitude of the neighborhood as a whole.

"Happy pumps people up," says Rebel, giving his own analysis of the dynamic. "Since he's out, people are putting in more work"— meaning crossing out and shooting. "If somebody messes with the homies they mess with them back. But nobody's, you know, shooting to kill. There's no real reason to, because none of the TMC homies has ever died yet."

This is a situation that is soon to change. But the situation with Oso changes first.

At seven o'clock on September 10, little Fernie of the *Pandilla Mugrosa* comes to tell Greg that Oso's younger brother Sleepy has just been shot in the head. It is rumored on the street that the shooters were from Primera Flats, the gang that claims territory at the western end of Aliso Village. A shooting of any kind is bad enough, but if Sleepy dies, and the shooter is from another projects gang, the resulting gang war will make life more dangerous for everyone. Before Greg races to the hospital he takes a swing through Flats territory, hoping to prevent further disaster. The streets are empty, which only means that forces are probably massing out of sight.

Greg arrives at the White Memorial emergency room just after 8:00 P.M. Oso has already been there and left. Evidently Oso barged past the ER guards to the nurse nearest Sleepy, and said, "If you don't treat my brother well, I'll kill you." Once he had determined that his brother would live, Oso blew back out of the hospital in a towering rage.

Standing next to Sleepy's bed, Greg's eyes meet in wordless communication with those of Maria, the boys' mother. "Sergio," says Maria, meaning Oso, her voice panicky.

Greg leaves the emergency room to begin the search. He goes to Pico Gardens first, where he can also do damage control. "After someone is shot," he explains, "it's important to get back to his neighborhood and say to everyone, 'He's okay. I saw him with my own eyes. His brains aren't falling out.' "

Each place Greg goes, Oso has been and gone. Everyone has seen him roaming through the projects like a freak storm, yelling for guns. Fortunately the Cuatro homies have the presence of mind to refuse the request. No one wants to get near him.

After nearly an hour of driving, Greg finally finds the huge gangster way at the back of Pico, alone, leaning against a lamppost. Greg parks the car and walks in Oso's direction. As he approaches, Oso looks up.

"I know who shot my brother," Oso says after a silence. "If they had killed him, I would have packed myself with all the guns I could find and walked to that guy's house and killed the motherfucker."

This is exactly Greg's worst fear. He begins speaking soothingly to Oso, as one might talk a suicide off a ledge. But Oso's expression has already softened.

"I gotta tell you something really weird, G," Oso says. "I was walking around the factories for a long time because I wanted to do something, you know, crazy. But I kept hearing this little voice in my head saying, 'Don't do it!' And, G, for the first time in my life, I listened to that voice."

Greg tells him he should always listen to the voice. Oso nods and keeps talking, his words, once started, streaming out like floodwater. He describes going to the hospital and how Sleepy's face was covered in blood, how when Oso came into the hospital room, Sleepy had burst into tears.

"I never seen him cry before, G!" says Oso, as if his brother's tears are the most terrible of signs. "This one teardrop rolled down his face and it separated the blood, G! This one big tear! An' that's when I realized what I done!" Now Oso's voice is full of anguish. "My brother looked up to me, G," he says. "And look what I do. I bang! I'm a gangster! An' he looked up to me!"

"Do you know what he was crying for?" asks Greg, hoping he can lead Oso to a level which will allow this moment to have more than mere transitory effect.

"Yeah," says Oso. "He was crying for him. For me."

Oso grabs Greg in an enveloping hug and gasps, "I've got so much stuff in me and there's no one to talk to!"

"Let me help you, Sergio," says Greg, grabbing for the window of opportunity. "You've never let me help you. I swear to you, I'll always be there for you."

Eventually Greg drives Oso home.

"I have to admit I haven't really liked Oso lately," Greg says afterward. "But tonight I found myself being converted to this kid. It's like that line from *Diary of a Country Priest*, 'Grace is everywhere.'"

Grace notwithstanding, back at his office, Greg begins worrying again. "We might get through tonight," he says, "but will we get through tomorrow night and the next night? And if it's not Oso retaliating, will it be somebody else?"

The next night, Greg has been invited to celebrate mass for the kids who are locked up at Kirby Detention Center, the most rehabilitative of L.A. County's juvenile probation facilities. He weaves the incident with Oso and the inner voice into his gospel homily. After the mass Greg stands outside Kirby's small chapel to greet the worshippers. Kids he has never met stand in line to shake his hand or receive a hug, touching him with a kind of awe.

One long-haired girl of fourteen with deep circles under her eyes makes a point of lagging behind the others to have a word with Greg. She first blurts that she is at Kirby for doing a murder. "I didn't do it, Father," she says. "But I ain't gonna tell them who did. I used to gang bang, but I'm changing. See!" She thrusts out her wrist toward him. He sees three scars the size of quarters on her wrist and lower arm, "I used to have my neighborhood tattooed on my arm," she says, "but I got rid of it."

Greg inquires of the girl if she had gone to County General Hospital to have the tattoos removed.

"No," she replies blandly, "I burned them off with a cigarette."

Greg starts slightly and his eyes tear up. He puts out both his hands and closes them about her wrist and arm in an unconscious benediction.

The next day is Thursday, Greg's day off. He is on his way to go to a much needed movie outing but swings first through Aliso Village to drop off a salary check to an East L.A. kid. All at once a community mother spots Greg and waves from her ground-floor apartment window for the priest to stop as he pulls over, she strings a phone on a fifty-foot cord out the window to him.

"For you," says the mother. "It's Pam. She says it's an emergency."

By Pam, she means Pamela McDuffie, the local VISTA volunteer and one of the projects' main activist mothers. Pam has a reputation for being able to find anyone, anywhere, anytime in the projects, and today she has evidently dialed her network of mothers and told them to call her if they saw Greg.

Greg sighs as he takes the phone, sensing his movie plans are about to evaporate.

"We got a problem," says Pam, then breathlessly tells him that Oso is in the middle of a fight with some Clarence over a tagging incident and that he ought to get over there.

By the time Greg reaches the scene, the fight is just breaking up. It seems that Oso has tagged all over a wall that falls within Clarence neighborhood boundaries. Greg pointedly ignores Oso, refusing to rebuke him or even to speak to him. Instead he makes a great show of getting paint from the church, then going to the wall in question and painting over the sprayed graffiti. Finally he drives over to Pam's house and instructs her to give Oso a message. "Tell Oso I will give him a job. But I need to know if he is a man or a boy. Because I only give jobs to men."

On Friday a chastened Oso comes to Greg's office and apologizes. He would like a job, he says. Greg tells Oso he can start work Monday. Oso also wants to know if he can be allowed to come to the funeral of Green Eyes' uncle, who has died suddenly and is to be buried Sunday. Oso's request for permission is appropriate gang etiquette since Green Eyes is TMC, Oso is Cuatro, and the two neighborhoods are presently at odds—mainly because of Oso's actions. Greg tells Oso he can come. When Oso thanks him, his manner is humble and desperately grateful.

The funeral is uneventful. TMC is present *en masse.* Oso sits quietly at the back of the church until the time comes for the mourners to file pass the casket. He then lumbers forward and embraces Green Eyes with untempered affection. Green Eyes embraces Oso back.

"Green Eyes is taking it real hard," Oso says to Greg afterward.

On Monday Oso shows up for work. Greg has placed him on the ever-evolving day care crew, which has become the first stop for homie job training in that crew members labor right outside Greg's office and thus are easily monitored. Surprisingly, Oso is an excellent worker, sporting his newly acquired construction worker's back brace as if it is a badge of honor.

———

For decades the cholo gangs have had unwritten rules forbidding certain actions: No shooting at an enemy when he is with his family or his lady, no shooting when children are around, etc. But of late, the ultra-violence seen elsewhere in the city is seeping into East L.A. Two days ago, someone opened fire in the direction of Dolores Mission Alternative, also the site of Dolores Mission Elementary School. There is a large-caliber bullet hole in the big metal door leading to the first-floor parochial school. Today someone else opens fire at Utah Elementary School, the public school a block from the church.

The next day, Greg hears via the grapevine that the shooter in the Dolores Mission Alternative incident is a kid named Alex who is a member of 38th Street, a non-projects gang. Greg sends a message to the shooter through a projects girl with ties to 38th Street. "Tell him to call me," says Greg.

In addition to school shootings, formerly uncrossable lines are now being crossed on a regular basis. There has been a spate of incidents in which the four main gangs packed tightly into Aliso Village have been shooting into houses. Every night, retaliations pile upon retaliations. Primera Flats shoots at TMC, TMC shoots at East L.A., East L.A. shoots at the East Coast Crips, and so on. No one has been killed, but there have been near misses. It's gotten so bad that some of the community parents are starting to shoot back.

"You read about stuff like this in the paper and it sounds like you're dealing with armies of teenage psychopaths," says Greg. "But all it takes is one desperate, messed-up kid, the one kid out of sixty who really should be locked up. He shoots into a house and pretty soon even the cooler heads feel they have to retaliate in kind or they're in a weakened position."

A week after the DMA shooting, Greg is at a stoplight when a brown station wagon pulls up next to him. The driver signals to him to roll down his car window.

"I'm Alex," says the driver. The Dolores Mission School shooter.

Greg looks the kid in the eye. The kid is small, young-looking, with a sweet, scared face. There is a short exchange and the kid assures the priest he will call. "Here I'm staring at a kid who shot toward an elementary school with all the fourth graders out," Greg says later, shaking his head unhappily. "And yet I have a feeling that if we knew his story, we'd have another Dreamer."

Near midnight, Greg is driving home when he sees a car he doesn't recognize with its lights off—a sure sign that a mission is about to take place. The driver, who wears a knit cap pulled low over his eyes, sees Greg and screeches away fast. Greg floors it in his own car and gives chase. Somewhere mid-block the driver reaches out the window.

BAM! BAM! BAM! The driver begins shooting in Greg's general direction. Greg keeps going, assuming the shots were fired only as a warning. The car peels around a corner fast. Greg tries to follow but the shooter's car has melted into the darkness.

———

Today the money issue has given Greg a tension headache. With the absence of any kind of jobs program for inner city kids, Greg just keeps on hiring more kids himself, or paying their salaries for employers who agree to take them on.

When Gumby, a hyperkinetic Cuatro Flats homie, hits Greg up for some *feria,* Greg takes out his wallet, turns it upside down, and shakes it with a look of exaggerated anticipation, as if hoping the wallet will suddenly spew bills like an ATM on a bender. Instead, a lone dollar flutters to the ground.

"As of today," he says once Gumby has exited, "I'm exactly $4,856 overdrawn. The woman at the bank was very polite." He imitates the female bank VP's well-modulated tone of voice. "'Father Greg? Were you planning on making a deposit any time soon?' " Greg laughs nervously. "I need a *milagro.* Big time."

Three weeks ago, Greg was heartened when an auto detailer called saying he had read about Greg's program and wanted to hire two homeboys at what sounded like a decent starting wage. Greg sent Spanky, whose job painting stereos has recently ended, plus a second Clarence homie, Marco. Every day since, the two have reported to Greg how the job is *firme!*—in other words, terrific.

It makes Greg nervous when, at the end of the first week, the detailer makes no move to pay his two workers. Greg directs Spanky and Marco to ask the guy when they'll be paid. When no clear answer is forthcoming, Greg calls the detailer, who assures him that he is on a two-week pay schedule. At the end of another week and a half, still there are no paychecks. Greg reluctantly tells the homies not to return to the job.

"Tell me something," Greg asks angrily when he calls to tell the detailer that the homies will not be back. "Did you think you were dealing with human beings?"

This same week, Greg has made the decision to send Cisco into a six-month residential alcohol detox program. In order to accomplish this, Greg must make a "donation" to the program. Cisco must also quit his job. "He's the best worker we have, bar none," says Greg, "but drinking's going to kill him."

———

The fact that the shooting in Aliso continues unabated has upped Greg's general stress level. Finally Greg calls a peace summit between TMC, the Dukes, and Primera Flats, with two representatives from each of the neighborhoods. He figures if he can get the three to agree, then he will go to the Crips separately.

Greg asks Rebel to represent TMC. Green Eyes might normally be the appropriate second, but he has been making a point of staying away from the projects and Greg is reluctant to drag him back in. Besides, Happy wants to go. Greg hesitates but Rebel talks him into it.

"Happy's a hard head," says Rebel later, out of Greg's hearing, "but I know if something gets crazy he'll be the best one to back me up."

"Rebel was at great risk to help organize this thing," explains Greg, "because he has sent out word that he doesn't bang any more. The double-edged sword is, just being there puts him back in it. But he's the one with the juice. In terms of juice, there's Rebel—and there's everybody else.

On the day of the summit, all homies are first searched for weapons by probation officer Ridgway before being transported to a neutral and secret location—the residence of the Catholic Workers, a liberal Catholic organization that serves the poor, with which Greg has a good relationship. Rebel horrifies Ridgway by helpfully giving her directions to the Workers' location as she drives, thus making it clear that he knows where the summit is to be held. Ridgway wonders if there will be an ambush.

There is no ambush. Instead, although the gang members glare and posture—particularly Happy, who goes into gang posturing overdrive—an agreement not to shoot into houses is hammered out between the three warring entities. Other than Greg, Rebel is the primary voice of reason.

"My insight," says Greg after the summit has ended, "is that all of them wanted to stop the escalation, but they needed me to give them a face-saving excuse."

That night Greg is standing in the parking lot of the church listening to small-caliber weapons pop-popping in the near distance. "You put out one fire and five explode," he says, his expression fatigued. Then he laughs. "Sometimes I feel like the guy that used to be on the Ed Sullivan show. You know the juggler who used to spin all the plates? I've got all these plates in the air spinning and I go back between this one and that one and that one over there, trying to keep them all going so none crash to the floor."

The next night the Cuatro plate is in danger of crashing.

Oso shows up in Greg's office. "Clarence is crossing us out," he says, "and the youngsters want to do something. But I said we should go to you first."

The next day Greg organizes a quick peace conference between Cuatro and Clarence. There is some tension, but unlike the TMC-ELA-Primera peace summit, little potential for serious catastrophe.

"There have been no deaths between Cuatro and Clarence," explains Greg, "and as long as there are no deaths between two neighborhoods there is always a road backward. Once there is a death, the toothpaste is forever out of the tube."

This time it is Oso who aids Greg, further cementing his transformation from raging bull to conciliatory leader.

By the afternoon Greg is feeling optimistic again. He has found a fabulous job for Spanky that will gain him entry into the construction union. Spanky is walking on air. Greg has also agreed to give him the church's oldest car, a beat-up beige station wagon. But first Spanky has to clear up a stack of old traffic warrants, including one for jaywalking.

"How come you are only twenty years old, and your sorry booty has managed to get all these warrants?" Greg asks in mild exasperation, as he leafs through the warrants. "And I am almost forty and I've never had a *single* warrant. Why do you think that is?"

Uncowed, Spanky slings an affectionate arm around the priest's shoulders. "That's easy, G!" he says. "It's because *you're* a citizen . . . and I'm a *terrorist!*"

Greg laughs in spite of himself.

"So all in all, things are good," says Greg later. He ticks off the names of the kids who seemed to have turned a corner: Spanky, Oso, Ghost, Wizard, Turtle, Rebel. Even Green Eyes. "I'd just about given him up for lost, but he's in better shape than I've seen in a long time."

———

Along with the sea changes that have occurred in the various kids Greg has named, there has been another change—this one inside me. I had come to the projects with the intention of chronicling the lives of Father Greg and his homies through the lens of an investigative reporter. But as the months passed, there came a point when I was no longer content simply to record the events I was witnessing. I began to want to affect those events.

The first time I noticed this slippage in objectivity was in May, when I interviewed Dreamer shortly after his day in court. I picked him up at his mother's house and we went to eat at a nearby Jack-in-the-Box, then drove around for a while to talk further. Finally, my questions ran out and I drove back to his mother's small, dark house. He hesitated before opening my car door, finding flimsy excuses to prolong the conversation. When he could find no more excuses, he just sat looking out of the car window, his body tilting slightly in my direction. It was as if I was a form of radiant heat and he had been cold for a very long time.

Driving home, I ruminated on what I had observed of his obvious desire for tenderness and caring from an adult—any adult. A week later I had a similar experience with Cisco.

The more I interviewed any of Greg's homeboys, the more I liked them and wanted to help them. However, I think the real point at which I crossed the line of objectivity was with Miguel Cisneros, aka Green Eyes.

Of all the gang members I had been following, Green Eyes was the one least likely to succeed. Even in the opinions of his probation officers, Tuchek and Ridgway, he was too angry, too hardened by the gang experience ever to be truly reclaimed. Certainly life had not dealt Green Eyes an easy hand. His mother was a PCP head, his father a junkie who rejected him outright, his aunts and uncles all gang members. And yet there was something about this kid . . . For all his surface cool, he always seemed eager for contact.

I had my own agenda for getting to know Green Eyes. I had gotten to know the Dreamers, the Turtles, the Spankys—but none were hardcore shooters, and Green Eyes was a shooter. Yet I could find no meanness about him. Nor any of the classic markings of a sociopath. I hoped that if I could penetrate his internal logic it would offer clues to the logic of the violence as a whole. I even interviewed his best childhood friend, an African American non-gang member named Marcus who had recently enrolled in city college. On the surface, the two had very similar backgrounds. Both had terribly dysfunctional families, no dads to speak of. Both were raised by grandmothers who were inattentive at best. They had been football players together, break dancers together—and then Green Eyes had been courted into TMC. What had made the difference? Why was Marcus saved while Green Eyes seemed so lost?

"I don't know," said Marcus. "I think about it all the time. And the only thing I can think of . . . this will sound crazy . . . but it might've been because I used to watch *The Brady Bunch*. I watched it all the time for a whole lot of years. And I would imagine that they were my family. It's almost like I was living it 'cause I could imagine it so clear. I don't think Mikey can imagine anything different than the life he got stuck with."

Green Eyes and I would usually go to lunch at some safe restaurant—"safe" meaning far from the neighborhood—and there we would talk in the presence of my tape recorder. I explained to him that the purpose of the interviews was to help him paint a picture of himself so that the rest of the world might better understand that gang members were human beings, not the monsters the public imagined.

From the beginning he took the task quite seriously, grappling with each question with great solemnity. He told me about the first time he fired a gun, the first time he shot at an enemy gang member, the first time his bullet hit its intended target. He talked to me about his secret dreams and his nightmares. Yet, whatever the subject, each time Green Eyes revealed to me another hidden, previously unarticulated part of himself, his sense of personal worth and value seemed to grow visibly larger.

Greg tended to banish kids for a while when they had pushed the boundaries too far. Since Green Eyes had been fired from Greg's crew, he had landed on Greg's bad list. Then a month into my interviews with Green Eyes, Greg remarked to me that he had never seen the kid so open and vulnerable. "Never underestimate how far a little caring can go," he said. Several weeks and several more conversations later, Green Eyes claimed to me that he had stopped gang banging for good.

Nonetheless, each day Green Eyes seemed to vacillate wildly between hope and the kind of trapped desperation that leads a kid to drastic acts. In one breath he would talk about his resolve to "make it" and how he wasn't going to ask Father Greg for help anymore. "I can't ask anybody for help. I've used up all my favors," he would say, his face grave and determined. "I've let G down too many times. I'm going to do it myself this time." In the next breath, his sense of determination and resolve would evaporate and his eyes would gaze into some bleak interior landscape. "I don't know if I can change it, you know what I mean? I don't know if I can change it."

———

Late in the afternoon on a Friday, Green Eyes' mood had been on the upswing and he was particularly full of plans. The week before, he had announced his decision to enroll in Rio Hondo Junior College. "I'm gonna make something of myself," he said in the general direction of John Tuchek, his probation officer. Tuchek reminded him that without a high school degree it would be tough going. Green Eyes set his jaw in reply. "Yeah, I know," he said, "but I gotta try it." I mentioned that Rio Hondo was a half-hour drive across town, that other junior colleges were closer. "But Rio Hondo'll be safe," he explained. "There're no enemies at Rio Hondo."

A snag had surfaced, however. As capable as Green Eyes was on the street, he was completely intimidated by the enrollment process. When I said I would be happy to help shepherd him through enrollment, he was elated. "That's great!" he said, shedding his habitual deadpan expression. "That's just great!"

That same afternoon, we began planning a trip to see the Mexican Art and Culture exhibit at the L.A. County Art Museum. I was surprised that Green Eyes was interested in attending the exhibit at all, but he was obviously delighted at the prospect, even offering to compile a list of TMC homeboys he thought should be included in the adventure.

As I was getting in my car to leave Green Eyes that afternoon—marveling silently at the change in this so-called incorrigible gangster—I noticed a new tattoo on the back of his neck. There, just at the collar line, in neat, almost romantic script, I could read the words, "I'm still here."

"It's the name of a song," Green Eyes explained with a wry smile. "I got the tattoo after I got shot." He was referring to the time in May when he had taken three .38-caliber bullets. "The song's a love song," he continues. "You know, a guy saying to his lady, 'I'm still here. I won't leave you.' But for me it means 'I'm still here in life. I'm still alive.'" He paused. "It's a good song," he said finally. "I play it every day when I get up in the morning. I'll bring it and play it for you if you want, next time I see you."

He never did play me that song.

A kid with no hope is dangerous. But a kid with a glimmer of hope is something almost scarier: incredibly fragile. That night Green Eyes decided to test the hope that had barely taken root inside him.

Green Eyes left Dolores Mission just after 6:00 P.M. He then drove his uncle—a grim-faced *veterano,* just released from prison—to the house where Green Eyes was staying with his grandmother and other family members. Once at home, he played for a while with his nine-month-old nephew, Leo, then showered and changed into a perfectly pressed white Penney's T-shirt and brown front-creased corduroy slacks. He snapped on the three slender gold chains—two rope-style and one link—that he wore when he wished to feel stylish. He splashed Paco Rabanne cologne liberally onto his face and neck.

At around eight-thirty, as he prepared to leave the house, his aunt Dolores, his mother's sister, reminded him that he had promised to help her the next morning with preparations for his uncle's welcome-home party to be given the following night. "Don't worry yourself, 'Lolo," Green Eyes reassured her, flashing his best smile. "I'll be back early."

From his grandmother's house, Green Eyes drove his lime-green Cutlass to the corner of Third and Clarence streets at the edge of Pico Village to meet a genial mix of TMC and Cuatro homies—Nomad, Romeo, Conejo, and Sleepy (Oso's now-recovered brother). The five of them decided to check out a party a few miles away with the idea of picking up some girls.

There were two possible routes to take to the party. Green Eyes had planned to take the one more roundabout, circumventing all enemy territory. Then at the last minute, to the surprise of his passengers, Green Eyes took the direct route. It was shortly after 10:00 P.M. when Green Eyes slowed his car at the intersection of Cummings and New Jersey streets and stared out his driver's-side window to where a cluster of gang members from the enemy Boyle Heights gang (one of the hundreds of out-of-projects gangs) were gathered. "TMC!" Green Eyes yelled. At this challenge, an unidentified homeboy from Boyle Heights pulled out a 9 mm pistol and fired a string of shots as Green Eyes gunned the engine. Several bullets punctured the Cutlass chassis. A single bullet hit Green Eyes in the head.

Panicked, Nomad took the wheel and raced Green Eyes to White Memorial Hospital, where the others did little more than roll Green Eyes out of the car at the emergency room entrance, then sped away, afraid of being questioned by the police. Emergency room surgeon Dr. Brian Johnson worked until midnight to determine whether or not Green Eyes' brain stem was functioning well enough to sustain life or thought.

As usual, Greg is the first one to hear the news. At 10:00 P.M. he sees Nomad and Romeo. Nomad's clothes look as though he's been doused with dark red paint. Frightened, the two spill out only a partial story. Greg races to White Memorial. While the doctors work on Green Eyes, Greg tries to reach boy's mother. Failing that, he tries for one of the aunts. He gets Dolores on the phone. She is unresponsive and vague.

"Do you think I should come down there?" she asks. "Yes," says Greg, suppressing anger. "I think you should come down here."

For a long time nobody shows up. Finally two of the aunts come. They take a look at Green Eyes, exchange a few words with Greg, then leave. All in the space of about five minutes. Greg paces after they exit. "Nobody's ever been there for this kid," he says. "Nobody. Ever."

The vacuum left by the absence of family is filled the usual way. Like doves lighting on a tree branch, groups of Green Eyes' homeboys and homegirls flutter into the ER waiting room to wait for news of his condition. Then around 11:30 P.M. Greg gets an emergency telephone call. The projects have gone crazy. Some people thought to be members of Boyle Heights—the same gang who shot Green Eyes—drive down Gless Street yelling challenges. TMC and Cuatro Flats, now hyper and well strapped with weapons, shoot at the car, which crashes near the church. Its habitants are yanked out of the vehicle and beaten so badly it is rumored that one kid may not make it.

Mini-riots have sprung up all through the projects like hot patches of brushfire. In Pico Gardens, homeboys are throwing rocks and bottles at housing police. When Greg reaches Pico, Cuatro homies shout something about Clarence driving by and yelling "Fuck Cuatro!"

"You see! You see!" screams Oso at Greg, his words ambiguous and shrill with hysteria.

Greg's presence momentarily calms the rioters. Then sometime after midnight, he has a bad feeling in his gut followed by a frantic desire to return to the hospital. Earlier, Greg had been made nervous by a car that circled past the hospital again and again, its occupants invisible from inside the vehicle's heavily tinted windows.

When Greg arrives back at White Memorial, the emergency room is in chaos. The mystery car had just come back filled with East L.A. Dukes. The Dukes opened fire on the hospital. A series of bullets have shattered the ER's plate glass window and slammed through the wall at the other side of the room to blast half-dollar-sized craters in a second wall beyond. Glass is everywhere. Peaches, the girlfriend of a Clarence kid, has been skinned superficially in the face. The ER personnel alternate between compulsive activity and a kind of immobilizing shock.

At some point, into the midst of this weird maelstrom comes Estrella, Green Eyes' mother, her emotional affect strange and dreamy, as if she is unable to fully comprehend what has happened.

After the mother is gone and the worst of the glass is swept from the emergency room, Greg's own mood becomes brittle. He makes a mental list of who he thinks has the right to cry if Green Eyes dies.

"It is a very, very short list," he says bitterly.

As bad as this night has been, there are still more lives to be ruined. Although Greg doesn't yet know it, a contingent of TMC's and Cuatros—some from the original group, some new participants—have taken Green Eyes' bullet-scarred car back to the scene of the shooting, where they open fire on the first Boyle Heights homeboy they find. The boy, named Danny Ortiz, dies within hours.

I don't get the news from Greg until early Saturday morning. "I've been dreading making this call," Greg says his voice flat and gray. "Green Eyes has been shot. He's brain dead."

I am completely undone. Not this kid, I think. I stash my own kid with a neighbor and immediately drive the forty miles separating my nice, safe residential area from the city and White Memorial. When I arrive at the intensive care unit on the hospital's third floor, Green Eyes hovers in the strange realm between dead and not dead. He is breathing, but his breathing has the eerily perfect rhythm that only a machine can produce. His face is badly swollen and although his head is bandaged, it is still seeping thin liquid. His chest is bare and looks terribly skinny and young. It is the chest of one you want to gather up into a mother's arms and keep safe from harm. But he is beyond the reach of safety now. Beyond the reach of any mother's arms.

There is no momentary illusion that this kid was an innocent. There are the tattoos, the one which spelled out his affiliation—TMC—scrawled without much skill on his right arm. His most prominent tattoo, which reads "Brown Pride," is written in a far more careful script across the right side of his neck. This was the tattoo that caused him problems on job interviews because no shirt could hide it. The new tattoo he'd displayed just hours before is covered by bandages. As I stare at him the title to his song plays like an ironic mantra in my head. "I'm still here, I'm still here, I'm still here."

But of course he isn't there at all.

Green Eyes

My name is Miguel Cisneros, but they call me Green Eyes, 'cause of my eyes, obviously. When I was a youngster, my homeboys who I looked up to used to call me by my real name. I didn't like that. It made me feel like I was a little punk. Like, "C'mere Mikey." So I said to myself, "I'm going to get my respect." And that's what I did. Because I took care of business for them, you know what I'm saying?

I was born and raised in Pico Gardens. My mother and my father, they were from the gang known as Cuatro Flats. That's where all my family's from. My uncles and my aunts. They were all in gangs. You got to be from a gang down in the projects. Most guys get into it for the protection. I didn't go with Cuatro because they were all the old *veteranos*. TMC was the gang with all the young guys. It was the new way.

My family used to all live in one apartment in the projects. There was five bedrooms, and three of us per room. It was pretty crazy. My uncles used to take a lot of drugs and freak out. When the cops would throw raids, everybody would run into my house. And then the cops would run in there, and get my uncles.

When I was fourteen, the police raided my house because my uncle had shot somebody. This time they found PCP and guns—three rifles and two handguns. So we had to move out. When I was a little kid, I used to say, "I never want to be like them." I mean my uncles and my father. But the saying goes, "If you leave the projects, they will never leave you."

I dropped out of school. The teachers said I had a good brain if I would use it for the right things. But you go to school and there's always an enemy there. And you're not going to punk out. You're going to fight with 'em. Then he's going to shoot at you. And you're going to shoot back, maybe. Then you can't go to school no more. I think the only place I was going to school where I was doing good is when I was locked up.

The first time I got locked up was for GTA, Grand Theft Auto. A basehead stole a car and had rented it to my friend, and I borrowed it from him because I wanted to learn how to drive a stick shift. That's why they caught me. I didn't know how to get the car out of first. You should have seen me. I slammed on the gas to get away. And all the car did was bounce down the hill like it had the hiccups. I didn't jack the car. But I wasn't going to snitch on anybody. So I just let 'em lock me up.

Another time I was locked up for selling dope. I saw this truck coming, this brand new Forerunner. And I'm thinking, "Hey, that's a big sale!" So I'm running up to this truck, and two of my friends are running right behind me. The way it is on the street, you got to jump in the window first, and take up the whole space, if you want to make the sale. So I jump in the window and open my hand I have all kinds of dope in it. And then I looked at the driver's face. An' it's my P.O., my probation officer. He started laughing. I went, "Oh man!" and I ran.

That night I called Father Greg, and I told him what I'd done. He said I should turn myself in. So I did it. I turned myself in. My P.O. only gave me twenty days. He gave me a chance. To this day, I can't figure out why he gave me that chance.

I been shot twice. The first time I was shot, I shot myself in the hand. We had went on a drive-by. Our enemies kick it in two places, so we had two guns. My homeboy had a gun in the back of the car, and I had one in the front. At the first place we stopped, I got out of the car and started shooting. BAM! BAM! Until I ran out of bullets. Then when we got to the second place, my homeboy froze up on me. He didn't want to shoot. So I tried to take the gun from him. I cocked it back, and I heard it click. But you had to cock it back another click. So when I was getting out of the car, I shot myself. I thought they shot me. Then I seen the gunpowder, and I felt all stupid.

The other time I got shot, I was looking for it. The guy who shot me came into Pico Gardens. He was coming to buy dope. But I came at him all wrong. I was showin' him, you can't just walk into the projects. I said, "Where you from?" And then I laughed at his neighborhood. So then he asked me, "Where *you* from?" An' I told him and *he* laughed. And I got mad. So I socked him.

He didn't want to fight me. He just walked away. All my friends were around, and so I figured he didn't want to fight me because of my friends. So I said, "I'm gonna go over there and fight him by myself." And I went over there, and told him, "What's up?! Just you and me. Right here." That's when he brought out the gun. BAM! BAM! BAM! But it was my fault, you know what I'm sayin'? If I woulda never tried to be all Mr. Bad, I woulda never got shot.

You know the crazy thing? I didn't know if I was dead or alive. I fell to the ground. After that, I got up and I started running. Then I noticed that I was shot. An' I looked around and I saw everyone looking at me. I thought, "Shit! I must be dead, an' no one can see me!"

Everything was quiet. I could just hear the bullet shot. I couldn't hear nothing after that.

Then my cousin came up and said, "Are you all right?" and I snapped out of it. I saw that I was breathing. Then I started saying to myself, like in the movies, "Hurry up and get to the hospital before you die."

At the hospital they didn't really do nothing. The bullets went right through me, which was good. Otherwise sometimes you get paralyzed later. They cleaned the wounds and bandaged me. They didn't give me no pain pills. They sent me back out to the street with the bandages and no T-shirt.

I had to walk to the neighborhood. But I wanted to go, to tell you the truth. I wanted to go back to my neighborhood and show my homeboys that I was alive.

Nobody from my neighborhood has ever passed away. Friends, yes. A lot of friends. A couple of guys from Clarence Street and from Cuatro. But nobody from my neighborhood. And for me to be the first one . . . Damn! See, I'm one of the main ones from my neighborhood. So that would've been bad.

I'll tell you the truth: I never went back for revenge. I just squashed it. I told my homeboys, "Let it go." It was my fault. He was just defending *himself*. You know what I mean? I was responsible. So I told 'em just to kick back.

My homeboys, that's my family right there. Because they're there for me. The last girl I was with—the girl who is the mother of my son—she gave me a choice: Either her or them. And I picked them. Because they've been there all my life.

My father, he was into heroin. He died about five years ago from a heroin overdose. I used to see my father. I used to say "Hi" and "Bye." But I never got into a conversation with him. I guess you could say I never had a dad.

My mother, she was a good mother, but she had problems with drugs—PCP. She tried her best to raise me, I give her that credit. But that drug just fuckin' takes her away. She would let people in the house . . . you know, *people*. And I would bring my friends to the house. And she would be all high. And I was sad for my friends to see that, you know what I'm sayin? I would talk so good about her to them. And then to bring them to my house and have 'em see her like that . . . It used to hurt me. I used to want people to say, "Damn, he gots a nice mother."

The worst was once when I saw my mom's boyfriend beating her up. I was about nine. I was scared, man. I thought he was going to kill her. Then I thought he was going to kill me.

My little brothers, they're in foster homes. I got three little brothers. Adam's five. Evaristo's seven. An' Armando's nine. I talk to my brothers every Sunday. When I had a car I used to go visit them. But I don't like seeing them. It makes me too sad. I see them and I think, "I'm going to get my life together and get a house and take them out of that foster home." But then I go back to the projects and I just forget about it.

Right now I'm writing to my mother. She's in Mira Loma, the women's jail. She's locked up for being under the influence of PCP. She's been locked up a lot of times. But sometimes when people are locked up it might change their lives. I can tell from the letters she wrote me, that she's trying to change. When she's out in the projects, she would always be smoking that shit and it wouldn't give her mind time to think. Now that her mind is clear, she can think better. She says that when she gets out, she's going to try to get my little brothers back and, hopefully, we can be a family. She's taking up some kind of training so when she gets out, she can try to get a job. I just tell her, "Make that time in there worth it." But something tells me that she's just going to get out and do the same thing. Because that's what she said last time, how everything was going to be different. And it's never different. See, she's just like me. She's in the game.

If I could change anything about my life, I would've wanted to've grown up in another neighborhood. Then I would have never been in a gang. I barely started gang banging in the tenth grade. I used to play football in high school. The position I played was receiver. I used to be smart, you know what I'm sayin'?

The best night of football was the night I played in the Big Game. Roosevelt High School plays Garfield every year. That's the Big Game. Everybody from the projects goes. That year Garfield won. They had the better team. But I put my all into that game. I did everything I could do. And I did all right. I was proud of myself. I miss that. Being proud of myself.

My favorite subject was math. I had a good teacher and there was a lot of pretty girls in there. And I used to want to show them how smart I was. You know how it is when you're young.

When I was going to school, at first, I was staying away from gangs. But I started needing money. See, my mother stopped having any money, so I used to go out there and make it myself. That's when I started selling dope. I started getting closer to the gangs because they were the, you know, connection. That's when I started getting their ways, being like them. I picked TMC to kick it with because they were the gang that was running things at the time. That was the number one gang. They had the most respect.

You could say I was forced into the neighborhood. I was in the part one time when the homies came up to me and said, "Are you ready?" And I said, "Nah. I'll be down with you guys. But I don't want to be from a gang." I was from a football team, Pico Stoners. We played football in the park. I was into sports, like I said. Then *boom,* my homeboy Freddie, socked me in the back of my head. I got dazed. From then on, I just let 'em fuck me up. They would keep asking me, "Where're you from?" And I'd say, "I'm from nowhere, man." And they'd hit me again, and then ask me where I was from again. The way I figured it, they were gonna keep hitting me until I said I was from TMC.

At first I was upset. Then a couple of days later I told myself, "This is what you're going to do for the next couple of years." But then it started getting crazier. I started getting tattoos. I got locked up. That's when I really changed, when I got locked up. I had to defend myself. I didn't have anybody to call on to help me fight somebody. I learned not to ask nobody for nothing. I learned how to hold my own. That helped me. It showed me not to depend on nobody. Because I never had no visits. My family never came to visit me. I never had nothing. Whatever I got I had to get on my own.

Here's the thing: I can tell I'm different from everyone else. I got a lot of respect. Not everybody in the projects have that kind of respect. A lot of old veteranos—the guys that always hang around my father—they give me respect. Even my homeboys see it. And that's crazy, an older guy giving a younger guy respect. But it's how it is.

I meet girls from other neighborhoods at parties and they tell me, "This guy wants to kill you" or "That guy wants to kill you." So I'm always looking over my shoulder. I don't know if I'm scared of dying. I wouldn't mind dying if I knew I'm gonna go to heaven. But I don't know that.

I don't try to hurt people. I just do it when they've hurted me or mine. I'm nice to a lot of people. Like the baseheads, everybody disrespects them. I try to help them out. A lot of my homeboys don't see the baseheads as people. But the baseheads out there—a lot of them were the ones that raised me when I was a kid. I see it like this, they took care of me when I was little; they wouldn't let nobody pick on me; so I'm going to take care of them now. Like my uncle. He's one of them. I got respect for him because he supports his habit. And my homeboys don't fuck with 'im because they know I'll fuck with *them*.

I'd like to change the way I think. Now I just got one thing in my mind—selling dope and gang banging. I don't wanna think like that. I never used to think like that. I used to think about going to school and being somebody. Helping the world in some way. Like what Father Greg does. I don't think like that anymore. I just think about hurting my enemies, and that's it. And making money at the same time.

I think about my son too. That's who I love more than anyone. My son. I don't see him as much as I would like. But I love him. I was locked up when he was born. I was in camp. When I got out he was three months old. It was hard to get a letter that my son was born two weeks ago.

If I had a, like fairy godmother who said I could have three wishes, then my wishes would be to have a job. Something where I could use my muscles. Something that would make me sweat. I wouldn't want to work in an office. That's not my style. Number two wish, would be to be a good father. And then the last wish would be to stop hurting people. Because the people I hurt, other people are hurting too. Their families. I think about that. Then I tell myself, they ain't worried about what they do to us. So why should I worry about it?

I never killed anybody. I've run up on people and shot them. I wanted to let 'em know who it was that did it. I don't try to kill 'em. Now—I don't run up on people. I do it the right way. I do it where no one's around. Where nobody knows nothing. Do it and don't tell nobody. That's why I have the respect, because I'm the one who always does it. Some people say I call some of the shots for my neighborhood.

I don't know about that. But if I say something—you could say that people will listen.

I never cry. Except when my father passed away, that made me cry. Somebody came up and told me, "Your father passed away." I took it cool for a while. But when I went to his funeral, I went up there to the casket and all that pain came out. It really hurted. I started crying.

I never knew my father. He wasn't there for me. He could have brought me up in a different way, helped my mother bring me up in a different way. But he just wasn't there for me. He did his own thing. But he's still my father. He's the one that brought me into this world.

I want to be there for my son. Teach him how to grow up the right way. So you don't grow up to be a mess-up. I'd tell him, "Be a good man. Go to school. Get a job. Be somebody for this world. Stay away from all this shit down here." But the truth is, I'm not there for him. Not really. I'm on the street.

It seems like I'm following in my father's footsteps. Everybody says that the things he used to do, I do now. I always told myself I'd never be like that. All my life, my father was the person I hated the most. And look, I turned out just like him.

Chapter 6

In the days following the
shooting of Green Eyes, a thick mood comes on the parish. For those
living in a war zone—and Pico Aliso is undeniably a war zone—
death is the uninvited visitor whom everyone has learned to expect.
Yet all the dire expectations that daily fill this community fail to
lessen the shock when a death finally comes.

Green Eyes is shot on Friday, but is not declared brain dead until
Monday. He is kept on life support until Wednesday, when he is
transported to surgery for organ donation. Saturday afternoon
Turtle calls from San Jose wanting to know if it is true, is Green Eyes
really dead? Greg says yes, he is really dead. Turtle begins sobbing.
He is coming back to the projects. "I don't want to disrespect you,"
he says, "but there's nothing you can do to talk me out of it." Greg
tries to talk him out of it anyway, knowing it will be futile.

Later that same afternoon, Greg receives a postcard from
Turtle postmarked a few days before. The card describes how
happy Turtle is in his new life. "I like it here!" he writes in elaborate gang script.

Greg flips the card to his desk, worrying aloud that with Green Eyes dead, Turtle's "safe life" will go up in smoke. "Three steps forward, four steps back," he says.

———

If getting to know Green Eyes had shoved me firmly over the line from objective to subjective as a journalist, his death began to tilt my life as a whole subtly off its axis. The night after he was shot, just subsequent to my visiting him in the hospital, I attended a birthday party for a friend, a terrific women who is the mother of one of my kid's classmates at school. It was a perfectly nice party. Good food, good wine, excellent company. And I hated being there. Talk about the next PTA fundraiser, or who was working on what Hollywood movie, seemed intolerably trivial next to the shooting death of a kid.

The feelings of alienation that began that night continued to grow as the weeks and months wore on. I became the dinner party guest from hell, interested in little else other than what I was seeing and experiencing in East Los Angeles. Greg and the projects were where *real life* resided. Everything else—everything other than my son— began to seem like a pale imitation.

———

There is a frail, revisionist myth making the rounds among the younger homies, that Green Eyes' death was an accident, that he had gotten off on the wrong freeway exit and found himself, by terrible mishap, at the fatal street corner where he was recognized by enemies who seized the chance to get the infamous Green Eyes. This wrong-exit story is an attempt to deny the most obvious fact of his death: Super-cool Green Eyes had not gone out in a blaze of glory. He had gotten himself blown away in circumstances both ignominious and unheroic. He had ended with a whimper, not a bang.

Tension also emerges around the question of who will be picked up and charged with the crimes attendant to Green Eyes' murder. At this point, even Greg doesn't know exactly who was originally in the car with Green Eyes, who got out after he was taken to the hospital, who else got in for the mission that resulted in the murder of the Boyle Heights kid.

Rumors are everywhere. The night Green Eyes was shot, a kid from BMS, a gang affiliated with the Dukes, was killed in South Central. There are rumors that the two shootings are somehow related. There is said to have been a second TMC/Cuatro mission, this one against the Tiny Boys, another out-of-projects gang. There is a companion rumor that the Tiny Boys have threatened to hit the church during the funeral mass. There is even a rumor that the Tiny Boys are out to get Greg.

Mary Ridgway takes the last rumor seriously enough to suggest that Greg take extra precautions.

"Like what should I do?" Greg asks, shrugging his shoulders.

Green Eyes' funeral is scheduled for Sunday night, with the burial to take place Monday morning. Greg is hoping that after the funeral, the rumor factory will slow and tension will lessen. "It feels like a long time until Sunday," he says.

In this kind of a crisis, Greg is grateful for the presence of Mary Ridgway. In the last several years, he and the probation officer have developed a friendship that seems to provide a measure of emotional sustenance to both of them.

Ridgway is a heavyset woman with a tired, intelligent face and very few personal indulgences save a penchant for fashionable shoes from Nordstrom's department store and good jade jewelry. Once a UCLA sorority girl, she chose probation work after her ambitions of working for the State Department were thwarted because of gender. Now she is one of the two best known and most respected P.O.s in the city, the Mother of All Probation Officers, whom even her superiors are disinclined to cross.

Although Greg often goes to Ridgway to plead on a kid's behalf, and Ridgway inevitably takes the harder point of view, they have come to respect the other's position. There is an affection between them.

Every Friday afternoon, Ridgway holds her probation meeting in the Dolores Mission School cafeteria. At this time all gang members who are on her or her partner's caseload must check in. Ridgway's partner, John Tuchek, is a tall looker with a diamond earring in his left ear, an amused, cynical demeanor and lengthy juvenile record of his own. The kids like Tucheck, but as P.O.'s go, Ridgway is the main event.

Between 4:30 and 5:30 P.M., twenty or so gang members straggle in and strew themselves among the rows of Formica cafeteria tables where they fill out slips of paper in order to report their weekly activities—whether they have missed school or days at work, if they currently have a job. The gang members from "the other side"—i.e., East L.A., Primera Flats, the East Coast Crips, and Al Capone; all the gangs who are shooting enemies with TMC, Cuatro, and Clarence— Ridgway will see separately in Aliso Village after this meeting is over.

Tonight, in addition to the usual check-in, Ridgway hands each kid a second piece of paper which he or she must sign. The paper says that the undersigned understands that for the duration of the weekend, "all gang association conditions will be enforced" and that a 9:00 P.M. curfew will also be in place throughout the projects.

When kids are placed on court-mandated probation, they are read a set of rules and regulations that will govern their actions for as long as probation lasts. The rules include such directives as: "No fraternization with known gang members," which technically means a kid can't associate with anyone who claims a neighborhood.

"Now, obviously, if I were to enforce this rule," says Ridgway, "all of the guys in this room would be locked up all of the time."

However, at crisis points, Ridgway can use the fraternization rule as a legal excuse to ask the cops to pick up any kid whom she considers to be temporarily in danger or dangerous.

The homies rumored to be involved in the death missions straggle into today's meeting with uneasy attitudes. The first to enter is Nomad, the tall, gaunt-eyed TMC homie who drove Green Eyes to the hospital. With no father, a drug addict mother, and a crazy grandmother, Nomad had always been a hard case. Yet for the past few months he has been showing up for both school and work with a sense of near-compulsive punctuality that has astonished Greg and the Dolores Mission staff.

"I'm just trying to make something of my life," he would say, the expression in his eyes questioning, not affirmative, like some gangster Pinocchio desperately wishing to become a real boy.

Today the wishful persona has disappeared and Nomad's face is chalky and expressionless. Romeo, another of the rumored passengers, greets Ridgway cheerily, covering whatever angst he may be feeling with sense of jovial bravado.

The third homie with an odd affect is Angel from Cuatro Flats. Angel is the older brother of little Fernie the PM'er. As children Angel and his two younger brothers—Fernie and Richard, an older PM'er—have each worn the nickname Cavity because their overwhelmed mother never had the time or money for adequate dental care. Even now Angel's smile is shadowed by dark spots of decay.

Sweet and peer-driven, Angel seems much younger than his eighteen years. Today he is jittery and so needful of caring attention one gets the feeling that, if it was socially acceptable, Angel would climb on the nearest lap and ask to be rocked to sleep.

Tuchek, who had been Green Eyes' P.O., is also pale and withdrawn today. Two weeks before, he and Green Eyes had argued because Tuchek had refused to let him off probation.

"You tell me to stay out of the projects," Green Eyes had said, furious at the restrictions probation demanded. "Which means you're telling me I'm not allowed to come down and see my lady and my baby! You make me feel so fucking trapped!"

"I'm just trying to keep you alive, Miguel," Tuchek had shouted after him as Green Eyes stormed from the room. After he had gone, Tuchek raised a cynical eyebrow. "That kid's not going to make it to twenty-one."

Today when I remind Tuchek of his prediction, he looks away. "I didn't want to be right," he says.

———

The mass is set for 7:00 P.M. Funerals are events for which gang members are unerringly punctual, and tonight homies are massing outside the church from six o'clock on. A *60 Minutes* crew, which has been filming a story on Greg, has requested and received permission to film the funeral. The cameraman has his equipment set up near the altar in order to film the entrance of the homies, who include as many Cuatros as TMCs, all sporting their latest memorial sweatshirts. In addition to the usual "IN LOVING MEMORY OF . . ." inscription, the homies have attached, "I'M STILL HERE."

Fernie, Jaime, and a half-dozen other PM'ers have scattered themselves at the back of the altar as Greg delivers an emotional eulogy, telling stories about Green Eyes working on the day care center, braiding the "I'm still here" refrain into an urgent message of redemption.

"Miguel knew what the solution was, because he told me," Greg says, winding up for a close. "And the solution is this: The solution is one person saying for himself, *'Y'a estuvo.* For me, it's over. Never again. I don't do this anymore. I won't do this anymore.' Miguel knew that is the answer. That's what he wanted for himself. And if you have a sweatshirt on tonight that says 'I'm still here,' *that's* what he wants for you."

Estrella, Green Eyes' mother, comes late to the mass dressed in a black leather jacket and docs not sit down in front with the grandmother and the aunts, her sisters. Instead she takes a seat midway down the aisle with the rest of the mourners. Estrella is overweight, bleached blond, and sexy, with an expression that suggests she rarely expects good luck to come her way. Her three younger sons have been released from foster care for the occasion. They sit next to her in a row, three sad little boys silent with shock.

"I tried to be a good mother," Estrella says dully after the mass. "But I wanted to get high all the time. I was just so miserable. I was stuck with all the kids with no father to ever help. Mikey helped me. He showed me how to get on my feet—how to get out there and hustle. He'd always give me a couple of dollars. We were both homeless for a while. But he always fought to help me get on my feet. He would say, 'Mom, if you love somebody, you've got to fight for them.' Maybe I shoulda fought harder for him. I never really felt I had the strength. But maybe I shoulda found the strength."

Green Eyes is buried on Monday at 10:00 A.M. The casket has been opened for viewing since much earlier. Turtle stands the longest at the casket, staring down at Green Eyes' waxy face. Jesús, Turtle's small nephew, stands off to the side watching his uncle. Since he has returned, Turtle has dressed only in full gangster regalia, his normally ungreased hair now glassy and black, combed to the furthest reaches of cholo perfection. After a few moments, Jesús puts his head on his arms and begins crying very hard. Greg walks into the church in time to take note of the tableau.

On the way to the burial, Greg sees cars full of TMC's and Cuatros throwing up signs at each other. In irritation Greg throws up his "sign," to the homies in the cars: he gives them the finger. Then in the afternoon, after everyone has returned from the cemetery, Greg pulls Turtle aside to tell him about the scene with Jesús.

"Jesús didn't even know Green Eyes," Greg says. "So who do you think he was crying for?"

"I know," says Turtle.

"He was crying for you, homes! And the PM'ers, they were crying for you too. And for themselves. What kind of a future can they see for themselves? What kind of a future have you shown them? All it takes is one person to change. That's all it takes."

As soon as Green Eyes' mass and burial are over, homies who had previously managed to hold it together start to come unglued. Monday night Happy goes on a tagging binge, then doesn't come to work on Tuesday morning, calling in sick. At the same time, Rebel has come out of retirement and is back on the street, armed and dangerous. Of the big heads in the two neighborhoods, it is only Oso who is still showing restraint.

On Friday, when Happy doesn't show up for work for the fourth day in a row, Greg goes to look for him and finds him kicking it with a group of homies. Seeing Greg, Happy doubles over, clutching his stomach as if in pain. When Greg doesn't buy the theatrics, Happy straightens up, apologizes profusely, and pleads with Greg not to fire him.

"All day long today, G," he says to Greg, "I've been up in the air and I've been looking down on all of this here. I could see everything, G. It was like with drugs or a dream except I wasn't asleep."

"What did you see?" Greg asks.

"I saw people really hurting other people," replies Happy.

"Were you hurting people?"

"No," says Happy, "I wasn't. And I don't want to."

———

Although the crisis precipitated by Green Eyes' death is not over, it has plateaued. Now the community's attention turns to a new and larger source of panic.

Although for months word of Greg's impending sabbatical has been leaking out, no one has wanted to believe it. Like an illness in the family that is mentioned only in whispers, Greg's departure has been a subject few have been willing to discuss openly.

Now, as the time draws closer, denial gives way to a rising apprehension. Suddenly everyone seems to asking the same question: "What's going to happen when G leaves?"

―――

Ghost shows up in Greg's office as he often does after work, usually just to joke and hang out. Today he is not in a joking mood. "My whole goal is to get out of here before you do," he blurts. "It's gonna all break loose when you leave."

Greg is testy. "I think hell is breaking loose right now."

Ghost just looks at him. "Wait 'til you leave," he repeats. "We have respect for you and it holds us back—even if some people just hold back a little bit—they still hold back. But when you're gone and the other priests tell us to kick back, we're just going to say, 'Fuck you' to them."

The conversation depresses Greg. "This is all I keep hearing lately," he says after Ghost leaves. "If the truth be told, I'd love to be here 'til the day I die. But part of me says, "That's not very Jesuit.' It's part of our charism that you don't get attached. We're supposed to be detached and mobile and willing to be sent anywhere."

When it is pointed out to Greg that he is anything but detached, he blinks unhappily.

"No," he says, "I'm not. This is my life. It's my joy. It feels complete. And that's a big part of my own spiritual journey. Probably for the last two years, my spiritual task has been to prepare myself to leave here."

―――

Greg starts out the day cheered by a distinct bright spot in his gloomy relations with Hollenbeck Police. There is a new guy named Mike Marchello heading up the night patrol. Marchello is of Italian and Mexican descent, speaks fluent Spanish, and has been making a point of walking around and chatting with community members. Moreover, instead of bad-mouthing Greg, Marchello has been spreading the word to whomever he talks to that he has a good relationship with the priest.

Although there is much worry about Greg leaving, some of the homies seem to be using their concern as an excuse to get their lives together. Wizard and Ghost have both gotten themselves jobs, as have various homies from the others neighborhoods whom Greg helped early on.

Yet there are too many kids who still seem to be swimming against an invisible current. A few kids are coming dangerously close to being swept away altogether. Right now there are four such *red alerts:* Angel, Cicso, Happy, and Turtle.

Midway through the evening, Greg is confronted with red alert number one when a fight breaks out between Cuatro Flats and TMC. Punches are thrown, guns are drawn, shots are fired. Eventually the police arrive and arrest fourteen guys, including Oso and Silent from TMC.

Just as the police are shoving handcuffed homeboys into cars, Angel bursts from the shadows and begins circling the cops, skipping about like an addled bird, begging them to arrest him.

"Please take me too!" he pleads frantically. "Please let me change places with somebody! Please arrest me too!"

Ever since the Green Eyes shootings, Angel has been slipping visibly downhill. Although it is still uncertain whether or not he was present at any of the missions, something is having a distinctly disintegrative effect on his spirit.

After the black-and-whites drive away, Angel walks slowly back to Greg, his face collapsing.

"I don't want to live anymore," he says. Greg tries to comfort him, reminding him that his two little PM'er brothers, Richard and Fernie, look up to him and need him.

Angel shakes his head. "So much has happened," he says.

———

Number two red alert is Cisco. When Green Eyes was shot, Cisco predictably AWOL'd from rehab. Now Greg is having a hard time getting him back.

"I just want him to walk through this one door," Greg says. "He needs to start his life over. I'm afraid if he doesn't do this soon, something awful will happen."

Happy is an even more urgent red alert. Almost daily it reaches Greg's ears that Happy was seen brandishing weapons here, crossing out graffiti there. This hyper-gang-activity has made him the new prime target of many of TMC's enemies.

The fourth red alert is Turtle. Turtle has not yet gone back to San Jose and sometimes seems to be struggling in a realm of internal demons that Greg can never completely penetrate.

"I shouldn't tell you this," Turtle said to Greg, flopping into one of the office chairs, "but you know I've got to tell you everything." He then relates an experience from earlier in the day in which he walked a young girl named Lucia home right past where all of East L.A. was gathered.

"I just didn't care what they did to me," Turtle says with an unnerving flatness of tone.

"What do you think I would feel if something had happened to you?" Greg asks.

"You'd feel bad."

"And why would I feel bad?"

Turtle thinks a moment. "Because you've done so much for me?"

In the last year, Turtle has become one of Greg's favorites. He is a smart kid, loaded with humor, capable of a high degree of self-reflection and insight. "It has nothing to do with what I've ever done for you," Greg says sorrowfully. "It's because I love you. If something happened to you it would break my heart in half."

Turtle pauses, taking the thought in. "I think of that," he says.

"But you don't think about it always, do you?" asks Greg.

"No," admits Turtle, "I don't. Sometimes I don't care."

———

After two weeks of near catastrophes, Greg decides that the only way to keep Happy alive is to get him out of the state. Right now Texas is the most accessible destination, since Happy has family there.

However, despite days of trying, Greg has not been able to get in touch with any family members to find out if they will actually take him. When Happy has one more close call, Greg decides to just put him on a plane in the hope that if the kid turns up on the relatives' doorstep they will have no choice but to do the right thing and take him in.

Greg calls me at home and wants to know if I can drive Happy to the airport. Ridgway can't do it, he says, and he is needed at the church. There is no one else. Besides, I have interviewed Happy several times, and Greg figures he will be comfortable with me. I have come to take seriously Greg's worry that unless Happy is gotten out of the projects, he may not live out the week. So I alter my day's work schedule, get somebody else to pick my kid up from school, and agree to take him.

Ridgway is waiting at the church along with Greg when I arrive. She has threatened Happy that if he doesn't leave today she'll have him arrested, and now wants to make sure she actually sees him get in the car.

The minute we leave the church, it's obvious from Happy's body language that he is looking for any excuse to bolt. His first move is to try and get me to stop at a friend's apartment so he can "get some music tapes I forgot over there." I tell him no, that we don't have time if we are to make the plane. From that moment until we reach the airport, I try never to slow the car to any more than a rolling stop.

"You know this is really bad for my self-esteem!" Happy mutters sullenly as we race up the on ramp of the Santa Monica Freeway. For the next fifteen minutes he glowers furiously out the window, his muscles tensed as if to spring. On my way to the church I'd stopped by a bookstore and picked up paperback copies of the two books Happy had told me were his favorites, Kipling's *The Jungle Book* and Hemingway's *The Old Man and the Sea*. I break the silence to tell him I have brought him a gift, that he should look in the bag in the back seat. Happy drags the bookstore bag forward and peers into it. He carefully pulls out both of the books and stares at them wordlessly, one after the other, reading what I hoped were encouraging inscriptions that I'd hastily scrawled inside each cover.

"Thanks," he says at last, and seems unsure if he should allow himself to be affected. He still looks like he'd like to jump from the car. I chatter mindlessly to him, mustering up dumb axioms about turning points and having the courage to change one's life, hoping to keep him distracted enough that I can get him to the airport before he does something crazy.

It is only when Happy watches the two cardboard boxes containing his few earthly goods disappear into the gaping maw of the baggage conveyor that his shoulders sag mournfully, and he seems to finally give up the possibility of escape.

Later, as we are standing at the departure gate, waiting for boarding to begin, Happy turns to me and blurts, "I thought of pushing you out of the car and driving away. I really wanted to do that."

"I know," I say, both horrified and touched by his admission. "But you didn't do it."

"But I wanted to."

"That's okay," I say, having by now absorbed some of Greg's strategies. "What's important is that you didn't."

That I have not freaked out at his confession seems to set Happy's mood in another direction. Like a preschooler clinging to his mom's skirts for safety, he now barely strays six inches from my side and, just before actually boarding the plane, he gives me a surprisingly emotional hug and thanks me. Then he heads toward the boarding tunnel. However, just before entering, Happy balks once more, performs an about-face, and heads back to me, his expression one of ill-concealed panic.

"Did G get ahold of anybody? To find out if it's okay that I come?"

"Sure," I say, although I know no such thing. "And it's fine."

After Happy is safely on the plane, I call Greg on an airport pay phone. He tells me he has just talked to Happy's sister. "They're going to take him," he says.

"Do they want him?"

Greg hesitates. "Well" he says, "that isn't entirely clear."

⸻

During the month of December, the shooting hasn't stopped but is has slowed. Then, four days before Christmas, Greg is walking back from a *posada* in Aliso village with Fernie, Jaime, and two other PM'ers. The *posadas* are a Latin American tradition in which community members stroll from house to house singing songs in a symbolic reenactment of the drama of Mary and Joseph finding no room at the inn. The singers are "rejected" at the first two houses they visit, then finally at the last house, they are "accepted." Hot chocolate and *pan dulce* are served to all. Bags of candy are distributed to the kids.

This night, Greg and his charges are approaching the small neighborhood market when a shootout begins between TMC and East L.A.—Rebel smack in the middle of it. The priest and the boys freeze. One of the smallest drops his bag of candy in the street as he throws his arms around Greg's legs, refusing to let go even after the shooting has stopped.

Finally Greg is able to unstick the little boy. The five walk the rest of the way to Pico Gardens in distressed silence. When they get to Fifth Street, Jaime is the first one to speak.

"Sometimes I wish that everybody that had a gun would come outside and hold the gun up to the air," he says, eyes as huge as a meerkat's. "And then the guns would float up to the sky and we'd never see them again."

A few yards later, Fernie, Angel's little brother, asks Greg to lean over so he can whisper in his ear. "You know what I want for Christmas, G?" he asks. Greg shakes his head. "I want my brother to get out of Cuatro Flats. That's all I want." Greg hugs him, thinking sadly that neither of these wishes is likely to come true.

———

Christmas comes and goes without incident. Greg is pleased when Oso shows up for midnight mass at the church, but less pleased when he notices that Oso is drunk. On the Friday after Christmas, Greg drives Turtle back to San Jose, where he will stay with his cousin. Greg has also extracted a promise from Cisco that he will go back to rehab right after New Year's Day. Cisco seems relieved that the decision has been made and assures Greg he won't even drink on New Year's Eve.

On New Year's Eve Greg gets a call around 11:00 P.M. It's Cisco.

"Hey, G! I need you to do me a big ass *paro!*" In other words, a favor.

"What?" asks Greg, immediately suspicious. "Where *are* you?"

"Where am I?" shouts Cisco to someone other than Greg. A male voice in the background answers, "Downey Police Station."

"Oh, yeah," says Cisco without a shred of embarrassment. "Downey Police Station."

"What'd they get you for?" asks Greg, beginning to become irritable.

Another shout by Cisco to someone at his end of the line. "What'd you get me for?"

The same male voice, "Drunkenness in public."

"Yeah! And I'm not even drunk, G!" Cisco informs Greg cheerfully. "They say they'll release me to you! You can pick me up in two hours!"

Greg is now entirely annoyed. "No," he says, "I'm *not* going to pick you up." Then he all but slams down the phone.

It's Friday and the day has not started well. Cisco fails to show up for his appointed 8:30 A.M. drive to rehab. Finally, at 9:30, Greg goes to Cisco's mother's apartment and finds the homie fast asleep with the rest of the family blissfully unaware that there even was an appointment.

Midday, Greg's mood improves somewhat when Turtle calls from San Jose to say that he is once again working and happy. "I don't have to watch my back up here, G," he says. "It's nice."

The activities of the afternoon are intermittently interrupted as Greg leaves his office to move load after load of raggedy white towels from the church's washing machine to the dryer. Towels for the homeless men are among Greg's ongoing bêtes noires as there are never quite enough to go around. This week, the towel supply is particularly low. So, in addition to making calls to get more towels donated, Greg alternates with Father Tom doing daily laundry duty. Today is Greg's day.

It is a bit after 3:00 P.M. Greg has just closed the dryer door on the final load when Oso wanders into the small patio where the appliances are stored. Greg is struck by how calm and serene Oso seems. For better and for worse, Oso is normally loaded with energy.

"When I die," Oso says in a non sequitur, "I want you to do my funeral mass. There's a certain song I want you to play, 'Someday We'll Be Together,' by Diana Ross. Okay?"

"Don't even talk like that," Greg says, shrugging Oso's statement away. "You'll be around to go to my funeral when I'm eighty."

Later Greg hears that Oso had made similar remarks earlier to a group of homies who were relaxing in the church's front office, telling them he wanted mariachis at his burial. The morbid talk had particularly upset Blue, a cherubic-faced sixteen-year-old from TMC, who had been hired part-time by Greg to do cleanup around the church. Blue idolizes Oso, all but sitting at his feet many days after work, listening as Oso tells war stories and dispenses veterano wisdom.

At around seven, just after the border brothers are fed, Greg gives a walking tour around the projects to a new Jesuit novice. The night air is clear and crisp and the distressing moments of the day fail to linger. Everywhere Greg walks the homies are unusually playful.

Oso is effusive in greeting Greg and the new Jesuit. In a spontaneous movement, Oso affectionately scoops up another Cuarto homie much smaller than himself and carries him, cradled like an oversized infant, over to Greg.

"Homeboy here wants a job and is too shy to ask," grins Oso. There is much laughter as the homie wriggles down from Oso's grasp. Greg gives Oso a happy, back-slapping embrace.

"*Tú eres lo máximo,* homes! You are the best!" says Greg.

———

It is around 10:00 P.M. when the homeboys from Eighteenth Street first come to the projects on what was intended as innocent business. There are two of them in a parked car flirting with some girls, among them Raquel, Rebel's currently estranged girlfriend. One of the Eighteenth Street homies is a *primo*, a cousin, to Romeo from TMC, giving his social foray into the projects even more legitimacy.

Nonetheless, the TMC's cannot resist seeing what these interlopers are about. Shadow from TMC begins to pump up his homies to go sweat the guys from Eighteenth Street. "Let's make sure they got respect" is the phrase he uses.

Shadow, born James Easton, is an interesting character. Like Rebel, Happy and formerly Green Eyes, he is one of the select few who is able to move TMC to action. Shadow is handsome, clever, and hotheaded, with a family predisposition for slanging—he was raised in the one of the most active crack houses in all of East L.A.—and has a personality strong enough to earn him a second nickname of "The President." Shadow is also black. Certain of the projects gangs have traditionally had a couple of African American kids numbered among them. Right now there is Shadow, Shady, and Terence Garrett from Cuatro.

Accompanied by a dozen or so TMC's, Shadow approaches the Eighteenth Street car, his pistol on prominent display. At first Shadow does most of the talking. He runs it down to the Eighteenth Streeters, asking them if they know where they are. The Eighteenth Street guys know the drill and are appropriately respectful. They explain that they are just there to party and want no trouble. Satisfied with this response, Shadow and most of the TMC's are ready to leave.

Suddenly, off to the side, something appears to go wrong. Words are exchanged between one of the Eighteenth Streeters and Blue, the freckle-faced boy who had earlier been alarmed by Oso's funeral talk. A short fight ensues. Shadow still brandishes the gun as all other players move back to give the fighters room. Both of the combatants are small, and the fight ends quickly. Although Blue seems to inflict the most damage, the battle is deemed fair and, once again, it appears that everyone is ready to leave. All at once Pato, another of the "Termites," the younger clique within TMC of which Turtle, Blue, and Romeo are all members, leaps forward and grabs a gold chain off the neck of the Eighteenth Street kid who is the cousin of Romeo.

This kind of move is considered bad form and lacking in honor. But no one appears to know how to rectify it. "It was my fault," Shadow says later after everything has happened. "I had the gun and so I should have been the one to stop him. I take the blame."

But Shadow doesn't stop Pato. Although no one from Eighteenth Street says anything, their faces go dark with anger at the insult. Finally the TMC's allow Eighteenth Street to leave. As the outsiders roar from the projects, everyone agrees that Eighteenth Street will be back.

During the next short while, there is much scurrying about in preparation. Raquel goes looking for Rebel to warn him, but he has already heard. Rebel runs into Oso and tells him something is about to come down. Rebel is planning to leave the projects to go to a party in order to avoid the trouble he knows is coming. Oso says he will be along in a few minutes. First he wants to go to the store, meaning the market at Fourth and Gless.

"You got a gun?" asks Rebel. Oso assures him he does indeed have a gun. For reasons that will never be understood, Oso is lying.

A few moments later, Oso has a similar exchange with Silent from TMC. Silent is Oso's first cousin and they are as close as brothers. Oso trots across Fourth Street to scoop Silent up, much as he had the Cuatro homie earlier in the evening. Silent sees that Oso is drunk, and is concerned to leave him alone. Silent also emphasizes that something is bound to happen and tries to get Oso off the street. Like Rebel, Silent asks if Oso is armed. Again Oso lies. He agrees to borrow Silent's black jacket as it is a cold night, and Silent is swinging by his grand-mother's apartment and can get another. Oso shoos Silent away, saying he will meet him in a few minutes.

———

No one knows for sure why they picked Oso. Maybe it was because he was the one who was out there. Some are sure it was because they mistook him for Midget from TMC, another large homie who was among the *bola* who sweated the Eighteenth Street guys when the gold chain was jacked.

What is known is that just after midnight, two vehicles come through the projects, a car and a truck. The car comes through first. TMC's fire on it thinking it is the only threat. They don't notice the truck stopped at Fourth Street until they hear the shots. BOOM! BOOM! BOOM! Big noises from a big gun.

The first shot hits Oso in the chest, knocking him to the pavement. But Oso is strong and gets up again. The shooter then exits the truck and fires again, this time nearly at point-blank range, hitting Oso in the head.

Maria, Oso's mother, hears the shots and rushes out of her sister's apartment where she has been visiting and finds other community members already in the street. One of the mothers tells Maria it was Oso who was shot, but no one will let her near him.

Rebel is one of the first to the scene. Together with Shadow he loads Oso into the car of a third TMC homeboy who speeds Oso to White Memorial Hospital.

By the time Greg gets to Fourth and Gless, although there are large bloodstains on the cement, Oso is gone. Greg drives straight to White Memorial with a shell-shocked Silent in tow. Greg talks to emergency room surgeon Brian Johnston. "We did everything we could," says

Johnston. Silent apprehends what the words mean and starts crying uncontrollably. Community mother Pam McDuffie, who has rushed to the hospital in her own car, also hears the words. Her knees buckle and she falls to the floor.

It is lightly drizzling by the time Greg gets back to the projects, Silent still with him. Maria has moved out to the front porch of the apartment, where she sits without moving as Greg parks his car and proceeds up the walkway toward her while Silent waits at a distance. On the porch, Greg takes one of Maria's hands and leans over to whisper in her ear.

"He's dead."

Maria's body begins rocking involuntarily as she opens her mouth to scream. "No-o-o-o-o-oooooooooooo!" She screams. "NO-O-OOOOOOOOOO! Sergio!" The sound of Maria's screams are at once terrible, primal, indelible.

"Sergio! Don't leave me alone!" Maria screams longer than seems possible. She doesn't stop screaming until she faints.

"Look at it," Greg explains later. "Oso's oldest brother is locked up. His brother Frank is locked up. Now Sleepy's locked up." Oso's father—who has never really been a father to him, and who is one of the five drunks who live in the park—even he's locked up right now. "So Oso was it for Maria! He was the man of the house, the provider, on that little salary I was giving him. That's why the job meant so much to him. He was it!"

The Cuatro homies are gathered about twenty-five feet away from the house. They stand stock still, listening to Maria's screams.

"I'm glad they're hearing it," says Greg, himself frantic and grief-stricken. "They never hear it. They see the crying. But they never hear that scream. I've always wanted them to hear that scream!"

For more than an hour, a group of neighborhood women minister to Maria. They shake rubbing alcohol into their open palms and pat it onto her skin to cool her. They break onions under her nose whenever she starts to faint again. As the women work, several drunken husbands circle about them, their movements jerky and misdirected, like blind moths darting toward a porch light. One man weaves up to his wife and slurs that she ought to come home right now. "I'm very, very busy," she snaps to him in Spanish, then turns again to Maria. The husband attempts another foray. This time the wife ignores him altogether.

Cuatro homies plus a few TMC's are still milling in the shadows between buildings when Terence Garrett, a close friend of Oso's and a hothead, strides up. "What are we waiting for?" he says, his deep voice coaxing and angry. "Let's do what we have to do!"

With Oso's death, the torch of Cuatro leadership has naturally passed to Largo, a large, calm homeboy with the face and physical demeanor of a heavyweight prizefighter. Largo listens to Garrett, then shakes his head "no." Some of the other Cuatro homies shrug, but no one protests the decision. For once they heard the screams. And—in the moment at least—that has made all the difference.

Silent

My name is Carlos Santiago. When the homies were giving me my street name, I knew what I wanted. I said, "Just call me Silent."

At first I wasn't from TMC, I was from Clarence. I used to kick it with TMC but they weren't really a gang yet. When Gato, Toker's twin brother, got killed, I got out of CSL. We were really young. I'm seventeen now. I was eleven or twelve when Gato got killed. It was bad. We were both running together and we decided to split up. He ran one way and I ran the other. An' he got shot. He was the first one in the projects to get killed. I guess nothing was the same after that night. Anyway, a bunch of us got out of Clarence at that time. TMC showed us a lot of love. So we got in there.

There've been a lot of deaths that've been hard. But nothing harder than my cousin Oso passing away.

I think Oso already knew he was going. Oso had told Shady from Cuatro, "Let's go party." And Shady said, "Not now, homes, I got to stay in. I got to work tomorrow. I'll see you tomorrow." And Oso had said, "There might not be a tomorrow."

A week before that, we were drinking at my house on top of my roof, and that song came on, "Someday We'll Be Together." And he told me that same thing, he said, "When I die, tell G to play that song."

I said, "Don't say that shit."

The night that Oso passed away, G had took me with him after he came out from being with the doctors. I didn't go up with him when he told my aunt. I didn't want to be there when he told her. I stood in the car. I just heard her screaming.

I was filled with anger. I wanted to do something. I told myself to kick back. I knew if I did something crazy it ain't gonna bring him back. Maybe I get shot. Or maybe I get locked up and never see my baby again.

My aunt said, "If you guys are going to do something, just shoot me first. I don't want to go through it no more. I seen my son laying there. And I don't want to see you guys the same way. If you got to do something—shoot me first. Then do what you got to do."

I been shot twice, once in the butt, once in the back. The first time I got shot I was with Wolf. The second time I got shot I was with Oso. We heard the shots. At first Oso was laughing. He thought they missed. And then I got up and I said, "They got me."

"Nah," he said. He still thought I was playing around. Then I showed him the blood on my back. "Damn!" he said, "they really got you!" He picked me up and carried me to the car, and put me in. He was going through red lights to get me to the hospital. He carried me in and said, "They shot my cousin! They shot my cousin!"

I'm not scared to die. The only thing I say to myself is, if I go out there and I'm a target for somebody else, then my daughter doesn't have a dad. So I just go and drink and kick back. I don't go out and be crazy. I got to take care of my baby.

I'm trying to stop kicking it with the homies. But it's hard 'cause I grew up with them. I used to bang and stuff. But not no more. I got out of camp and I said, "No more."

Right after camp, I got locked up for something I didn't do. That was when I asked God to help me stop banging. I said, "If you help me out of this, I'll stop. I ain't telling you I'll come to the church every day. But I'll try my best to stop." I had a good public defender. He believed in me. And I got out of that case. Since then I've been working to keep the deal I made with God.

I met Joanna, my lady, at the church, in G's office. She looked different. She was *firme*. Other *hinas* were out late, kicking it. A lot of other girls would come after me. But they be tripping. They don't listen to their moms. And her, she has a mom that she listens to. She's smart. She's pretty. She'll be a doctor if she tries—if I keep beating her ass to go to school. I kept making her go to school even when she was pregnant. I said, "You got a brain."

When she got pregnant, in a way I was happy. She didn't want no abortion. I wanted the baby. I wanted to leave something behind if I go.

I was there when Maritza was born. I seen her head coming out an' I got all happy. I was making Joanna laugh when she was in labor. She kept telling me to shut up. But I was trying to take her mind off it.

In terms of friends, Popeye from Clarence was my best friend from forever. He taught me how to fight. He taught me everything. He taught me how not to be scared of nobody. He said, "Hit 'em back. If they beat your ass, they beat your ass. So what." After that, I said to myself, "They're gonna hit me anyways, so I'm gonna hit 'em back." And I did hit 'em back and I found out that I could beat their ass. And they'd never ever wanna fight me again.

I was thirteen when I first pulled a trigger. The gun went BOOM! really loud. I just shot up in the air that time. I used to practice shooting. I would shoot at trash cans. I'm a good shot. Most of the homies don't practice. So they're not good shots.

My dad's never been there. He's in prison. He writes me for my birthday. And he remembers Christmas. Hopefully he'll be out soon. My mom's in Juarez. I was raised originally by my mom. But she was using drugs. She was in jail too. My grandma raised me the rest of the way.

I was happy though, 'cause I had my cousins. Oso, Sleepy, Alfred, Frank—all of them. We used to do trick or treat at Halloween together. I was closest to Frank and Oso. Now Frank's locked up and Oso's dead.

G is like our father, not a priest. When I was small, like age eleven, and G was first there, we'd always go to the church. We were the age the *Pandilla Mugrosa* is now. So he's been like a father for a long time. It's going to be hard when he leaves. I probably wouldn't be right here, right now if I wouldn't'a met G. I woulda been out there messing around. If he tells me something, I listen to him. Like, when he was telling me that the homies killed my cousin, that gang banging killed my cousin, at first I was saying, "That's not true." But then I thought, "Yeah. It's true."

They're taking all the down ones. All the down ones are leaving us. They took Green Eyes. They took Oso. Those are the ones you could talk to, and they would listen. Green Eyes was stubborn. He was hardheaded. He wanted to be out there. He said, "My uncle's locked up. My dad's dead. My mom's all fucked up. Fuck it. I don' give a fuck." The only thing that probably kept him from tripping big time was his baby. If he'd been locked up it woulda been better. Green Eyes' death was hard for all of us.

When they killed Popeye, his family had just paid bail so he could get out for his birthday. Everybody was planning a party for him. That day, before the party, he went off with the homies but he said to me, "Do me a favor, homes, iron my pants." So I ironed his pants. And then he left with the homies. I didn't go with him. I had just got back from Juarez. I came back 'specially for Popeye's birthday. I said, "I'm just going to kick it here, homes. I just got back and I want to check out the 'hood." He said, "All right then," and he left.

Then homies came and said they shot Popeye. I started crying. I jumped in the truck and I went to the hospital. His mom was crying there. And I said, "What's up with my homeboy?" They didn't want to tell me nothing.

He wasn't dead yet. They just said, "We got seven doctors working on him." So I went back out. I was just waiting and waiting. And they came and told me he was gone. His mom was hugging me and screaming, "They took Eduardo!" which was his real name.

It was terrible. Like I said, they're taking the *down* ones. They're taking the warriors. They're all going down.

You got to move away from the projects if you want to stop gang banging. But it's hard to leave your homies, just like, stranded. Only if you hit the lotto and just become rich and take all the homies with you.

When I think of what I'd be doing in ten years, it's hard. I don't know if there're going to be ten years more in my life. In ten years— if I have another ten years—I'd like to be kicking back with my family. Have another baby.

I don't know if I'll be with Joanna. I know *I'll* be there. I don't know if she will. Probably she'll get tired. Joanna is one girl I really respected out of all the girls I've ever been with. I seen something in her. She was the quiet type. We were so young when we were first with each other. At first I just likeded her. I didn't love Joanna at first, 'cause I didn't know what that word meant. I asked her, "Do you want to be my girlfriend?" And she said, "Why?" And I said, "I want to see if something could really work." And then she asked me, "Do you think it could work?" And I said, "Yeah. We could try. If you want it to, I think it could work." And I gave her a kiss right there in Father Greg's office. Afterward I was all happy and my homeboys saw me and said, "Man, what happened to you?"

Once I started seeing how Joanna really was, then I started loving her. We used to walk shoulder to shoulder and not say a word to each other. I never wanted to push myself on her. I never touched her. I never tried to have sex with her for a year and a half. All the other girls I wanted to kiss 'em and whatever right away.

One time I heard that the homegirls wanted to jump her into TMC. And I told the homegirls, "I'll beat the shit out of all you guys if you touch her."

At first we would be together out on the streets. Then I began to think that this was wrong to have her out there. So I would take her home. I was always embarrassed at her house. Her mom was nice. She would always ask me if I wanted to come in the house and have something to eat. And I would tell her, "No, that's okay, thanks. I just finished eating." Even if it wasn't true, I would lie. I felt uncomfortable in the house. I felt unwanted. I don't know why. I felt like her brothers were thinking, "What the fuck is he doing?"

The only time I felt comfortable is with her father. Other fools are scared of her father. He asked me, "Do you love my daughter?" And I said, "Yeah. I love her a lot."

Joanna and I argue sometimes. And sometimes I know I'm hard on her. I don't know why. I sometimes say wrong things to her. Then I think, why did I say those things to her? And I cry. Maybe it's 'cause of how my dad was, I don't know. Probably that's the reason I'm the way I am. I can't blame nobody. I had my grandmother there. But maybe you need a father.

I love my daughter more than anybody on this earth. I never told my mom I loved her. Or my dad. I told my grandma, though. I told her last on New Year's Day. It made me feel good to tell her.

Like I said, my mom was a drug addict. My dad got her into that. Once I told my mother, "You ain't my mother. If you don't straighten up, don't call me your son." To this day I think of it and it makes me cry. But I had to say it to her 'cause she was killing herself.

We used to visit her in prison 'cause we loved her a lot. 'Cause she was our mom. And then when she got out, she went to Juarez to recover. She wanted us—me and my brother—to come with her. But we couldn't. We couldn't leave my grandmother 'cause she raised us. She can't come back because of her parole. They'd arrest her. I had to tell her not to come back. I know it hurt her. But I knew if she came back she'd mess up. I came back from Juarez 'cause I love Joanna and I love my grandma.

One thing I told my dad, I'll never be like you. I'll never be in jail. But sometimes it seems like even if you try and try, even if you do good, things still don't work out. I just want to make something of my life for my family. That's all I want.

Chapter 7

Every death hits the community at a slightly different angle. Green Eyes had been the toughest, the coolest, the most impossible to kill. His death stunned, whispering messages of mortality to every kid on the street. Oso was big, crazy, infuriating, beloved. Grief in his name is enormous, extravagant, voluptuous.

Turtle cries and cries. Greg keeps checking in with Cisco, with whom he has set a new date for rehab, reminding him that this is what Oso would have wanted him to do.

Sunday, the morning after Oso is killed, Greg goes to Juvenile Hall to say mass. He makes a point of going early so he can first visit Oso's brother, Sleepy, who will not yet know what has happened. Sleepy shows no external response to the news. He just sits there staring blankly.

Sunday afternoon, Blue comes to Greg's office with the pressing need to talk. When they are alone, Blue breaks down. "It's my fault," he says of Sergio's death. "I caused it." He then confides in Greg how he had picked the fight with the Eighteenth Street kid. Although it was most likely the stealing of the gold chain, not the fight, that was the actual precipitating event, Blue either does not know or does not believe this and is inconsolable.

Oso's death hits Greg very hard. "Most of the twenty-six kids I've buried have been in the past two years. It used to be about one a year. And now there've been . . . so *many*."

Two nights before the wake, Greg dreams he too is shot. In the dream, Greg feels two bullets go into his chest, one to the side, and the second next to his heart. He looks down and sees his shirt redden and wonder if he's going to live. Somehow he gets to the hospital.

At the emergency room it seems to Greg that all the Mexican American poor of Los Angeles are there, bleeding and in need of medical attention. Greg's parents are also at the hospital in the dream. To Greg's horror, the parents muscle their way past the other wounded and demand attention for their son. "Don't do this," Greg pleads with his parents.

The dream gives Greg a feeling of peculiar unease. "It was so vivid. It felt so real that I thought it was going to happen today," he says.

During the period after a death, Greg struggles for equilibrium so he can effectively minister. This time the equilibrium is eluding him. "I feel much more distressed by everything than I used to. So many kids have been killed. I'm *embarrassed* by the sameness of it. The routine of it. The here-we-go-again of it. I feel helpless, angry in a way I never felt before. I feel, 'Why don't they stop?' Somehow the weight of the deaths becomes cumulative. It's like each death becomes more than itself. It calls up all the others. I keep thinking here it is *again. Again. Again.*"

"And I just dread tomorrow night," he says. "I dread it."

Greg had gone to everyone in Cuatro and asked them not to drink before the funeral. "You'll drink afterward," he told them. "But please don't drink before."

He wants them to be sober so that he can preach to them. A wake is an opportunity like no other to reach the homies at their most vulnerable. However, today he wonders if he has anything left to say to them.

Greg's other task immediately after a death is to isolate the person who is most likely to feel an obligation to avenge the killing. In this case one of those most at risk is Silent, Oso's cousin.

With his mouth frozen into a perpetual Elvis sneer, Silent, who is seventeen, so rarely shows emotion it might seem to the casual observer that some essential connection between his head and his heart was somehow severed. In truth, the bad dude demeanor masks an agonizingly deep wellspring of feeling.

Silent is madly in love with sixteen-year-old Joanna, who works as a part-time secretary at the church. At Roosevelt High School, Joanna tested in the highly gifted range, and she is movie-star gorgeous. Silent is tormented by the thought that this girl will eventually leave him for a better life. Some days, when insecurity overtakes him, he forbids Joanna to curl her hair or wear makeup or even to stray from the apartment where they both have lived with his grandmother since their baby daughter was born in October. On better days he will good-naturedly badger Joanna to study hard in her high school classes. "You'll think of me when you're a doctor," he says.

Silent's best self comes out when he is in a helping, almost paternal, position. So Greg's strategy is to make Silent his first lieutenant in all of Oso's funeral arrangements, putting him in a position that would normally be occupied by family.

It is rare that a projects family has enough money to cover the costs of a funeral, even with the addition of funds raised at car washes and food sales. Maria has nothing, so Greg kicks in whatever remains of the burial costs.

This week there seems to be no end to the unexpected drains on Greg's checking account. He has sent money to Happy in Texas, who still doesn't have a job. A well-connected Texas friend of Greg's family has been helping Happy with the job search, but has thus far found no one willing to hire a gang member. Then, two nights ago, the mother of a Cuatro homie calls crying, "You've got to come over here," she says. When Greg arrives, the mother hands him a twelve-by-twelve-inch plastic case, obviously containing a gun. Back in his office Greg opens the case. Inside is nestled, like a mean metal bird, the most high-tech, compact little Uzi Greg has ever seen.

The gun had been in the possession of Oscar, a Cuatro big head who is known more as a "street entrepreneur" than a shooter. Oscar says he thought he saw enemies creeping through Cuatro territory, so he borrowed the Uzi from a drug supplier.

Greg has become exceptionally skilled at getting weapons out of the neighborhoods, and uses every opportunity to do so. He then turns the guns in to the police, who have learned to accept them from Greg without questions. Normally when Greg (or a mother as his proxy) snatches a gun, the homies simply chalk it up as a lost. But this is a different situation. The Uzi is valued at $1500 and if Oscar doesn't return it, the drug dealer is going to do what they do in the movies.

Oscar is genuinely frightened. "This guy's going to pay somebody two hundred dollars to hurt me," he says.

After talking to Oscar, Greg sighs resignedly. "What's the guy asking for the gun?"

"Six hundred," says Oscar.

Against his better judgment, Greg decides to give Oscar the money. Before he does so he lays down a list of conditions: "Number one, *nobody* will know about this but you and me. Nobody. Two, you stop banging. You don't write on walls. You don't throw up your sign. You don't fight. You don't touch a gun. Three, you stop slanging, effective immediately. Four, you show up to work at the church at eight Monday morning."

Oscar agrees to all conditions.

"What am I going to do if you violate any of these conditions?" Greg continues, trying to come up with some meaningful consequence that will put teeth into his stipulations. After all, what exactly *is* he going to threaten? To hire the same bad guy for two hundred dollars?

"I'll tell you what I'm going to do," says Greg, attempting to load his words with great dramatic weight and import. "I'm going to be *very disappointed.*"

Failing to see the humor in the situation, Oscar tries one more time to persuade Greg to solve the problem more directly.

"If you'd just give me the gun, everything would be all okay, G."

Greg shakes his head. "What kind of priest would I be if I did that? What kind of man would I be? You're worth the six hundred dollars."

"What was I supposed to do?" Greg asks later, defensive. "It's a kick in the teeth. But I don't want anyone to hurt him. In many ways, Oscar's a kid who's waiting to get out. Maybe this is all he needs." Certainly that is the hope. However, now Greg is not only out $600, he has one more new worker to pay.

Greg is consciously aiming at getting as many homies as possible on their feet, employed, and away from the projects before his impending July departure date, seven months from now. "My goal," he says over and over again, "is full employment. My other goal is for the majority of the homies to weary of gang banging, and for those two events to dovetail before I have to go."

The Friday before the Oscar and the Uzi crisis, Greg has a scene with Spanky. The priest comes up to Spanky's room in Casa Pro and finds Spanky still in bed. Greg is furious. "Get up immediately and go to work!" he shouts.

On a seismic scale of fights, this was the big one. "I have gotten him the best job I've ever gotten for anyone!" Greg says. "Eleven dollars an hour with union benefits. He did great at first, but now he isn't going to work."

Some time after Greg has shouted at Spanky, he has an insight: Two weeks ago the priest informed Spanky that now that he had a good job, it was time for him to leave Casa Pro and find an apartment. Greg also remembers a remark Spanky had made two nights ago. "If I have a job and have money then I have to leave," he had said. Clearly Spanky didn't *want* to leave. Therefore—no working equals no money equals getting to stay.

———

The night of Oso's mass the church is completely packed. The balcony is also full. Cuatro and TMC are there. Even Clarence is there. Although most of the homies have on black sweatshirts, there is a smattering of snowy white commemorative sweatshirts, each spray-painted with the message, "In God's Loving Hands," together with an air-brushed picture of Sergio.

Angel is one of those who wears the white sweatshirt. He doesn't sit with the rest of the homies, but instead stands at the church's side door in a state of jittery suffering.

"It happened for nothing," he says. "He died for nothing."

All three of Oso's brothers are still locked up, and thus unable to attend the wake. However, since Sleepy is in a juvenile facility, Ridgway is able to pull enough strings for him to be able to see Oso today at the funeral home. He came, escorted by a police officer, his feet and hands shackled, and stared at his older brother's body without a word.

Tonight Silent stands in the place of the brothers, his eyes entirely wrapped in jet *locs*—sunglasses—his demeanor quiet, his expression so careworn and weary that the grief-creased corners of his mouth resemble those of a middle-aged man.

The choir members are wearing the white sweatshirts instead of robes and are sobbing so vigorously they can barely get through their first song. Pam McDuffie rushes around getting water for the criers and the fainters, her high-heeled spring-o-laters clicking rhythmically against the church floor.

Greg is vested in pure white with a Guatemalan stole woven of primary brights draped across his shoulders. He waits until the loudest of the sobbing has subsided, then takes a deep fast breath, as a cliff diver might before a jump.

"The night Sergio died," begins Greg, "he wanted to kick it with one of his homies. And the homie told him he had something else to do, that he'd kick it tomorrow. Oso said, 'You know, tomorrow might not come.'" A pause. "And sometimes it doesn't."

With this, the homies' attention locks onto Greg's words.

"Sergio had a *sweet* heart. He had a heart as big as his body. I have many stories and memories about Sergio. But I have my favorite . . ."

Greg unreels the tale of the night that Sleepy was shot, about how Oso listened to the little voice, about how it had changed him.

"You and I know how many times I've had to stand here in a situation like this. So I asked a lot of people this week—homies, kids, mothers, girls—what I should say to you tonight. And they all said the same thing: Tell the truth.

"Today I didn't know what the truth was. But I sat at my house and I prayed to the voice that spoke to Sergio. I said, 'Tell me what the truth is.' And this is the truth: *Gang banging is killing us.* This is the truth: If you listen to the voice in you that says, 'Don't do it,' then you love Sergio. If you ignore that voice, I don't think you do. Because if you bang, you participate in what caused this."

Greg runs his fingers lightly over the big coffin that holds Oso, simultaneously trailing his gaze over the homies. "And that is the truth. And it hurts me to say it, but that is the truth."

After the mass, Greg experiences some relief. "At least they were sober," he says. "I realize I didn't mention God once. Or Jesus or the resurrection, which is what you're supposed to do. But I thought, 'Oh fuck it.' I was talking to them. This was for *them*."

Greg's homily has the desired effect, at least in the short run. Later that night two Cuatro homies—Droopy and Weasel—creep over to Aliso Village with the idea of shooting. They are stopped by Turtle, who has returned from San Jose for the funeral. He dashes up to intercept the creeping twosome.

"Don't do it," he says. "Remember what G said. Listen to that voice inside."

Remarkably, the strategy works. "Yeah, you're right," says Weasel to Turtle. And with little more than that he and Droopy turn and walk back to Pico Gardens.

———

Oso's grave at Resurrection Cemetery is a few graves away from that ·of his best friend Night Owl, the kid killed by sheriffs. After Greg does the burial ceremony, he takes the Cuatro homies aside one at a time, hoping to cement the effect of last night's sermon. First he beckons to Droopy, putting one arm around his neck and bending close, so his mouth is right next to his ear.

"You know how much I love you," Greg whispers. "I'd die for any of you guys in a second. But I know you went out with a gun last night. And you need to know that if you participate in this, then you're part of what killed Sergio. The blood of Sergio is on your hands when you do that."

"But the homies . . ." begins Droopy.

Greg interrupts sharply. "I don't give a fuck what your homies are doing. This will end when you want it to. You can change this for yourself."

Droopy begins crying. "I know, G," he says. "I know."

Next Greg grabs Champ. After Champ is Oscar. Then another three after that. By the end each one cries. All the time he talks, the mariachis that Sergio had wanted are playing.

"Something good is happening," Greg says later, his mood calmer than it has been in weeks. "It's sort of like Saint Sergio is out there. Like all that's good in him has been having an effect on everyone. Even for me . . . when I was talking to the homies . . . I felt like the Holy Spirit was talking through me."

That afternoon, at Ridgway's Friday meeting, homies are still in the thrall of the burial. Angel and Romeo sit next to Ridgway, who holds a hand of each kid in each of her own hands.

At the end of the meeting, Romeo bursts into tears.

As he is leaving, Angel looks sorrowful and urgent, as if he is operating under an emotional deadline no one else can perceive. "Everybody needs love but they don't got it," he whispers.

"Romeo and Angel are right on the edge," comments Ridgway.

———

For nearly three weeks there has been peace. Occasionally, there is the sporadic sound of gunfire, but nobody has gone on missions. Even East L.A. has been affected by Oso's death. Danny Boy from ELA calls Greg from jail to say how well he'd known Sergio and how sad he was about his passing. "And Danny Boy is public enemy number one," says Greg.

Greg is sure the situation is greatly helped by the fact that he has a record number of kids working. He hires still more trying to maximize the momentum.

And, once again—he has no money to pay them.

Greg is rifling through the handmade dark wood collection box fishing out checks. "I love the 9:00 A.M. mass," he says, finding one more check near the bottom. The nine o'clock mass on Sunday is in English, and tends to bring a group of wealthier white people who usually give checks that Greg decides are earmarked for his jobs program. The rest of the collection, which runs about six hundred dollars a week, goes for the normal operations of the parish in addition to a $10,000 monthly subsidy from the Archdiocese.

A few minutes later, Greg stares dolefully at his checkbook, the balance of which he has just finished calculating. Greg has a separate checking account into which he deposits all the donations that come to his designated for his work, an arrangement which is a mild source of contention between him and Father Tom, his more bottom-line-oriented associate.

"I'm two thousands dollars in the hole. I'm hoping I can make it up before the bank notices." He laughs. "This is a variation on the Irish blessing, 'May you be an hour in heaven before the devil knows you're dead.' Mine is, 'May all your checks clear before the bank figures out they're rubber.'"

Next Greg opens his mail hoping to find more checks to fatten the anemic bank account. He opens a Publisher's Clearing House envelope, inside which a solicitation shouts in huge black letters: "GET READY TO GREET THE WORLD AS GREG BOYLE MULTI-MILLIONAIRE!!!" With a straight face Greg hands the piece of paper to Mouse, an energetic Cuatro homie who just wandered into his office.

"What d'you think, homes?"

Mouse stares at the announcement, printed to look like a check with an impressive string of zeroes. "Is this for real, G?" he asks hopefully.

Greg takes back the "check" and tacks it up on his bulletin board next to a collection of similarly exclamatory solicitations from Ed McMahon, one in Spanish. "Nope," he says, "unfortunately, it's not for real."

The next letter Greg opens is from Dreamer, writing from camp. Dreamer writes that Monica, his fifteen-year-old girlfriend, is pregnant and due in February. Greg puts his hands to his eyes and makes a pretense of crying.

"Just what we need," he says. "Dreamer a father!"

Greg is forever telling this kid or that to be sure and "wrap that rascal," his way of urging them to use a condom. Yet he sees the soaring numbers of teen pregnancies as more than just the result of adolescent carelessness. "It's another symptom of despair," he says. "Think about it. If you don't believe you're going to live till you're twenty-one, then you want to see junior *now*."

━━

When Turtle returned for Oso's wake, his job in San Jose dried up, so he is back in L.A. for good. However, he appears to have temporarily stabilized. Now the real red alert is Rebel.

Wild, handsome and full of drama, nobody walks the walk or talks the talk better than Rebel. Unlike some of his other homeboys, Rebel took a long time to warm up to Greg, refusing to trust the priest's intentions. It wasn't until Greg literally stood between Rebel and a group of East L.A.'s whom Rebel had every intention of "blasting" that he was willing to take the priest seriously. "I'm not going to let you shoot anybody," said Greg to Rebel then. "You're going to have to shoot me first."

"I couldn't believe that he would die to keep me from killing some people he didn't even know," Rebel said much later. "After that I gave him respect. He wasn't like anybody else I'd ever seen."

I met Rebel a month after Green Eyes' death. I was driving down Gless Street toward the church to meet Greg. I had with me a girl named Claudia, the sister of Raccoon, a Cuatro homeboy. We stopped to chat with a few TMC homies who were milling about in their usual Friday night location. Suddenly a kid I had not before met half flung, half draped himself through my passenger side window. I recognized him as Rebel, whom I had heard much about but never been introduced to face to face.

In this moment Rebel was all high cheekbones and charm. He alternately flirted with Claudia, my fifteen-year-old companion, and made intense and intelligent inquires about the book he said he's heard I was writing. I cannot remember encountering a kid who oozed more charisma on a first meeting.

Twenty minutes later Rebel was running down Gless Street, a gun in each hand, shooting with abandon.

Greg always says that all it takes is one fool tripping to set events in a tragic direction. Right now Rebel is that one fool. The fact that he had been Greg's most powerful peacemaker only a few months ago doesn't matter now. Since Oso was buried, Rebel has been withdrawing deeper into a state of anger and alienation that nothing, including Greg, seems to reach.

TMC and Clarence Street have long been allied. In fact, some of the TMCs used to belong to Clarence. The problem begins when Rebel picks a fight with Flavio, the second of the two brothers who are CSL shot callers, and Wizard gets into the *Kool-aid*—into the mix. Silent is in the mix too, but tries to cool the situation down. Nonetheless, the fight escalates and before the night is over, Rebel trashes Wizard's car—smashing in the windows.

Wizard is normally even-keeled and sensible, but has a formidable temper when finally filed. Initially Greg talks Wizard out of retaliation, saying he will help him with the cost of window replacement. But a few hours and quite a number of beers later, Wizard begins to feel his honor is at stake, and perhaps even the honor of the Clarence Street Locos. The calls go out, the guns come in. Two kids on whom Greg's influence has already had a more permanent effect decline to participate. Still, two cars full of CSL's head out to find TMC's generally, and Rebel specifically.

Whether by unconscious intuition or stupendous luck, Greg happens to drive down Gless just in time to intercept Wizard and company at the outer borders of TMC territory. Wizard sees Greg, screeches around the corner, then pulls over to think. He decides to abort the mission. There is some protest from the ranks. "No," he says firmly. "We're going back. I'm not going to dis G."

"Now I've got all this anger inside me and I don't know what to do," Wizard says to me later, then characteristically turns his angst into humor. "Now don't suggest that I try jogging to work off my anger. That won't work around here. If you start running in *this* neighborhood, pretty soon somebody'll start chasing you!"

———

With few exceptions, the kids who tend to rise to the top of the gang hierarchy are those with the most intelligence, social skills, leadership capacity, and the ability not to blink in the face of danger. Rebel has all these qualities, plus an almost artistic temperament and a sensitivity to both political and emotional nuance that, had he been born into a different circumstance, might have led him to do well as an actor or politician.

However, his emotional side, which is the key to much of his charm, potentially holds the seeds of his undoing. Rebel reels disastrously from the one-two punch of Green Eyes' and Oso's deaths, in addition to his recent breakup with his girlfriend, Raquel. Now it appears something critical has dislodged inside him.

———

In the wee hours of the morning after the aborted Clarence mission, two housing patrol officers respond to a call that someone is breaking into a car in the Pico Aliso projects. The cops call for backup on their way to the location. When they arrive they find Rebel inside the car, stark naked, his clothes nowhere in sight. The officers motion Rebel out of the car at gunpoint. At some point one officer tosses him a blanket. The officer holding the gun on Rebel is a rookie and in the four minutes it takes for backup to arrive, his gun hand begins to falter. Four minutes is a long time to hold up a two-and-a-half-pound police-issue 9 mm Beretta. As the rookie officer's hand falters, Rebel's street reflexes combust with his despair. He lunges catlike at the cop, grabbing for the gun, all the while crying, "Shoot me! Shoot me! Shoot me!"

The cops do not shoot. Instead, the utterly unnerved rookie and his partner struggle to wrestle Rebel to the ground, finally subduing him with repeated blows from a nightstick.

"Rebel wants to die," Greg says, standing in the church parking lot staring out into the night. "In middle-class neighborhoods, people talk about an epidemic of teen suicides. Here in the barrio, there's no such thing. They do it another way. When Smoky got shot, he was the only one who didn't duck. It was the same with Shotgun from Clarence—everyone ducked but him. Look at Oso and Green Eyes; both of them all but called it to them. So maybe I haven't buried twenty-six kids killed by gang violence. Maybe I've buried twenty-six suicides." A pause.

I don't want to bury Rebel. I couldn't stand it."

―――――

With Rebel safely locked up, Greg turns his attention to Spanky. He walks over to Casa Pro with the intention of nagging him to set a move-out date. But before Greg can find Spanky, Spanky finds Greg.

"I got an apartment, G. I moved out last night," Spanky announces this with a kind of self-possession Greg has never before seen him display. Then, having nothing more to say, Spanky starts to get in his car to drive away. Greg calls him back.

"Congratulations," Greg says. "I'm *really* proud of you." Surrogate father and surrogate son look at each other, both lacking words to adequately express the moment.

"How do you feel?" Greg asks finally. Spanky thinks for a second. "I feel scared," he says. "But I feel okay."

When Spanky drives away, Greg looks nearly out of his mind with pride. "It feels like birthin' a baby!" he says. "It's amazing! Spanky's just a new man. No, it's like, finally he *is* a man. That's the difference."

The next night, Greg empties out the little guest apartment over the garage at the Jesuit residence, snatching for Spanky's use a bed, a refrigerator, and kitchen table plus chairs. All without permission from his fellow Jesuits, of course. "I learned long ago," explains a guiltless Greg, "that it's easier to ask forgiveness than to ask permission."

———

Although the community is panicked about Greg leaving them, they have never protested his sabbatical. This is in part because they know his absence won't last forever since he has recently requested that his superiors return him to full-time gang work at Dolores Mission, and his superiors have agreed to do so. But also, everyone can sense that Greg is emotionally depleted, particularly since the last two deaths, and that he needs a break.

It's now five months until his departure date and Greg is working like a madman to somehow assemble a network of people and jobs that will aid the homies in his absence. He is enthusiastic when Officer Marchello organizes a series of basketball games, the first of which is to be the cops versus the ELA Dukes. An outsider might suppose that the gang members might be too aloof to participate. The opposite proves to be true. The Dukes show up in full force sporting nice new white and green ELA T-shirts. The game is close. First 20–25. Then 33–37, with the lead passing back and forth.

"We're the home team and they're the homies," jokes one officer sitting in the bleachers. The joke is delivered with warmth. Greg sits in the bleachers using the time to write payroll checks as he cheers for the homies.

Marchello is jubilant. "Whoever wins or loses, we all win!" he says. In the end the cops win by a few points. But everybody comes away satisfied.

———

Greg's *60 Minutes* segment is scheduled to show soon. He has been profiled by Tom Brokaw and the *L.A. Times,* and now there is a movie about his gang ministry in the works with Columbia Studios. Greg is jumpy about the publicity since it inevitably makes other Jesuits uncomfortable. However, each time Greg shows his face on TV again, more donations arrive in an over-the-transom flurry, allowing him to keep his jobs program afloat financially. Greg is now using his days off for speaking engagements, and gets some civic award or other on nearly a monthly basis. The only entity that seems slow to recognize Greg's growing reputation as a national expert on Latino gangs is the Catholic Church.

That there is a bit of underlying ambivalence toward Greg and his gang work first comes to public light in late February when Los Angeles Cardinal Roger Mahony holds a press conference on the subject of gang violence. The cardinal announces the launching of a new multi-million dollar gang prevention program called "Hope in Youth" which will involve prominent clergy from all over the city. Only one name is conspicuously absent from the list: Father Greg Boyle.

At the press conference, the cardinal uses the same battle vernacular already favored by law enforcement: Stamp out . . . war on . . . wipe out. Cisco happens to catch some of Mahony's speech on the local news.

"Why does your boss want to declare a holy war on us?" he asks Greg afterward.

When Mahony is asked by press members why Greg was not involved, the cardinal replies that Greg had been invited but "Father Boyle had other commitments."

Greg is stung by the exclusion.

———

Greg is getting creative on the job front. He talks an organization named L.I.F.E.—Love is Feeding Everyone—into hiring and training eight homies, four from Cuatro and four from TMC. Greg will still pay their salaries but at least someone other than he will be providing the day-to-day oversight. Greg also keeps adding members to his own crews.

A spot on Boyle's job crews is more than just gainful employment for a homeboy. It is intended as a training course in the realities of the job world. Sometimes here too, Greg feels for every two steps forward, there is a step-and-a-half back. When Bandit, a TMC homie, is late two days and doesn't show up a third, Greg is determined to fire him. However, when Bandit is called into Greg's office, he begins speed-talking before the priest can read him the riot act.

"I'm sorry I didn't come, G, but it was terrible! I was kidnapped!" "Kidnapped?" asks Greg, annoyance increasing. "Yeah, by them space people. They got me right up there by Fourth street and took me away to their planet! And they made me work, G! That's why I couldn't work for you! Actually, they were pretty nice to me. They even paid me for working. Only, G, they don't pay you in dollars. You know what they use for money on their planet? Rocks, G. Like you know, stones. But they ain't worth nothin' down here, so I really need to go back to work for you! So don't fire me okay?" With this, Bandit gives Father Greg a pleading look.

It works. Greg is laughing too hard to fire anybody.

Romeo and a new kid just out of camp, Wolf, are currently two of Greg's most enthusiastic day care crew workers. Wolf is from TMC and was most recently locked up at Camp David Gonzales with Dreamer. He is very personable with an ingratiating smile, an ease with small talk, and the kind of boyish good looks that girls take to immediately. Wolf is also extremely smart, scoring measurably higher in math and science than anyone ever to come through the testing system at Camp Gonzales.

Street gangs typically attract a broad range of intellects from well below average to highly intelligent. Mary Ridgway has long contended that if across-the-board testing was done, TMC in particular would be found to have more kids per capita who score in the gifted range than would your average suburban high school class. There's Happy, Romeo, Rebel, Midget, Drifter, Shadow, Cool-Aid, Stress, Creeper . . . the list goes on from there. In many cases, the smartest kids are the hardest ones to get off the street. It is an unfortunate truth that a high-energy kid with a 145 IQ isn't going to be engaged for very long by a job in a warehouse unloading boxes. The street will continue to call out to him, not just because the street is more exciting than the warehouse, but also because, in an admittedly skewed and tragic way, the street uses more of his talent.

Greg is invited to speak on Power 106, the city's largest hip hop radio station. Greg's speech is mainly an on-air plea for jobs. During the show he is deluged with calls. Unfortunately, not a single one contains a job offer. The calls are from homeboys and homegirls phoning from other parts of the city to ask if Greg can help *them* find jobs.

At the end of the afternoon, Power 106 management graciously steps up and offers to hire two homies and, better yet, to pay their salaries. Greg gives the jobs to Romeo from TMC and Shady from Cuatro, an African American kid and Romeo's best friend. The radio station personnel fall instantly in love with the two homies, who fall in love back.

A few days later a second company calls with a job offer. Greg sends two kids, although he has some concern when he hears it is a commission sales situation in a telephone boiler room. On the homies' first day at work, the FBI raids the place and carts everyone off to jail. Fortunately, the FBI men quickly ascertain that the terrified homies know nothing about the scam operation, and do not arrest them.

An outraged Greg calls the head of the boiler room to read her the riot act. "Hey," she counters, "your guys break the law all the time, so what's the problem?!"

As he gets off the phone with the boiler-room woman, PeeWee, a smallish ELA Duke, rings in on Greg's second line. "G," says PeeWee, his voice shy, "I got a question."

"Ask me anything, *mijo*," Greg replies, still coming down from the anger of the previous call.

"Would you adopt me?"

Greg puts his head in his hands after he rings off with Pee Wee. "Every day I feel more like the Ed Sullivan guy with the spinning plates," he says. "I just want to get as much as I can in place before July."

To add to Greg's already over-the-top pressure, the latest fool tripping is Angel. He picks a fight with Turtle, which Silent manages to pull apart. A day later, outside Ridgway's Friday meeting, the whole fight nearly starts up all over again.

"I have so much anger in me," Angel says still later as he leaves the meeting. "I don't know why. I don't know what to do. I just don't know. It's like I hurt inside and I can't make it stop."

Greg tries to reassure and steady him. Ridgway also tries on a separate occasion. I try on still other occasions. Yet it is as if his hopelessness is a force field, bouncing all the words of all the caring adults back out again.

In the early evening, I drive through Pico Gardens, where Angel flags down my car, as he often does, just so he can get in and talk for a while. Usually the talk is about nothing in particular, mostly an excuse to gather motherly warmth. Before he leaves my car he unfailingly collects a hug. After he waves goodbye to me this night, I reflect on how unsuited Angel is for gang membership. Certainly no kid is *suited* to be a gang member. But if one can conceive for a moment of gang membership as a profession for which one has talent or not, Angel does not have the talent. He is too gentle in nature. The violence that wears on the spirit of every kid in this barrio seems to weigh on Angel's soul in a way that daily becomes more injurious. Yet what is to be done? I say this aloud to Greg later, when I'm in the priest's office. I am not willing to take Angel to my house to live with me and my kid. So what is to be done?

"I don't know," says Greg. "He's slipping through our fingers."

———

The *60 Minutes* segment finally appears. The broadcast unleashes a small flood of donations—ten thousand dollars or so—exactly enough to allow Greg to pay salaries for another two months.

The influx of cash has put Greg in an upbeat mood as he sits in his office listening to some of the Clarence homies trade insults. Creative insults are a fine art among gang members, and they are flying fast and furious tonight.

Midget from TMC had wandered through earlier to remark that one of his homies dressed so badly that ". . . we got to put him out on the freeway ramp with one'a those signs, 'WILL WORK FOR CLOTHES AND TATTOOS!'" Much laughter.

The closing and best insult of the evening is offered by Wizard. "Oh yeah," says Wizard as a rejoinder to whatever insult had last been volleyed, "well you're so dumb it takes you *two hours* to watch *60 Minutes*!"

There is a serious shooting at Gless and Eagle. At first it is thought to be a drug deal gone bad. Now everyone is saying that it is gang-related, that homeboys from outside came into the projects and were fired on. A young woman aligned with a non-projects gang was hit, and her injuries may result in permanent paralysis. Very early in the morning Romeo is arrested and charged with attempted murder, supposedly on the word of an eyewitness.

By midday, there are dueling eyewitnesses. Romeo's mother goes to the police and says she knows who the real shooter is and it is not her son. The police soon arrive at the same conclusion. By the next morning they have released Romeo and gone in search of a second suspect: Angel.

Greg tries to locate Angel first, but he has vanished. Then, late in the afternoon, Pam McDuffie calls. You've got to come over right away," she says.

When Greg arrives at Pam's Pico Gardens apartment, she gestures upstairs to her bedroom. At the top of the stairs Greg looks to his left into Pam's room. Angel is on the bed curled into a fetal position, like an infant in deep distress. Greg softly says Angel's name. Angel rolls slightly to turn his head Greg's direction. "Hi, G," he says.

"They're looking for you," Greg says. "You know that." Angel says he knows. "And you know what you need to do, don't you, *mijo?*" Angel nods, still curled. Greg touches Angel gently on the shoulder. The tall boy obediently unfolds his legs and gets up, docile and dreamy, like a young child wakened from a deep sleep. He follows Greg back down the stairs and out to the car. Greg drives Angel straight to Hollenbeck Station.

That night, Angel's younger brothers, Fernie and Richard, hover miserably around Greg's office, wounded creatures who have lost their bearings. Despite Greg's non-stop attempts at intervention, their way of coping with Angel's arrest is to fight constantly with each other, sometimes throwing a punch, mostly tossing insults, each one upping the ante.

"Fernie wets his bed," hisses Richard at one point in the evening. Fernie bursts into tears. When Greg finally drives the two kids home,

Richard is still belligerent, stuttering like a jackhammer. Fernie is broken.

Extremely late at night, Pam calls me, unable to sleep, furious about Angel's arrest. "Those parents never did a thing for that child! Any of those children. They don't feed 'em right! They never fixed their teeth! When Angel was spittin' up blood last year, who d'you think he came to?! Me! Why?! Because his own mamma wouldn't do *nothin'!*"

———

Angel has been charged with two counts of attempted murder and he will likely be tried as an adult, which means if he is convicted, he's looking at a sentence of twenty-five to life. The same day the charge is announced, Greg hears a string of problems at the church. One woman, the mother of the tiniest PM'er, tells Greg she has just been evicted from the projects and doesn't know where she will go. A few minutes later, Greg must calm a woman who tells him she is going to kill herself and her two sons. Still later Joanna runs into his office, sobbing and talking suicide after a fight with Silent. She won't tell him exactly what is the matter, but Greg suspects Silent is hitting her.

"It's been bad since Oso passed away," is all she will say.

In the afternoon, Greg goes to see Angel at Eastlake. Angel clings to Greg as though drowning, then lets go. "I just wish I could've had a baby," he says crying. "I just wish I could've had a kid so I could've showed my mom and dad the way a kid is supposed to be loved by his parents. I know I could love a kid! I just wish I could show my parents so they'd know!"

When he returns to his office, Greg flops down in his chair, leans his head back, and breathes deep, as if grappling for internal balance.

"People's suffering here is so extraordinary," he says.

The suffering seems to weigh more on Greg as each week goes by. He rarely takes a day off and even when he does, he does not come back revived. He is beginning to have chest pains. "I thought I was having a heart attack," he says one day after making an audible gasping noise. Once the moment has passed, he laughs it off. "I'm probably just eating too many chilies." When he is pressed to see a doctor he drags his feet. "It's not like I'm having shooting pains into my arm or anything," he jokes, but it doesn't come off as humorous.

Part of the problem is that the homies come to Greg for everything, even their physical ailments. Sometimes he will make arrangements for them to see Dr. Barnes, a kindly and elderly M.D. in the neighborhood. If symptoms are more serious, he sends them to USC County General Hospital. Frequently the problems are sexually transmitted in nature. On almost a weekly basis a mortified homeboy will approach Greg to confess that he has a problem "down there."

"Down there is a pretty big area, homes," Greg will say, trying to coax more specific information out of the reluctant patient. Last night, Grande, a tall, generally monosyllabic kid, comes to Greg with a "down there" variety problem. Since Grande is obviously in tremendous discomfort, Greg drives him right away to the overcrowded County General emergency.

As they wait in line to see the triage nurse, Grande panics. "G! I don't know how to explain this to the nurse!" he says.

Greg tries to be calming, "Okay. You say, 'My right testicle is inflamed. It's swollen. And it really hurts me a lot.'" Greg adds that Grande should "throw a gang a' drama," that otherwise he might not be taken seriously enough. Grande nods, but he does not look as if he has a handle on this yet. Greg suggests they practice.

"All right," Greg says, "I'm the nurse." Then, in a nurse voice, "What seems to be the problem?"

By this time Grande is in so much pain that he is dazed.

"Uh . . . *my balls are in flames,*" he blurts. Greg is so far over the brink of exhaustion he gets the giggles and can't stop.

"Please don't laugh, G," pleads the miserable Grande.

"I'm sorry, homes," says Greg, still trying to get a grip. "But you can't say that! They'll bring you a fire extinguisher instead of a doctor!"

Later, when Grande has been treated, he repeats the ubiquitous refrain, "What're we gonna do when you're gone, G?"

It's not like I'll be gone forever," Greg replies. "I'll be back in ten months. Think of it like I'm away in long-term camp."

Two days later, Greg has a short go-round with Father Tom on the going-away issue, but the interaction has a very different cast. Greg asks Tom if he can leave some of his belongings in his current bedroom during the time he is away. He'll vacate the room and make it habitable for other tenants. But the arrangement will allow Greg to move into the same room when he gets back.

Greg is surprised when Tom tells him, no, that they will need all the space and cannot afford to have him leave anything except in storage.

"I *am* coming back," Greg says. "It's not like I'm not coming back."

"We really need the room," replies Tom.

Greg and Tom have always been close friends, and the exchange unsettles Greg. "They're probably right," he says. "But symbolically it was, I don't know, weird. It made me feel weird." He shrugs. "Maybe I'm just so stressed that everything's getting to me."

The conversation turns out to be prescient.

Rebel

I'm William Ayala. Rebel. I'm a good gambler. Any kind of game. Black Jack. Pinochle. Dice. Everything. It's instinct, I guess. And I'm lucky.

Perrito from my neighborhood is my best friend. He's my compadre, the godfather to my daughter. Danny Boy from East L.A. also used to be my role dog. We three used to be together all the time. The three stooges. But then Danny Boy got jumped into East L.A. and now we're shooting at each other.

I was with TMC when we started it. I was eleven. First we were all break dancers. Then the next step was selling drugs. I was about thirteen then. I made a lot of money in those years. I bought my mom a car. The rest went to pay for my baby—to get her a crib, diapers, that kind of thing. Babies are expensive. I went to camp when I was sixteen. When I got out of camp, I stopped slanging 'cause of my lady and baby.

I nearly had a professional soccer career. I was playing for this league. This promoter came to see a couple of games, and he liked the way I played. So he took me to, like, a minor league—like in baseball. We were about to make a deal. Then I got hurt and I couldn't play no more. I played from the time I was nine until I was fifteen.

If I was to say what were the three best days of my life, number one was when I had my little baby. I wasn't there. I was locked up. My probation officer called me. I felt great when I heard! When my lady, Raquel, was pregnant, I was the one who got sick—like morning sickness—not Raquel. I would always feel all this stuff.

Then when 'cause of Father Greg I got to go on a trip with Jerry Brown, who was running for President of the United States, that was the second happiest time. The best steak I ever ate was in Nebraska with Jerry Brown. It was a steak as big as a plate. And I ate every bit of it. It was so good to be with someone with his power who paid attention to us. It made me feel like I could be someone, not just a gang member, not just a person who could only handle a gun.

The third happiest day was when I got my own apartment. I'd never thought of having my own apartment. So that was like a real accomplishment.

Another time I was happy was when I was in Fire Camp. I loved Fire Camp. It wasn't like I was locked up. I had freedom. I was a fireman. That's how I took it, like I'm in fire training. I never took it as punishment. I just couldn't go home.

The first two weeks of Fire Camp is hell because you're barely getting used to it. You go through training camp. You climb mountains to get in shape. After training, I was fighting fires and getting paid. Most of the guys were getting paid ten cents a day. I was getting paid ten dollars a day because I became crew chief. I didn't like that job because I had to snitch on people. Like I was a cop or something. So I resigned. I became a sawman, working with the chain saw, cutting down trees and bushes to make fire breaks. We fought the big fire in Duarte in '87 or '88. We got dropped in with a helicopter to cut lines 'cause we couldn't use water to fight it. I was the first one on the firelines. I was face to face with the fire. Like almost actually *kissing* the fire. Like if I was to put my arm out, it would've burnt my arm off—the flames. But that was my job. I loved it! It keeps the cobwebs away from you.

I got out of camp two years after G got to Dolores Mission. When I met G, I thought he was just a regular person, a regular priest. But he wasn't. I never really went along with the homies talking to him about our problems. Not until I found out he wasn't no joke. That he was speaking the truth and he wouldn't go telling the police on us.

The time I saw he was different was when we was about to shoot at East L.A. and he was caught in the middle. It was like a movie. We were on one side and they were on another side. He was in the middle of us and he was mad. He was even cussing. "If you're going to fuckin' shoot, you've gotta fuckin' shoot me first." He had to be pretty mad for him to cuss. I was hesitating. Then I just turned around and told the homies, "Let's go."

Later he talked to me. He knew it was me out there even though I had on a beanie and a rag over my face. He still knew it was me. I guess 'cause the homies were listening to me.

When he talked to me, he said, "How could you do a stupid thing like that? Take somebody's life? How do you think their mother's gonna feel? How do you think their family's gonna feel? Their brother and sister?" He told me, how would my mother feel if they was to kill me?

It's true. People don't think that way. They don't think about the other person's family, how they're gonna feel. If they're gonna be able to afford the funeral and all that stuff.

I can't tell you I came completely to my senses right then. But it hit me. It gave me a lot of thoughts. My change wasn't in a flash. It came slow. But watching G that day made the first big change inside me, seeing how he stood there, that he was ready to lose his life for somebody else's life. He didn't know whether I was going to shoot or not. He didn't care. He stood up for somebody else. I know I wouldn't do that for just nobody. I think he'd do that for anybody. never met a person like him.

If it was not for G-Dog, I'd probably be dead. Or somewhere doing life for somebody I killed. Most likely I'd be dead, the way I was going. I was straight out a fool. All I cared about was my homeboys and gang-banging.

My brother Dino and I took the footsteps of my dad. He left when I was seven. I still see my dad sometimes. But I don't really like him. He's a Mexican gangster, that's all he is. The worst thing that ever happened to me was when my father and my uncle said they were going to kill my mom. I was there when they pulled the gun out. I was six, then. My dad and my uncles were drunk. My dad hit my mom. He kicked her, and my mom got a thing of hot water and threw it at him. So they came back in, and my dad grabbed my mom by the hair and my uncle pulled a gun out. All of us, all the kids, jumped on both of them. That's the only thing that made 'em stop.

I love my mother. She's been a mother and a father to us. I don't care what happens to my father. He's never been a father. Because of my dad, I never had happy times when I was small. We never had money. My dad had money but my mom wouldn't take money from him, 'cause it was dirty money. Drug money. That's why she left 'im.

I ain't going to lie, I'm scared to change. I've been a gang member almost all my life. One part of me's got a lot of hope, because I know I can change and make a good life for me and my little family. But I'm scared how things are going to be in the new life. It's like a little kid scared to go into the closet with the lights off. He knows nothing bad is in there, but he's scared anyway because he can't see what's inside it. The life I'm in is scarier than the new life. But I'm used to it.

It's not to say that I'm invincible, that I can't be killed. Anybody could be killed. No matter how big or how strong you are. All it's got to do is hit you in the right place. Look at Oso. Oso was a strong mother-fucker. He took a .45 in his chest. That's a strong caliber. He fell and he got right back up. When they killed 'im they had to shoot 'im in the head. You know what? He got killed because of us. When my homies came to me and said, "We kicked Eighteenth Street's ass," I said, "You all are bragging about it, but they're going to come back." I said, "We got to get all the guns out here."

The Eighteenth Street guy they robbed—I knew who he was. He's their trigger man. Raquel was looking to tell me, 'cause she knew what would happen. Right before they killed Oso, I was with him. I was trying to get him to leave. "I'm going to wait for you," I told him. He said, "All right then." A minute after I left, I heard about five shots fired. Then a car came through where we were. I shot it all up with the Uzi. Then I ran to the store and saw Oso.

It hurts a whole lot when a friend dies. Father Greg asks me why I got a tack of Green Eyes' name on my neck. It's 'cause I love him. We did a lot of stuff together. We went out with girls together. He had a way with the women, I'll let you know that. The way he used to talk to them, he had the right words to make them lose their minds. Of all the people in the world, he was not the one I ever thought would die.

I feel lucky to have the lady I got. Raquel is special. She's a beautiful woman. She's got a nice body. She cares for me. She's a special woman. She was my first love. I was her first love. When I was first with her, I was messing around with drugs and I was slanging, and I wouldn't care for her. I had a dope house that I set up. She'd come knocking at my house and I'd see her through a peephole and I'd say, "Tell her I'm not here." 'Cause I didn't care.

I'd always try and buy her love just so she would be with me when I wanted, and stay away from me when I wanted. I'd buy her a lot of gold chains and things. Then one day she threw all that stuff in my face and said, "I love you. When you get your life together we can see if things can work out."

And I said, "You know what? The drugs, all this stuff is ruining my relationship. This is the devil. I don't need this." So I gave 'em up. Raquel's a strong woman. Sometimes I think she's a lot stronger than I am.

The scariest thing that ever happened to me was a time when me and Raquel got into a fight. I was staying at her house, with her family, and she bleached all my clothes. On purpose. She put all my clothes in the bathtub and poured in about four bottles of bleach. Clorox. Ammonia. It was when I was making money. I had silk shirts that cost about thirty-five dollars each—about ten of them—and some nice cords. And a brand new pair of Nike Cortez's. Those she stabbed all up. Then she put everything in the bathtub. And when I came home she said, "Oh, your clothes are in the bathtub if you want them." I went in there and it stunk. The smell was so strong. And I was standing there just looking at my clothes, and I passed out, because the Clorox went so strong into my system. Her little brother walked in and came back and said, "William's asleep on the ground in the bathroom." And they came up and found me. They brought me downstairs and, like, wetted me down, and called 911.

When the doctor came he said I almost died 'cause of inhaling the Clorox. I knew I almost died. It was scarier than being shot at. I was just lucky. I most want to live for my daughter. Raquel was in shock for about two days, saying it was her fault.

The time I wanted to die was when I had financial problems—no money 'cause I wouldn't slang any more and didn't have a job yet, and Raquel said she was going to leave me and take the baby from me. I love that little girl more than anything. I figured I had nothing to live for. So I went out there and was a straight fool. I was gang banging. Just walking up to enemies and straight shooting at them. I always carried two guns.

I would change a lot of stuff in my past if I could. A *lot* of stuff. I regret getting introduced into selling drugs. I regret gang banging. If I could, I'd go back and try to live a normal life. It's too late now to change the past. And it's hard to change the future. I'm not saying I can't do it, but I'll tell you, it's hard. Even if you ain't gang banging no more, people will recognize you for what you did before. It's easy to say, "I could change if I go live in another state. Or change if I go live somewhere else." To change is the hardest thing in life—to leave your neighborhood, to leave your roots. If you wasn't really into it, then you could do it. But not if you're really into it like I have been. I've had a couple of homeboys who have left. But they were never down for the neighborhood. Stomper was gone for a little while, but then he called us and wanted to come back.

It takes a lot of responsibility to be a man. I don't think I'm a man yet. I'm a man in supporting my daughter. But a man doesn't hit a woman. And I've slapped Raquel. And that proves to me I ain't a man. A lot of people won't say that. But I know I ain't a full-grown man. G-Dog's explained that to me and I knew it was the truth.

I've told Raquel all the things I regret with her. The things I regret doing. The things I regret not doing. I've told her that I want to start all over.

I have a good friend, a black guy who's in the pen. He has a record that's so long, his stack of papers is probably as thick as a dictionary already. He's caught up in the system. He's going to be out soon, but he'll go back to the pen. He's a wonderful person, good-hearted, but he's caught up in the system.

I've still got a chance. I'm not caught up in the system. Last time I said I was gonna change, I feel I didn't really put no effort into trying. This time I'm going to put all my effort into it. I'm going to do it.

At Father Greg's last mass, I would like to make a speech for G-Dog. I want to tell everybody that when G leaves, it's up to the community what happens. We can make it. It doesn't have to be as bad as everybody says.

That's how I feel about myself. I'm gonna surprise a lot of people. A lot of people expect me to fail. But I'm going to prove a lot of people wrong. I'm not going to fail. I'm going to make a life. Watch.

Chapter 8

Reactions to Greg's impending departure grow in intensity as the days speed through spring and on toward summer.

Rebel is out of jail and seems, at least momentarily, to have regained his balance. He comes into the office with Joker, a wiry, dark-skinned TMC homie with part-Cuban lineage. Joker shoves his hands in his pockets, his normally terse manner overrun with melancholy. "Will this office still be open to us, G?" asks Greg. "I mean, can we just come into this office and *sit* when you're gone?"

"I guess that's up to the next occupant of this office, homes," Greg replies.

Rebel paces. "Everything's gonna change!" he proclaims with the melodramatic certainty of a street prophet predicting apocalypse. "Everything's going to change, just watch. It's all going to get way crazy."

Although Mary Ridgway is upbeat in front of the homies, in private she has also taken to making dire predictions. "When Father Greg leaves, it's going to be disaster. The jobs programs are going to die. Every neighborhood is saying the same thing—that as bad as it is now, it's going to be total war when G leaves.

The notion of a post-Greg war is now a shadow on the priest's psyche as well. "I don't believe it exactly," he says. "But if it's everybody else's perception . . . sometimes things have a way of becoming self-fulfilling. It just fills me with dread," he says.

The dread spurs Greg to an activity level that borders on the manic. The pace at which he now hires homies seems part social strategy, part anxiety-lowering device. The number of kids working climbs impossibly high—from twenty-five workers to close to sixty, if you count the part-time kids. Most of those salaries still come out of Greg's checking account. This brings him weekly to the brink of financial calamity. The *60 Minutes* money is almost gone. The priest is supposed to get film option money from Columbia Studios, but a check has yet to materialize.

Greg is like an Energizer bunny with controls jammed in the ON position, spending every spare moment working to generate enough cash to cover his payroll. He takes on ever more speaking engagements, does ever more media interviews, makes ever more pitches for money to any and all who will listen. Although Greg's popularity continues to grow, he finds the willingness of Anglo L.A. to donate hard cash for programs involving gang members to be spotty and unpredictable. When Greg gives an impassioned speech to a conference of L.A. high school teachers, teary audience members surround him afterward, filling his hands with nearly four thousand dollars' worth of personal checks written for amounts ranging from twenty-five dollars to two hundred—generous donations for those living on a teacher's salary.

However, when Greg speaks to the Beverly Hills Chamber of Commerce, although the applause is bountiful, the donations are not. During the question-and-answer period, a Warren Beatty look-alike who is a plastic surgeon by profession raises his hand to ask what he can do to help.

"Jobs and money." Responds Greg.

"Yeah, I know," says the surgeon, "but I mean besides that."

An annoyed Greg appears to think before replying, "Did I mention jobs and money?"

In lieu of an honorarium, a grinning Chamber officer presents Greg with a nicely boxed Mark Cross pen, "So you can write out all those salary checks!"

In private moments, Greg is able to step outside his actions enough to joke about them. "Stop this man before he hires again!" he laughs, then acts out a humorous parody of the kind of specialized twelve-step program he should attend: "'Hi. My name is Greg Boyle. And I'm helpless in the face of my desire to hire gang members.'"

Those who work with Greg also frequently comment on his behavior. "At Dolores Mission when we were trying to solve a problem, we used to ask ourselves, 'What would Jesus do?'" staff community organizer Leonardo Vilhis teases. "Now because of Greg we just ask, 'What would Santa do?'"

When Greg is pressed, he admits that there is a personal cost to all the activity. "I'm not really praying any more," he says, "which is a great loss to me. I've let a lot of things go . . . exercise . . . sitting a half-hour in my chair with a cup of coffee, thinking . . . praying. I know when I get to Detroit [where he will spend most of his sabbatical] I'll start praying again. And running again." He laughs. "I'll be running four times a day in Detroit in order not to go out of my mind."

Although he does not say so to the kids, in private he confesses that he is starting to look forward to his sabbatical.

As departure time draws nearer, more homies are added to the list of those who are using the impending loss as an impetus to shore up their lives. Turtle is one of those who appears to have had a breakthrough. Greg has bullied the director of a Jesuit retreat house in the hill community of Azusa into giving Turtle room and board and a job doing grounds work, with Greg paying the salary. Turtle takes to the rural quiet and soon gains a reputation as a hard worker. He spends little of the five dollars an hour Greg pays him, turning the balance over to his mother for safekeeping. When he has enough saved, Turtle says, he is going to buy a car and enroll in the local junior college. "If I had a car I wouldn't need to go to the projects," Turtle says, "'cause I could go do other normal things with normal people. Go to movies, or to the beach, or to clubs to, you know, dance. I love to dance and I'm good at it too. I can see it—how it'd be to have, like, a normal life. This is the first time I can really see it."

After a few weeks, Greg sends Cisco up to join Turtle. While this means one more salary to pay, Greg is pleased that Cisco has agreed not to drink during the work week. In the beginning, at least, the arrangement works very well and both homies appear to have a positive effect on one another.

Rebel is another who seems determined to get his life squared away before July. His case was a D.A. reject and, having been yanked from the brink of destruction by his arrest, Rebel has emerged from jail a more mature version of himself. He and Raquel have reconciled. And although Rebel visits Greg's office at least once a day for father/son chats, he returns home to his lady and baby most evenings.

With Rebel becoming a family man, Silent has become Greg's main conciliator for TMC. Silent is especially useful in keeping the younger, crazier TMC's in line. "More and more I find myself really counting on Silent," Greg says.

Although there is a growing list of homies who seem somewhat settled and working, Spanky is Greg's most dependable source of pride.

"I got a savings account now," Spanky announces to Greg when the priest comes to visit Spanky's pleasantly decorated one-bedroom apartment on a quiet street in the suburb of Montebello. "And I got a . . . whatd'youcallit? . . . a budget!" Father Greg observes to Spanky that the apartment is spotlessly clean. The homie bobs his head modestly. "I do most of the cleaning 'cause I don't mind cleaning and that shit," he says. "I even kinda like it."

A few weeks later, Greg makes another trip to Montebello to meet Spanky's newborn son, Juan Carlos Jr. For several hours the formerly anti-family homie regales the priest with wonderstruck descriptions of the birth process right down to detailed accounts of dilating cervixes and the virtues of Lamaze breathing.

"I don't know another kid," says Greg as he leaves, "who has so connected to this river of grace that is down deep inside of him. He's able to draw from it always. With his background, he has every reason to be a complete mess. But he isn't. Instead he connects with this deep river which gives him his warmth, his kindness, and his wild sense of humor. There's no one like him."

———

While not exactly stable, Dreamer is out of camp and trying to come to grips with being a father. One Sunday Greg is standing on the church steps greeting the parishioners before the noon mass when he is surprised to see Turtle and Dreamer heading toward the church's front door.

"Dreamer and I want to receive Communion today," says Turtle, "because we've really fucked up."

"I've hardly ever seen Turtle at mass," Greg remarks when they have walked away. "And I've never seen Dreamer. So whatever kind of theology this is, it seems like a good idea."

After the mass has ended Greg receives hugs from parishioners and little kids. One of the kids who comes up to him with arms outstretched is Angelina, the girl from the shooting incident with Dreamer. After she collects her hug from Greg, she skips away to swing back and forth under the church's front banister while her mother chats with other churchgoers.

Greg calls Dreamer over, then drapes an arm around him. "Now don't turn around yet," Greg whispers, "but the girl in the brightly-colored sweater playing on the steps is the girl you shot."

After Greg has gone, Dreamer turns and looks. He watches Angelina as she scoots up the banister then slides back down, up and down, over and over. For the next half hour Dreamer gazes at the little girl, his expression unutterably sad. From time to time, when the experience seems to become too intense, Dreamer looks away. Then a few moments later, he looks back again. But he never leaves. The spell is broken only after Angelina's mother takes her by the hand and the two of them disappear down the street.

"That's the most adult expression I've ever seen on his face," says Greg.

That night, Greg takes Dreamer and another TMC homie out to dinner.

"How did you feel today, looking at the little girl?" Greg asks Dreamer.

"Oh, G, why did you do that to me?!" says Dreamer. "It made me feel so scan'lous!"

"Good," says Greg.

By mid-April, the trouble spots have quieted enough that Greg decides to plan a much-needed two-day vacation. The occasion is Greg's older brother Steve's fortieth birthday. Steve is a junior high school administrator in San Diego, and has been pleading with Greg for months to help him celebrate the big four-oh by coming to Las Vegas. Finally Greg agrees and seems to look forward to the outing. Gambling is one of Greg's few secret indulgences although his speculative ventures rarely extend past a Thursday or two at the racetrack and a once-a-year foray to Vegas, for which he allots himself a twenty-dollar gaming stake.

"I'm not bad at poker," Greg says with a trace of macho bravado.

———

It is Holy Saturday, three days before Greg is set to leave town. A duo of extra-large garbage cans sit like fat plastic icons in the middle of the church parking lot, each filled with water that Greg and the other Jesuits have blessed. Since the 10:00 P.M. mass, the parishioners have been streaming in to scoop out cups of the holy water which they carefully bring back to their apartments. All year mothers will use the water to sprinkle around the house for protection, or to use in cooking, or to dab on their children's foreheads for a blessing as they scamper out of the front door.

Greg stands with arms folded observing the action from a distance.

"Oh God!" he exclaims suddenly. "Here come people with some dogs! Damn!" Greg has never been an animal person. His pet experience as a child was limited to goldfish won at the school carnival that turned belly up in a week and were summarily flushed down the toilet. "I always tell everybody I don't *do* animals. No dogs! No exorcisms! But nobody *listens*."

As another Jesuit goes over to head off the dogs, Romeo hobbles into the parking lot on crutches. He greets Greg affectionately, then leaves a few moments later with a car full of TMC's, ostensibly headed for a party out of the projects. Greg looks after him, brow furrowed.

"Something happened last night," says Greg. "I'm not really sure what the implications are yet." It seems that Romeo got into what he euphemistically described as a "small discussion" with a Crip, a guy just out of the pen with the unlikely street name of Pontiac. Romeo told Pontiac in particular and the Crips in general to stay out of TMC territory, at which juncture Pontiac pulled out a gun and shot Romeo in the foot. Rumor has it that Shadow had a gun trained on Pontiac from a nearby apartment roof and fired a couple of warning shots. This had supposedly discouraged Pontiac from shooting further.

"You should've taken me out," Romeo reportedly said to Pontiac after the shooting, "because I'm going to come back and take you out."

"But I think he's okay about it," says Greg now. "I don't think it's going to go any further than this. I *hope* it isn't going to go any further than this."

When Ridgway hears about the Pontiac/Romeo incident, she is less optimistic. "If someone comes up and shoots you in the foot and you don't retaliate," she says, "then you're punk from a gangsters' point of view. Now we have to wait for the other shoe to drop."

The other shoe falls on Wednesday night, while Greg is still in Vegas. At about midnight, Pontiac is sitting in what is known as "the archway," a landmark at the center of TMC territory, when someone comes up and shoots him three times from behind. An execution. Pontiac is pronounced dead after three hours of surgery at County General Hospital. The Crips, who do not know that Greg is out of town, express fury when the priest never turns up at the hospital.

"If it was a Mexican he'd'a been there," says one angry Crip.

When Greg gets home there are frantic messages all over the place: Something has happened. In the few minutes before Greg learns who has died, he has an irrational thought: What if it's Spanky? Then he has what seems to him an even stranger notion. "I thought, 'If something happened to Spanky, it's the only time that nobody else's grief would be more important than mine.' No matter how broken up I am by a death, no matter how close I am to a kid, I always have to hold somebody else's grief. He's the only person for whom nobody would be in greater grief than me. No one else would be higher than me."

———

Following Pontiac's death the community is thrown into a panic that centers on two elements. First, because the murder crosses the brown/black color line it risks blowing into a racial conflict. Second, the East Coast Crips are but one set of a large network of Crip sets that are all aligned from First Street to the hundred blocks in South Central—easily a thousand strong if they ever wanted to mobilize.

Greg has no one he can pressure or plead with to ameliorate the situation. Pontiac's family lives elsewhere, and the main shot callers for the Crips are kids from out of the area with whom he has little or no influence.

In the first days after the murder, scores of Crips from elsewhere in the city drift into the projects. Everyone expects the worst.

The murder is cold, and it has slammed Greg to the floor emotionally. He is less affected by sorrow for the dead kid (whom he did not know) than he is unstrung by the creeping realization of who may have committed the murders. Although no arrests have been made, Greg has a good idea who is involved—two TMC's who are his workers.

"I don't want to think about it," he says. "It's too awful. I'm in such denial. Nobody believes more than me about jobs working, saving kids' lives. And most of the times it does work, but . . ." His voice trails off.

As the days after the murder pass, the threats from the Crips become more virulent. Romeo is obviously a prime suspect because of the earlier incident, whether or not he was actually involved. Even the police hear that the Crips are saying if they can't get Romeo they'll get his family. This kind of warfare is unheard of in the projects. Families are considered untouchable under the code.

Pam McDuffie comes into Greg's office and announces that he can't possibly leave in July as planned. "You'll just have to wait until September," she says. "With all this shit happening, we can't do without you that soon!"

Greg laughs when she leaves. "I just hope I can *hang* until July," he says. Then he quickly corrects himself. "Of course I can. But sometimes it *feels* like I can't."

On Saturday, Greg is scheduled to speak at a job-a-thon organized by the radio station Power 106. Greg goes with Romeo in tow, but leaves early. "I couldn't do it," he says. "I was supposed to stand up there and convince everybody how jobs stop violence. And I didn't have the *ganas,*" the will. "I have unshakable confidence in jobs as a strategy and sometimes it does the trick, like with Ghost. But the cycle of despair goes so deep that sometimes a job is only a drop in the bucket. Romeo's a perfect example. He has a terrible family background, an alcohol problem, and any number of other complications. A job brought him halfway out of the water but not completely."

Boyle asks Romeo if he had anything to do with the murder. Romeo says no. Boyle wants to believe him.

Drifter from TMC calls Greg when the priest is feeling particularly low. "What do we do now?" he asks. Greg tells him to just take care of himself and not worry about the problems of the neighborhood.

"Sometimes," Drifter tells Greg, "I feel like I just want out of everything." By *everything* Drifter means life. But Greg deliberately misinterprets the statement and tells Drifter he thinks it would be great if the homie left the projects and the neighborhood.

"But I knew what he meant," Greg says later, his voice hollow, despondent. "I feel like that too sometimes."

———

At Ridgway's meeting, she announces she is not only imposing a curfew, she is putting everyone in the projects on house arrest for the entire weekend.

When Silent comes in, she pulls him aside. "Can't you do something?" she asks. "Can't you talk to some of these fools?"

"Ain't nobody who can do a thing to stop the Crips," replies Silent. "The Crips want payback, and that's that. Everybody should just stay off the street."

Wolf is one of those whose name has been mentioned in connection with the murder. When he saunters into the meeting, he affects a remarkable lack of concern, considering Crips for a hundred blocks want to kill him. When Ridgway suggests he might have reason to worry, he smiles a slow, dimpled smile.

"You got me all wrong, Ridgway," he says. "I'm a lover, not a gang banger."

"There's not much that phases Robert," says Ridgway after she has given Wolf permission to leave. "I have to hand it to him, though. He had a lot of courage when he showed up at his cousin's wake a year or two ago. Shy Boy from Primera Flats was his cousin. Wolf had enough presence, enough respect on the street, that he told Flats, 'I'm coming no matter what.' Tuchek and I stood outside that night and we were scared to death. And that kid walked alone into a room of two hundred enemy gang members. He was really broken up. Stood at the casket and cried. It's the only time I've ever seen him display that kind of emotion."

For nearly a week, through the combined efforts of Ridgway, Greg, and the police, there are no serious retaliations. Everybody hopes that an arrest will be made before luck and energy run out. Then, on a Wednesday afternoon, luck throws a curve ball in the form of the Rodney King verdicts.

At exactly 3:16 KFWB all-news radio announces each one of the verdicts separately: *Not guilty. Not guilty. Not guilty. Not guilty.* The content of the announcement is momentarily confusing. How can one be found not guilty of something that the whole country saw one do on video? The radio announcer says that there may be unrest. However, as I drive toward Dolores Mission to meet Greg, the likelihood of citywide violence seems a distant concern. Pico Aliso currently has its own unrest, which feels infinitely more up close and personal.

At the church, a group of Comite Pro Pas mothers plus Leonardo have gathered with the idea of marching to Parker Center to protest the King verdicts. Instead, I accompany Greg to Kirby Detention Center where he is scheduled to say mass every first Wednesday of the month. During the mass, kids are more agitated than we have ever seen them. After mass, Greg always visits various "cottages" in order to talk to kids individually. Tonight each cottage has a TV on and, although the kids seem glad to see Greg, they can barely wrench their eyes away from the violent, balletic images which careen across the screen. A news clip of a white man being pulled from a truck and horribly beaten is being replayed over and over, in an eerie reverse image of the tape of the King beating. In the cottages, the Kirby kids are even jumpier than they had been at mass, their bodies twitchy, unable to light anywhere for long.

From Kirby we drive to Manresa Retreat House in Azusa, where Turtle and Cisco are working. Greg has promised to pick up the two homies and bring them back to L.A. for a short visit. We take them to dinner before heading back to the projects. The food is good and both kids are in high comic form. For the first time in weeks, Greg relaxes, the crazy images of the television are briefly forgotten.

We head back toward the projects around 9:00 P.M. As we near Los Angeles, we hit a colossal traffic jam. The sky is bright to the northeast of us and also to the south, and there are veils of smoke. For the first time since the afternoon we turn on the radio and learn what the rest of Los Angeles already knows.

When I finally drop Greg and the two homies at the church parking lot, Pico Aliso is quiet and dark, a seeming haven from the storm which is quickening everywhere else. That there is danger in the nearby shadows is not immediately evident. After I leave the church, Greg goes to get something out of his office, after which he intends to drop the two boys at home and head home himself. Just as he is closing his office door, he hears shots coming from farther down the street. Then the phone rings. It is Pam telling him it's not safe to take the TMC's out of the church. Seconds later Joanna calls. "They're shooting!" she says. For the next two hours, cars full of Crips roll up and down Gless Street, the dull shine of gun barrels visible out open car windows.

I hear about none of this until the next day, as I am now fully occupied trying to imagine a safe route home. To my right is Hollywood, where the palm trees are fantastic firey torches lining the freeway with furious light. To my left is South Central—the epicenter. Using the radio news as a guide, I decide to head west across the First Street bridge, straight through the middle of downtown.

The first sign of trouble is at the New Otani Hotel. Most of the windows have been smashed and there is evidence of fire damage. A few blocks farther is Parker Center, LAPD headquarters, which is protectively surrounded by a shoulder-to-shoulder string of a two hundred officers all top-heavy with riot helmets.

"Get over to Third Street," one of the cops yells to me. I take his suggestion, not realizing that the insurrection is a live thing now, which no one can track or predict. Although I see signs of mayhem, at first the Third Street route seems clear. Then, as I round a barricade at the corner of Flower and Third, I run smack into everything I am trying to avoid: As far as my eyes can see, crowds of people— brown, black, many white—race and twirl in zigzag patterns across streets like whole teams of football runningbacks turned crazy. The sound of glass erupting in a musical clatter repeats from all directions.

Gunfire is close but sporadic; the bullets, I think, spent more for effect than for injury. Flames slash angrily from the inside of certain stores and only barely sequin the facades of others. All trash cans have been lit on fire as if every rioter has seen the movie *Blade Runner.* I weave from street to street, no longer stopping for anything. Everywhere I turn there is madness.

I am not scared when I am in the middle of the downtown craziness. Nor am I scared once I get on the Santa Monica Freeway, nor later on the Pacific Coast Highway, or still later snaking up the curvy road that leads to my rural L.A. canyon. Only when I am actually in my house and with my child again do I allow myself to be scared. It is safe here. My kid is safe here. As safe as safe gets, anyway. Tonight that is all I care about.

For the next forty-eight hours in Los Angeles, everything stops and everything is in motion. However, in Pico Aliso, there is no rioting, no looting. Although some residents are known to have made forays into other areas of the city, most of the community huddles together like a family riding out a hurricane—Crip/TMC conflicts momentarily forgotten.

On Thursday, as Greg walks the projects trying to calm people, hoping the National Guard will arrive soon, a frightened Cuatro homie approaches him.

"This is the end of the world, isn't it, G?" says the kid.

"Don't be silly," reassures Greg, "of course it's not." Inside, he is thinking that he is not so damn sure.

Greg is more expert at emotional compartmentalization than most anyone I have ever met. While he experiences great grief and great discouragement, those emotions are tucked into separate rooms of his psyche, distinct from his day-to-day workings. It's how he survives.

However, today the controls are loosed. In reaction to the psychic earthquake which has taken place around him, Greg's protective barriers have broken down and all the emotions are running together.

"It took everything in me to muster up the right response to that kid," he says later. "I have never felt so, I don't know, dark. And it's not just because the city's out of control It's that the city feels like a paradigm for the neighborhood. The neighborhood feels out of control. *I* feel out of control." He pauses. "It makes me wonder how much I hold myself together with magical thinking all the time—to keep myself from feeling this terrible."

———

The TMC/Crip conflict stays forgotten for almost two weeks while the city reels in shock. In the first days that follow the riots, politicians make obligatory pilgrimages down to the poorer sides of town, including to Dolores Mission Parish. Greg agrees to allow then-presidential candidate Jerry Brown to hold a press conference at which gang members will speak to the media about the needs of the barrio. Rebel, and Bandit from TMC, and Champ—one of the big heads from Cuatro—are among the most articulate. Champ talks with eloquence about the need for jobs and opportunities, while the photographers snap photos of his muscular, resplendently tattooed body draped in a white tank-top T-shirt.

Rebel is the most poetic. "See, if you look you'll see that Dolores Mission is surrounded by three hills," he tells the reporters in a velvety cadence. "And no matter where trouble starts, even if it starts up on those hills, it always rolls down to the projects."

At the end of the press conference, Brown announces he will take two homies on his next out-of-state campaign swing. A forest of hands go up to volunteer. Greg selects Champ first, then suggests Largo, Champ's best friend, as a second.

Champ objects. "I think the other person should be from another neighborhood," he says. "How about Rebel?" This is a particularly generous gesture coming from Champ, who prides himself on being the downest of *vatos*.

So Rebel and Champ it is. There is a mad scramble to pick up belongings in time to make the scheduled plane flight. Rebel asks if he can wash his clothes in the church washer since he doesn't have one at home. Greg volunteers to do the wash himself.

As Greg drops Rebel's small pile of worn T-shirts and pants into the washing machine, he is startled by the paucity of the garments.

"Here's a kid who used to sell drugs like crazy. But now he doesn't want to slang and he doesn't have a job yet. So this is it. This is all he has."

When Rebel and Champ return to Los Angeles two days later, they are met at the airport by a mass of journalists who pepper them with questions which the newly media-wise homies field skillfully.

"We did things we couldn't dream about," says Champ. "People invited us into their houses and they treated us like kings."

"We got out of the projects and away from the gang banging and violence and into the world," says Rebel. "We were scared but we liked it a lot."

A reporter asks Rebel if he and Champ will vote for Jerry Brown in the upcoming presidential primaries. Rebel smiles. "We would if we could. But we're felons. We can't vote."

The same reporter asks Champ if he would like to take another such trip. Champ looks the reporter straight in the eye. "We'll never do anything like this again in our lives. We know that."

———

Friday afternoon. Another Ridgway meeting day. Whenever Ridgway is late, like today, Father Greg always waits out front until her white custody car pulls up so that the various gang members won't be left alone together without the mitigating influence of adult supervision.

The unease that had temporarily dissipated is creeping back into the projects bit by bit. There has been a small meeting of African American residents in Aliso Village to discuss racial tension. One of the meeting's participants, a gang consultant named Kenneth Wheeler, begins criticizing Greg. "We'd be a lot better off if a respected leader wasn't harboring the person who killed Pontiac," says Wheeler. By this he is referring to the fact that Wolf is now one of those on the suspect list, and he's still on Greg's work crew.

Greg is infuriated when word of the comment circulates back to him through parish gossip. "What am I doing? Hiding him in plain sight?" Greg says. "Look: I asked Wolf if he did it and he said he was there, but he had no part in it. If Robert had said he'd done it," continues Greg, "I would have done everything in my power to get him to turn himself in. And obviously I couldn't have him working for me. But he *didn't* say that. And the police haven't arrested him. So what exactly am I supposed to do?"

Greg looks anguished. "Whoever *did do* it, I just hope the police get them before someone else does. God."

When Ridgway arrives, she speeds through the meeting, then dismisses the homies to spill outside into the vivid late afternoon sunshine. There is marked apprehension in everyone's face, but it is only displayed indirectly. Shadow from TMC launches into an accelerated monologue about how terrible everything will be when Greg leaves. He and some of the other TMC's have named Father Pete, Greg's successor, "Greedy Pete," a sobriquet which Shadow now lobs into the conversation, like a series of water balloons.

"You think Greedy Pete's going to care about us? You think Greedy Pete's going to try and get us jobs? It's not for me I'm worried. It's for my younger homeboys who haven't had the time with Father Greg that I have."

Since Shadow is black, this whole Crip thing has put him in a particularly vulnerable position. Suddenly his manner seizes up. "For me it doesn't matter," he continues, still ostensibly talking about Greg's departure. He breaks open a smile. "See, I'm dead already."

Across the street in the church parking lot, Romeo, showing off his recently shaved head, chatters animatedly about how the Power 106 job is *firme*. Wolf, dressed in freshly washed gray sweat pants and a bright blue Gap brand pocket T-shirt, alternately gives his opinion of presidential politics and teases Rebel about his jeans shorts, which are average in fit, rather than the normal size 44's.

"I've never *seen* somebody wear pants so tight," says Wolf, affecting outrage. "That style just don't look right, homes!"

For once, Ridgway has talked Wolf into allowing her to drive him to his mother's apartment for safety's sake. She says she will leave as soon as she makes one more phone call. A minute or two after Ridgway disappears into the rectory office, three black-and-whites screech into the church parking lot. Several officers efficiently handcuff Wolf and Romeo, then move them quickly into the police cars.

Mike Marchello is one of the arresting officers. When he is asked what the two will be charged with, he responds without rancor, almost apologetically.

"It's a one-eighty-seven," he says. "Murder."

After the cops drive away, Rebel spins over to confront Ridgway, screaming that she called the police so they could arrest Romeo and Wolf. Ridgway denies this, but only perfunctorily. Greg grabs Rebel away from Ridgway and herds him into the rectory.

"What the hell difference does it make?" Greg yells to Rebel. "Do you really think it would be better if the police broke down the door to Romeo's mother's house at five in the morning and traumatized his little sisters? The point is that *one* of your homeboys killed a kid! Open your fucking eyes!"

"I don't have any patience for this any more," Greg says as he walks away. An hour or so later word drifts back that Housing Police have just arrested Shadow for selling drugs.

———

Greg decides to send Rebel to a job that has just opened up at Tri-Star Motion Picture Studios. Knowing Rebel's wardrobe firsthand, Greg also determines that a shopping trip is in order and takes Rebel to the May Company over the weekend.

Rebel and his dramatic personality are an inspired match for the movie business job. In the afternoons after work, he shows up at the rectory to regale Greg and anybody else willing to listen with his latest observations of life on the film business fast track.

". . . And then I came in to this woman's office with the scripts like she asked, G, and there she is with her *bare foot* up in the air with all these little *white cotton guys* between the toes! And this other person was like painting her toenails an' everything! And she just took the scripts, G. Like it was nothing that she had all these little *cotton guys* between her toes!"

Every day Rebel seems to grow more solid, as if a real future is for the first time tangibly within his field of vision. Midway through Rebel's second week of work Greg gets a letter typed on Tri-Star stationery. It reads in part:

Father, I would like to thank you for all the things you have done for me and my young family. Father you have done so much for me that I owe you my whole life. G, if it wasn't for you, I don't think I would be alive today. And don't tell me that it is drama because it isn't, okay?

Father I never typed a letter in my whole life so if I fucked up somewhere I hope that you will understand.

Well G-Dog I've got to get back to work. Okay?

Love truly, crazy ass Rebel, William Ayala, Puro DMC [Dolores Mission Church] not TMC

————

One evening, Rebel stays in Greg's office after everyone else has gone, his mood thoughtful.

"Are you part Mexican?" he asks the priest. The fair-complected Greg tells him that he's pretty much all Irish.

"Why'd you become a priest?" Rebel asks next.

Greg thinks for a few seconds, "I don't know," he says honestly. "I guess I thought I could help change the world."

Rebel nods. Then the two men sit quietly, content in each other's company.

————

The days move fast now, and although Greg still seems hell-bent on getting as many homies working as humanly possible, the frantic quality has faded. Maybe it is the combined effect of fatigue, the riots, and the strain of the episode with Pontiac's shooting, but something has pushed him past the breaking point.

"I can only do what I can do," he says now on a regular basis.

Father Greg also is beginning to look forward to his sabbatical. He will have time to rediscover himself as a Jesuit, he says, time to renew, time to start praying again.

One evening, when he is in a reflective mood, Greg reminisces about how he came to make the choice to join the Society of Jesus. He talks about how he was drawn to the notion of service by his Jesuit teachers at Loyola High School, whom he saw not only as inspiring and cutting edge but as genuinely happy, when happiness seemed to him to be a foreign and rare commodity among most other adults he knew. "Nobody around me seemed to get joy and life out of what they did."

Greg comes from a large Catholic family in which all male family members were expected to grow up and find work at Western Farms, a commercial dairy founded by Greg's great-grandfather. "I paid for my whole high school education loading trucks," he says. "I guess I thought, 'Is this what I want for my life?' Although Greg's own father had aspirations of being either a high school coach and teacher or a priest, he too dutifully spent his adult working years at the dairy, as did all but two of Greg's many uncles. "My dad's a great man who loves his wife and kids," says Greg. "But I think there was a real sadness in terms of his choice of occupation."

Not wishing to repeat what he viewed as his father's mistake, the adolescent Greg gravitated instead toward the men around him who seemed the most intellectually vital and vocationally fulfilled—his Jesuit teachers. Before he turned eighteen he announced to his parents that he was joining the Society of Jesus.

There were periods early on when Greg says he came close to quitting. He says he fell in love several times in the course of his theological studies. "I think celibacy is an anachronism and somewhat out of step," he says. "There are times when you think it would be great to be married and to have a wife and kids. There was a time when that was the most negative side, where I thought, 'This is really a sacrifice.'"

After college and divinity school, Greg was assigned to teach at his old alma mater, Loyola High School, where he got swept up into apostolic fever.

After Loyola there was more study in Boston, then Bolivia. "Bolivia freed me. I thought, 'I want to do this kind of work for the rest of my life. I want to live the Gospel.' And I just couldn't do it and have a wife and kids."

Outsiders, particularly non-Catholics, are inevitably intrigued by the conundrum of Greg's calling. He is after all a cute-guy priest with a winning personality and a sexuality that doesn't seem entirely unavailable to him. (At Dolores Mission there has been the occasional parish woman who has flirted openly with Greg, although he is adept at gently deflecting all advances.)

"It's still difficult," he admits. "It's hard on the intimate sides, in terms of wanting to share your life in a way that's more intimate than the way you can as a priest. But I guess what I'm trying to say is—it's been more difficult when I'm not at a place that fills me with life. Dolores Mission fills me with life. The strongest feelings in my life have all happened here—the most joy, the most sadness. Dolores Mission is a great place if you have an appetite for living—if you love what all those feelings do to you. In the end, even the sadness—it breaks you open. You go where the life is. And the life for me is here in this parish—especially with these kids. The happiness they bring me is beyond anything I can express in words. Even now, after everything. In the truest and most absolute sense, this work is a vocation. And for good or ill I can do no other."

———

Yet, he is about to do "other"—at least for a year. The sand in the hourglass has almost run out. In the last two months that are left, some homies remain stable. Others hit downswings. One afternoon, Dreamer, who had been staying out of trouble, decides to stroll into the multipurpose center on First Street, where several of the Dukes are working. As the startled Dukes scramble for guns, Dreamer insists he just wants to go head up with one of them—any one. The Twin, recently released from camp himself, steps forward and a gigantic brawl ensues.

A few days later, Turtle takes an even more disquieting nosedive. It seems he finally asked his mother for the eight hundred dollars he had saved toward a car. She told him she had spent it. "She said she didn't have no money to pay the bills," he says, "because my brother who lives there didn't give her no money and my dad didn't give her no money." More likely the mother drank the money, although Turtle will not admit to this possibility.

"Now I've been working all the time for nothing," is all he will say.

As more days go by Turtle's state of mind deteriorates further. The betrayal seems more important than the cash which, even he admits, can be saved again. When he is in Azusa at the retreat house, coworkers report he sometimes cries on the job. At other times he works so frantically his supervisor has to tell him to slow down. On weekends he talks friends into picking him up and bringing him back to the projects, where he goes on suicidal tagging expeditions. Sometimes he just stands on First Street daring the Dukes to shoot him. In retaliation, the Twin and others from East L.A. tell his girl-friend Liliana, who works at the multipurpose center that they intend to "light up your *pinche* Tamale boyfriend."

"When G leaves," Turtle says, "I'm really not going to care no more."

For once, Turtle's desperate behavior doesn't send Greg into a tail-spin. "I really love that kid. But I can't make him care for himself."

———

There are other omens of trouble to come. Even though Rebel contin-ues to do spectacularly well at his Tri-Star job, there is one ominous sign. He has gotten a bunch of new tattoos, the most unnerving of which is on the back of his neck—in the same location and in the same script as Green Eyes' "I'm Still Here." Worse, it reads, "Green Eyes R.I.P."

Virtually the same week, Wizard too gets himself newly tattooed. Wizard's tattoos include a giant Clarence Street Locos right across his stomach, and a large CSL crawling prominently down his forearm. Greg is particularly perplexed by Wizard, since he has pulled way back from CSL and is only a week away from moving to Texas together with his lady and his babies.

"You know," Greg says, "on the surface, these would all seem to be different circumstances, but there's a similarity between all three kids. Deep, deep inside they each still say to themselves, 'This will never happen for me. A good life can never be mine. So I'll mess it up myself before it gets messed up for me.'"

———

A week later, Rebel messes up for real. Early on Sunday, Greg gets a call that Rebel has been arrested. At 3 A.M. the night before, he had been talking on the pay phone located near the market at the corner of Fourth and Gless—the same corner where Dreamer was shot and Oso was killed. A dark, newish car approached the corner and slowed down. Rebel assumed someone was about to do a drive-by. Rebel says he did not fire at the car. Suffice it to say that *someone* fired in the direction of the car. They were warning shots, fired high. But shots nevertheless.

The good news is that the dark car did not belong to enemy gang members. The bad news is that it belongs to an off-duty police officer—Metro Division. The officer and his partner were on their way home from work. Twenty minutes after the shots were fired, the police returned in force and arrested the only gang members in evidence—Rebel and Cisco—who were blithely sitting together on the front stoop of an apartment near the church.

It is unclear why Rebel did not leave the area after the shooting incident. Within an hour after his arrest, Cisco has been released and the two cops riding in the dark car have positively ID'd Rebel as the shooter.

Talking on the phone from jail, Rebel starts to cry. "Just when I was getting my life together so good . . ." he says.

As discouraging as Rebel's arrest is, Greg is less knocked for a loop than he was by, say, the threat of Ghost's arrest.

"Whether Rebel actually shot the gun or not," Greg says grimly, "he shouldn't have been there at 3:30 in the morning. If you're out in the projects at 3:30 in the morning, sooner or later shit happens. Period." He sighs. "So often it's like this. Things start going well and the kid has to hit the self-destruct button. Sometimes they're lucky and the self-destruct doesn't happen. Rebel wasn't lucky."

As he says this, it is certain Greg doesn't care less for Rebel than for Ghost. They are both kids for whom he feels a deep attachment. But day by day, the threads of his attachment to Dolores Mission and all it encompasses unbraid just a bit more. Perhaps by July 31, they will have unbraided enough that the separation won't tear him apart.

Noticing his fatigue and his new found detachment, a number of people—Jesuits and staff—remark that Greg is leaving just in the nick of time because he is clearly burning out.

"I hate when people say that!" Greg says in reaction. "I think what's happening is the organic thing that *keeps* me from burning out. *Burn out* is if Wizard's jokes don't make me laugh, if Spanky's tenderness doesn't fill me with joy, if Rebel's or Turtle's or Happy's dilemmas don't catch me in the throat—then that's burnout. But that has never happened. Not even close. I guess what I *am* doing is whatever one does to make it hurt less. To make the leaving hurt less."

July is a month of goodbyes. There is the last mass at Kirby Detention Center, the last mass at Juvenile Hall. Father Greg is asked to be the graduation speaker at the local elementary school. When he steps onto the stage a choir of high sixth-grade voices sing to him, "You Are the Wind Beneath My Wings."

Each of the four main neighborhoods insists on throwing parties for Greg, as do the various mothers' groups. The homies of TMC, CSL, and Cuatro, plus Joanna and some of the girls, make a goodbye video for him. With the help of one of the producers on the Columbia movie project, they shoot endless footage of gang and community members talking into the camera, saying what Father Greg has meant to them. The edited video is quite stunning, the highlight of the community's big going-away party. Joanna reads a long lyric poem she has written for the occasion. Greg is overwhelmed.

During the last weeks, there is a flurry of baby baptisms in addition to the parties. Dreamer, Spanky, Joanna, and Silent all rush to get their babies' ceremonies in under the wire before Greg is no longer available.

Predictably, even up until the last minute, there are new crises for Greg to solve, disasters for him to mitigate. Happy has returned from Texas and has already gotten himself shot in the upper arm. Turtle is more and more marked by East L.A. In rebellious reaction, he pushes himself to make ridiculously foolhardy tagging forays into Dukes' territory. He also gets himself newly tattooed. The tattoo reads "I'll make it easy," written in longhand right over his heart.

"It's the name of my favorite song!" he says to Greg.

The self-destructive symbolism bothers Greg. "Did you ever think," he asks irritably, "that you might not have the same favorite song when you're thirty?"

———

Father Greg's last Mass at Dolores Mission is held on July 26, 1992, out in the church parking lot under a blazing midsummer sun. The parking lot is chosen because the crowds who have come to say goodbye can't possibly fit into the church. The media is also here en masse—print reporters, crews from six networks, plus CNN. Pam's husband Bebee is videotaping from the church's bell tower. The PM'ers are perched along the rectory roofline like rowdy baby crows. Word goes around that East L.A, Cuatro, Clarence, and TMC have, of their own volition, put aside their enmity for the day to honor their surrogate father.

The homeboys themselves are the last to arrive. When they do show up it's with remarkable theatricality. Each neighborhood enters the parking lot in its own single-file line, resembling four hard-eyed *corps de ballet* making tightly choreographed entrances onto an enormous stage. After everyone settles in, the choir sings some hymns, and several of the other Jesuits make introductory remarks. When finally Greg gets up to speak, the moment is electric as the crowd is suddenly swept by visible waves of emotion spanning a range from searing grief to love that borders on the ecstatic.

Greg first speaks in Spanish to the community at large. Then he breaks into English to speak directly to the homeboys.

"*Mis* homies," he says, his tone choked and intimate, "you know what's in my heart for you right now. I'm a richer man because I know you. But you also know the pain it's been to bury you. I'm going to talk to you straight out because I love you. You know I do. Many of you have told me, 'When you leave, we're going to *loc* up! It's *on*.'"

He pauses, his gaze sweeping from kid to kid. "Well, if you love me . . . if you respect me . . . it's *off*."

It is at this point that Greg's composure fails him. "You know where I've been for you," he says, tears streaming beyond his control. "Well, here's where I want you to be for me: Please stop banging. *Please stop banging*. I had one of the homies say to me the other day, 'I owe you everything.' I said, 'No. You owe me one thing. Please have a good life.' I want to know your children. And I want to know your grandchildren. And I want to baptize 'em. And I don't ever want to bury one of *La Raza* again. Never. I don't ever want to do it again."

By the end of the speech, homies from all neighborhoods are sobbing, their arms around each other for ballast.

Right after the mass, three of the four gangs in attendance—Cuatro, TMC, and CSL—organize a spontaneous peace conference with Happy skittering between neighborhoods as prime organizer. The homies celebrate their negotiated truce with a game of touch football in the field between Cuatro and TMC territory.

The morning fades into afternoon then into evening in a mood of piercing brightness. There is a huge block party in the park. Greg stays there for hours, salsa dancing again and again with every community woman who asks him. After nightfall, he drifts in and out of his office and around the projects. Well-wishers of all ages float around him, swooping in and out like swallows, wrapping themselves in the moment so intensely that it seems they are weaving even these last seconds into a cloak of protection to shield them from what is later to come.

———

On July 31, Father Greg's final day, homeboys, community members, and PM'ers start gathering in the church parking lot at 5:00 A.M. Pam McDuffie brings the hot chocolate at 5:15, by which time I have already set out the pan dulce. The original plan was to meet in the school cafeteria but no one wants to go indoors and risk missing a second of this uneasy morning. When Greg hasn't arrived by 5:25, Lupe Loera and I decide to go to the Jesuit residence to fetch him. His beige car is parked in the driveway, trunk open. Spanky's beige station wagon is parked behind Greg's sedan; Patricia, his lady, and their baby curled up sleepily in the back seat.

Greg is still in his bedroom closing suitcases. The mattress on his twin bed has been stripped. His dresser, small side table, and chair are completely bare. When the room was decorated with Greg's belongings—fabric wall hangings from Bolivia and Mexico, miscellaneous drawings, posters, and photos—it looked warm, full, ample. Now it looks pinched and meager.

Little Fernie and Jaime ride with Greg to the airport, the rest caravanning behind. Greg and entourage arrive at LAX two hours early for the 8:30 A.M. departure. Greg is recognized twice by admirers en route from the baggage check area to the boarding gate.

His parents are already at the gate when we arrive. Even Mary Ridgway is there, dressed more formally than usual in a deep purple long-sleeved dress with a hat. Normally stoic, she blinks back tears for the whole two-hour wait.

At 8:25, homies, girls, Ridgway, Pam and Bebee McDuffie, Lupe Loera and the other mothers, plus a half-dozen PM'ers all stand in a helpless line waving and sobbing as Greg raises his hand one more time to his community, then turns and walks his duck-footed walk up the ramp and out of sight into the boarding tunnel.

From there, everyone moves in a clump to the boarding gate window to stare at Greg's plane. Soon the jet wheels out toward the runway, still within sight of the crowd at the window. There is a delay. The delay stretches into minutes and then past a half hour, but no one is willing to go home until the plane actually leaves the ground.

"Maybe it's never gonna take off and he'll just have to come back," says Joker, his forehead knocking rhythmically against the window. "Yeah. I think that's it. God isn't gonna let G leave!"

Shortly after 9:15 A.M., the United 747 begins to accelerate. "He's leaving!" yells Pam's seven-year-old son. Those who have straggled away momentarily run back to the window to stare transfixed at the now racing jet.

Then, with the speed of a breath, Father Greg Boyle is gone.

Happy

My name is Alfonso Trujillo. They call me Happy 'cause I've got a positive attitude. There's five in my family. The other three live with my aunt in Texas. But me and my brother grew up in foster care. We lived in the countryside in Texas until I was about six. Then my mom wanted to get away from her family because there were problems. So she came to Los Angeles and we lived in Bell Gardens. My mom had little problems here and there, drug problems. Heroin. So my brother went into a foster home. And I went to live with my uncle. I was eight and my brother was six. I really hated not being with my brother.

I started getting into the system when I was fourteen when I went to camp. I was sixteen when I got out. When I got out, the first thing I did was I went to get my brother from the people where he was staying. I snuck into the house and said, "You want to go?" And he said, "Yeah!" so we left. And we came to the projects. We been on the street since then. We stayed here and there. We sold drugs to get money.

I'm not the type of person who would go out and steal or rob to make a living. I would rather sell drugs. I watched my homeboys sell drugs so I knew who they got 'em from.

I have a good relationship with my mom. No matter what she does, me and my brother, we still got love for her. An' she got love for us. She still is having a very, very hard time. She used to have problems with the law. But she's over that. Right now she's just trying to patch the holes that she made in her life. Drugs are the main reason for all her problems. I think, if I was to say, she got into them to get away from her true feelings. I don't know. I never got personal with her. If she would talk to me I would know. But she hasn't ever talked to me in a personal way.

When we were little, my mom did do some stuff for us, like she used to read to us. My favorite book was *The Jungle Book*. I liked how the little boy survived in the jungle. I sort of put myself in his place.

I read when I can. My favorite book now is *The Old Man and the Sea*. It's about courage. I like that. I like the faith that the old man had. He went fishing and he never caught a fish in his life. But he caught that fish and he stuck with it, you know? A lot of problems happened and he still stuck with it.

I got a criminal justice book at my house because I like to study about the law. The law is my big problem, now. Obeying the law.

It's hard to explain why I joined a gang at first. I didn't really know what was going on. It wasn't to be different from others. It wasn't to feel wanted. Nothing like that. It was more something I wanted to do for myself. With TMC, we all began it, so we all jumped each other in.

There's two ways out of this mess. One way out is that you do the right thing. That's the individual thing. You got to look into yourself, and not care what other people are doing. The other way to get out is to go out backwards. I mean, to get shot.

I do carry weapons. I don't have them on me. I just have them in a place where I can get hold of them. If someone shoots *at* me, I'm not going to retaliate. I don't do that. If they *shot* me and I lived, then I would take that into consideration. I would go back.

Some police, they like me. Some police they don't. The time I broke out of the hospital, it started when they arrested me for having a gun. It was an automatic rifle. I was going across the street, taking it across from one side of the projects to the other. We had heard that this other neighborhood was going to come down and shoot at any of us that they could find. The police chased me because they were looking for one of my other homeboys and they thought I was him.

So they got me, and took me to the alley and they beat me up. They were trying to make me say the gun was mine, but it wasn't.

You could say they beat me up a lot. There's not much you can do when you're handcuffed. But when we got to Juvenile Hall I made out that my ribs were broken, which was not true. But I was mad that they'd beat me up so much. So I was playing a little role, like I couldn't breathe. So they had to take me to the hospital. Then at the hospital, they were about to give me an X ray so they had to take the handcuffs off. I asked the doctor if I could use the bathroom, and he said okay. The police were rookies so they were just sitting out in the hall like stupids. So I went inside the bathroom and stood there a little while trying to figure out what I should do. Then no one was around so I just got out. I ran across the freeway and right through my enemy's neighborhood. And they were just looking at me, whistling. I just kept running.

I called Ridgway up and she started laughing. I was on the run for about two weeks. I was going to stay on the run till New Year's and then turn myself in. I picked New Year's because I've been locked up for three Christmases already, and three New Year's. So this was going to be my first Christmas out.

They were sweating G-Dog and sweating my homeboys about where I was. They were causing a big ol' scene. When they finally caught me they beat the shit out of me.

I've done quite a few crazy things. The craziest thing I've ever done was fighting with the police when they caught me that time after I was on the run. When they apprehended me I refused to be cooperative. The officer hit me. So I hit him back. Then the other one comes in and starts fighting, so I started fighting with him too. Then there were four of them altogether, trying to restrain me. But I just refused. I tried to jump out of a window. I had run into a house, right there on Gless. Really, though, I'd do anything to get away.

I guess I'm a good fighter. But I kind of got tired. We were fighting for about five minutes. They were trying to hold on to me because I was going for the window. Finally they arrested me. But they didn't take me to the police station. They were pretty mad so they kind of drove me around for a while and gave me the treatment. They beat me down pretty good. They were putting guns to my cheek and saying,

"We'll kill you right now." And I would say, "You can't do that. Everybody knows that I'm going to jail."

When Green Eyes passed away it hit me hard. Green Eyes had a good personality. He was cool. He trusted me and I trusted him. We didn't hide nothing from each other. I was in the projects when I heard he'd been shot. I heard because my homeboys came straight to me after they went to the hospital. When I found out how it happened, I felt like it was for nothing. When you realize what went on that night, you realize it was for nothing. The guys who shot him'd probably never even seen him in his life. I feel like I'm guilty for what happened. Everybody's guilty. For not, you know, giving him advice. For not doing positive things that he could take into consideration—so he could change his life, you know. I wish I done a lot of things differently about Green Eyes. So many I can't even say them all.

People think I'm crazy, but I'm not. I don't do things unless my back's against the wall. To tell you a truth I don't have big grudges against any of my enemies. If there would be a day that we could get along, I would get along. But I don't know what's in their minds. If they would get along with me.

My problem is I got a temper. Like one time I ran across Father Tom when he had two East L.A.'s in his truck. And I recognized 'em. One of 'em was this guy who shot at me one time. When I saw him, I got so angry I wasn't thinking. I did have a piece on me. And I pulled it out and I started waving it around. Then I caught myself. I realized what I was doing. I wouldn't shoot him.

When G heard about it, he got very mad at me. He was cussing an' everything. It made me all nervous. I thought, "I made a priest sin!"

I'll tell you how it works. It's like flashbacks. Somebody tries to kill you and then all the time afterward you think about what happened. And you keep saying to yourself, "I'm gonna get 'em. I'm gonna get 'em." And then after a while you forget about it. But then you see that person again, an' you remember. You get a flashback and you get all crazy.

The closest I came to getting killed was when this guy shot at me at just about point-blank range. He was pretending he wanted to buy a twenty. Then when I walked over, he pulled out this big old gun.

He shot BOOM! BOOM! I started zigzagging, running away. I don't know who it was. Obviously he's an enemy.

If I wanted to, I guess I could be one of the ones who calls the shots because all my little homies look up to me. I guess when I'm around they think that more will happen. When I got back from Texas, all the homies were saying, "Hey man! We're deep now!"

I can't go back to Texas. I was very unhappy there. Very unhappy. It's hard to explain. There were miles and miles of trees. It smelled good, that was true. But the people I was staying with, I didn't feel like they were family. It was embarrassing too. I felt like I was in the way. There wasn't too much money to go around. And I didn't want to be a burden. They didn't say it, but that's what I felt. An' there were no jobs. Here at least you can slang or work for G to make some money if you can't get another job. At least that's how it was until G left.

There were four neighborhoods at G's last mass. And I called a meeting because everybody was there. That's the best time to hit on everybody because some of those people are hard to find. So if you want to get something settled, occasions like that are a good time. The reason why I wanted to have that meeting was for Clarence and Cuatro to squash it. And for us and Cuatro to squash it. And for us to each put all of our little youngsters in check. I was trying to pump everybody up to get everything off their chests, let their feelings out, because there ain't no second chances. But things didn't go as planned. Everybody started backsliding into their own little world. Now look what's happened. There ain't no second chances

Everybody's got a role in the drama here in the projects. When these certain people died—like Green Eyes and Oso—things got messed up. Things wouldn't be happening between us and Cuatro if Oso was alive. 'Cause he was always kicking it with us. Also, if Green Eyes hadn't passed away, things wouldn't be so messed up 'cause his whole family was Cuatro.

I don't know what my role is yet. I'd like it if my role was to make everyone realize that to kill people for that little piece of ground is crazy messed up. The thing that's made it get so bad is how everybody abuses that word "love." People say they care for each other in their neighborhoods but they don't. People say, "I'm your homie. I got love." But they also say "Trust no man." You can't have both. I think most of the problem—why people gang bang—is because they ain't got nothing else better to do.

You know what I would want to do, if I could do anything? Work with a veterinarian. Once I knew an owner at a pet shop and I used to help him clean up and stuff. I'm good with animals. One time I had a rattlesnake for a pet. It was a baby. People say the babies are the most dangerous, but this one was cool. I would hold it in my hand and it never tried to bite me. I guess it got used to me. I would carry it in my pocket. I even let it go inside my shirt. I liked it. It was *firme*.

The best thing about Texas was that I had a dog. She was a puppy—part golden retriever—and I named her Brandy 'cause of her color. She was a good little watchdog. I used to sleep with her. She comforted me. She wasn't judgmental of me. See, all that time, everyone in my family was always deciding where I was going to stay. They would, like, fight about it in front of me, talking about who was going to be made to have me at their house. You could say there were no reservations made for me in Texas. You could say I wasn't wanted. But I loved that dog and she loved me.

Then one day I couldn't find the dog and nobody would tell me where she was. Then finally I went around the side of the house and there was Brandy, lying there dead. She had eaten some chicken bones and choked. When I found her, it was raining, and I kept thinking about how bad it must have been for her, to die alone in the rain. I couldn't get that thought out of my mind. I came back to the projects pretty soon after that. After I lost the dog, I figured there was no reason to stay.

I need for people to have faith in me. I know I got talents, that I've got to live up to my potential. I'm trying. Sometimes I feel like giving up on myself. Father Greg never gives up on us, an' that's what we need more than anything. If people will just have faith in me, then I'll never give up. It's the faith that makes the whole difference.

Chapter 9

Like music suddenly removed,
Greg's absence leaves a startling silence. On this first afternoon, and certainly in the days that follow, homies and community members react with varying degrees of drastic emotion.

All day Jaime and Fernie wander around the church, lost little birds, occasionally gazing toward Greg's office, which is closed and locked against its emptiness, like a patch placed over a missing eye.

Within a week of Greg's departure, TMC and Cuatro have broken the truce and begun tripping. "See," says TMC's Joker, explaining the phenomenon, "it's like the homies feel really sad. But they don't like feeling sad. So then they start doing crazy things, so they won't feel sad anymore." He pauses. "And it's going to get worse."

Father Greg's absence knots me into a different shape as well. Because I have followed Greg around Siamese-twin-like for nearly two years, and have interviewed so many of the homies in depth on my own, I find myself in the odd position of knowing more kids than almost any other adult in the projects, save Ridgway, Pam McDuffie, and Leonardo—and knowing certain kids better than anybody else. Moreover, in trying to understand Greg's workings from the inside out, I have, without noticing it, come to inhabit a version of his strategy and emotional point of view, in such a way that it has begun to flow out of me as if it is my own.

I tell myself that the reason I drive to the projects every weekend is primarily for purposes of research, since I no longer have Greg to fill me in on events for which I am not present. But my motives are far more diluted than pure research, far more intricately wound. Although I don't then admit this to myself consciously, I am drifting increasingly into a position of temporary parent attempting to fill in for the father who is away from home.

Greg's Tertianship, as his sabbatical is called, doesn't formally begin until September 1. He is spending all of August on a Jesuit pilgrimage, a thirty-day, five-country, if-it's-Tuesday-it-must-be-Lourdes sort of tour that he is taking with another Jesuit. Part of the reason for the trip is to help Greg make the emotional break from the projects. However, after two weeks away, Greg can't stand it and calls for news of the 'hood from a pay phone in the Spanish countryside.

"Do I sound like an addict getting a fix?" he asks.

Back in the parish, the other Jesuits are attempting to keep the various programs going, including the jobs programs. However, without Greg's charismatic solicitations, donations drop off precipitously. The number of gang members working has been cut well below half and keeps dwindling, and there is little ministering to the kids. Father Tom, on whom most of the burden has fallen, is teetering under the new pressure.

Of the Jesuits, Father Tom also seems to be having the most vivid personal reactions to Greg's absence. Some of his stress has morphed into a growing anger at Greg. When he attempts to explain his emotions, all he can point to is his dislike of Greg's profligate spending habits for homies' salaries.

By the three-week mark, there have been several shooting incidents, but nothing with long-lasting implications. Drifter is shot in the leg as he is walking in broad daylight in front of the local Four Square church.

The shooters are rumored to be Crips. Drifter, trying to honor what he believes would be Greg's wishes, does not pursue the matter. Player from TMC is shot more seriously, the bullet passing between ribs near his heart. Yet he is out of the hospital in under twenty-four hours.

When Player is shot I am the first to get to the hospital, and the only one available to go back to Clarence and TMC and do damage control—i.e., to do what Greg always did, to say to the homies, "I've seen him. He's going to be all right. Stay calm. Don't do anything crazy."

From the hospital, I call Father Pete Neeley, the new pastor, who is obviously in bed when he picks up the phone. I suggest he come to the hospital. Neeley comes, but it is a short and grudging appearance.

———

When Greg would get discouraged at the hopelessness so deeply rooted in the homies' psyches that at times it seemed like a greater force than anything he could array against it, he would refer to *the darkness*. "It seems so dark down here right now," he would say.

I rarely was troubled by the darkness while Greg was still in L.A., perhaps because he seemed such a constant source of light. Now I feel the darkness is creeping into my skin, invading my dreams. I dream about murders one night in mid-August. Two nights later I am awakened by a dream about Player being shot all over again. Restless, I get up in the middle of the full moon night and worry drowsily that I should call Turtle because he always gets crazy when the moon is full.

I also begin to have irrational worries about my own safety. Ridgway has warned me that I shouldn't be alone in the projects after dark. I don't think she is right, but I don't know for sure. Perhaps sensing my fears, my little boy admits that he is scared for me. He is starting to wet his bed at night, and I suspect there is a connection.

"Maybe I just won't let you go down there anymore," he says in his kid's voice, as if he alone has the power to command me away from harm.

———

It starts over something stupid, just after midnight on the fourth Friday night after Greg's departure. Somebody from Cuatro shoots at somebody from TMC. Or maybe it is the other way around, that somebody fires over somebody else's head as a warning. Or maybe somebody blasts harmlessly at the streetlights, and some other homeboy, his perceptions altered by having just taken bad street acid, begins shooting back. Suddenly everyone runs for guns and the streets from Pico Gardens to Aliso Village explode in a rage of gunfire. Figures run in all directions, crisscrossing through the dark. The initial shooting occurs between Cuatro and TMC. But within thirty seconds of the first shots, Crips, Pimera Flats, and Dukes are shooting from Aliso. Everywhere, in every direction, bullets follow flashes of light.

I am just leaving the projects when I hear it begin. Rather than continue on to the freeway and home, I turn back, more out of mother's instinct than reason, not realizing the magnitude of what is happening. My only thought is that kids I know are shooting at each other and I can't possibly leave. Suddenly shots are coming from everywhere. Even at the church, bullets shot from high-powered assault rifles two city blocks away whiz past the metal gate posts—ZING! ZING! ZING! A few rounds hit the posts with high-pitched clangs and ricochet elsewhere. I have screeched my car into the parking lot for safety and, after a near-miss near the fence, I retreat up against the rectory wall where I am protected on three sides. I want to call the police, but the rectory is locked. The shooting goes on for fifteen minutes with several hundred rounds of ammunition expended. When at last the popping and booming slows to a silence, it seems impossible that no one has been killed.

For the duration of the shootout, several LAPD squad cars sit parked up on the hill at Pecan and First Streets, the officers afraid to intervene. Now the police roll from street to street, looking for casualties. Against all odds, although three people are wounded, the wounds are not serious; there are no deaths. Ted Gabrielli, an extravagantly bearded, sweet-natured Jesuit not yet ordained who worked closely with Greg, was nearby when the shooting started, and now walks around surveying the damage.

Nothing of this enormity has ever taken place in the projects. One of the most frightening aspects of this shootout is the size of the guns. Every neighborhood was using large assault weapons: M-16's, Mac 10's, AK-47's. TMC is even rumored to have an old-fashioned

Tommy gun. Too keyed up and shaky to go home, I walk around Pico Gardens with Pam until past three in the morning, picking up spent bullet casings.

Despite having been there, despite the body of knowledge about gang behavior I already possess, this shootout is incomprehensible to me. It appeared as a sudden, outsized vomiting of violence that dwarfed all previous collective symptoms of illness; a horrendous, deadly tantrum thrown by a hundred large children all at once.

I question various homies for explanations. "Everybody's been, like, stockpiling guns since before G left," says Wizard (who is back from Texas) the next day. CSL was the one neighborhood that managed to stay out of the shootout. "It's not that we plan to use 'em," he continues in a neutral, informative voice. "It's like it used to be with the Russians and Americans. If you hear the other side's got 'em, then you got to get 'em—just in case. Crazy, but that's how it is."

"Nobody was really trying to hit anybody else," says Happy in a faint attempt at rationalization. "See, it's like a game. Like playing army." More like playing Russian roulette on an enormous scale.

Other homies have other explanations, but they illuminate little. No one seems to know exactly why this monster shootout happened. And no one knows what would keep it from happening again—other than having Greg come back. However, after the shootout, things grow quiet for a while, as if the homies' grief-driven tantrum has frightened even themselves.

———

From Europe, Father Greg sends dozens of blue aerogram letters of encouragement to the kids he knows from experience are likely to now be the most at risk. Then at the beginning of September he flies to Detroit to begin his Tertianship, firing off a flurry of letters and birthday cards to the projects whenever he gets the chance. The Tertianship is a three-part process. First, three months in study and prayer, with the middle thirty of those days to be spent in silent retreat, starting October 1. Then five months of short-term ministry. Then back for a last month of wrap-up in Detroit.

Finally, if all goes as schedule, Greg expects to be home to Dolores Mission to work with gangs full time, by June of the next year.

The homies treat letters from Greg like wins at the lottery. "I got a letter from G," one homeboy will announce, waving it around. "Yeah," another will say, affecting great casualness. "I already got one yesterday." Letters to kids for whom he doesn't have addresses, Greg will send to me or to Pam. The same is true with phone messages. I drive to the projects unfailingly every Friday night, letters in hand, a routine that I notice markedly increases my juice. I am now the eagerly awaited mail boat coming to an isolated island with messages from home.

Turtle is especially buoyed by the letters. He is back in the projects but, when not working at the new job he has found as a short-order cook, he mostly stays inside the house of his new girlfriend Liliana, a young woman of fifteen who is working hard to have a steadying influence on him.

"I'm trying to do good for Liliana . . . and for G," Turtle says.

Abandonment is always an achingly real issue in the projects. As the weeks pass, the homies cope with Greg's absence in various ways. Jaime and Fernie collect photos of Greg and are making scrapbooks. Joker doesn't come out of his house for the first two months after Greg's departure except to work.

Even locked up, Rebel has a dream about Greg from which he wakes up crying.

Silent's yearning for Greg is particularly painful to observe. Night after night since Greg's exit, he stands on Gless Street unarmed, a sentinel, as if his candle-in-the-wind presence will persuade his homies to stay out of harm's way. Silent himself refuses to go inside his grandmother's apartment to be with Joanna and the baby. It is as if he has tried to swallow Greg whole—earthly detachment included—and is embodying the only kind of nobility his imagination can conjure.

By mid-fall, the conflict between TMC and Cuatro supercedes all other rivalries. There is no logical reason for this escalation except that a body once in motion tends to stay in motion—unless someone acts to intervene. And there is no longer anyone to do the intervening.

On yet another Friday night, the tension quotient shoots way up again. Everyone senses something is going to happen. I am, as usual, down in Pico Aliso. Pam and I decide to walk the projects together, hoping that an adult presence will have a calming effect. We have walked through Pico and are halfway down Gless when we turn back because two of the older PM'ers—Sal and Tomas, Jaime's big brother—are shrieking "*Puro* Cuatro Flats," an extremely dangerous activity in the present climate. As we are lecturing to the PM'ers we hear a single shot coming from the apartments along Gless, near the church. Since there is no return fire, we think perhaps someone is shooting in the air. A few minutes later, we hear sirens.

A Cuatro veterano named Eddie has been shot badly. He was drunk and talking crazy, and somebody shot him once in the stomach at close range. As Pam and I run down the street, a bola of Cuatros runs too, their expressions overcast and dangerous.

Several police cars are parked in a hasty pattern of diagonals. A crying Cuatro homie named Alfonso is pleading to be able to cross the yellow police tape to talk to Eddie, who is still alive and being loaded into the ambulance. But the police won't let him by. The kid, who is obviously unarmed, becomes increasingly upset. I take his hand and begin to coax him away from the scene. He tries to come with me, but now the police won't let him go. Two officers yank him from my grasp and struggle to wrestle him to the ground. When he resists, two more police pile on top of him, pinning his arms under him, one cop with a foot on the kid's head.

Meanwhile, out at the street, three cops have Pam's husband, Bebee, hemmed up against a car and are searching him. Pam sees this and races pell-mell to shout at the cops. Bebee is a forty-year-old former gang member who once spent time in the pen. Now he is president of the Pico Gardens Residents' Advisory Council and has recently gone back to school to get a degree. But he is black and street-looking, and is routinely hemmed up by cops from outside the area.

A nearby Housing Police officer named Kent Keyfauver stares at both scenes, looking pained. "Those guys are from Metro and they're scared because they don't know the projects. I wish I could do something," he whispers apologetically, "but I can't interfere."

While the Cuatro kid is being handcuffed and pushed into a police car, from a hundred yards away comes the sound of scuffling and screaming. A group of Cuatros have hold of a TMC named Penguin, and are attempting to drag him out of the apartment of Mama Terry, a sort of neighborhood Mary Magdalene, and off into the darkness with what looks like murderous intent. Although the police were quick to grab the unarmed Alfonso, now none of them moves to intervene. On reflex, I spring over to place myself between Penguin and the Cuatros, adding my own voice to the screaming.

"Is this what G would want?" I shout over and over, mainly because I can't think of anything else to yell. The Cuatros yell back, furious as cats who are about to be deprived of their mouse.

Then all at once my screaming match is solely with one homeboy, Santos Morales—known as Puma—who floats tall and fierce just above and behind the action. Time slows and it is as if there is a tunnel of light between us; everyone else has faded to gray.

For weeks Pam and I have been talking about who really calls the shots for Cuatro now. Largo has a job and has pulled way back. Both Oscar and Champ have long been among those with the most juice, whereas Puma had gotten himself locked up in the spring of 1991 and was only released the day before Greg left the projects. Yet in this moment I understand without doubt that *Puma is the one.*

I can't say how long the screaming goes on, but abruptly it is over. With one last piercing look, Puma turns and simply walks away. All of the Cuatros follow him without a word.

The immediate drama past, I become shivery and weak in the knees. I wonder if I have done the right thing, or if I have just made myself a hazardous enemy. But what else could I have done? I ask myself.

In the ensuing days, I learn what Father Greg has known all along: an honest confrontation rarely creates an enemy of a homie. In this case it creates a bond of mutual respect between Puma and me—one that proves to be of value in the months to follow.

Later the same night, when Pam and I and some other mothers are at County General Hospital waiting for news of Eddie's condition, an epiphany occurs: clearly somebody is urgently needed to step into the breach left by Greg. If it isn't going to be the Jesuits, it will have to be the mothers. It is decided that the community mothers need to be organized to walk the neighborhood in small groups.

The following day Pam talks to Comite Pro Paz mother Lupe Loera, who embraces the mother walks concept immediately. The idea isn't to patrol. Rather, it is for the mothers to communicate by their presence a message to all the homies of all the neighborhoods: "You are all our sons. We love you. And we're not going to let you kill each other."

"We could call it 'The Love Walks,' " says Pam. Notices go out that a meeting has been called for Tuesday of next week.

Before Father Greg left the projects he began institutionalizing his Jobs for a Future program in the form of three homie-staffed businesses. The first is a gardening crew staffed mostly by ELA. The second and third are a Tortilleria and a bakery, both to be operated under the banner of Homeboy Industries, staffed by a combination of Clarence, TMC, and Cuatro. Capitalizing on the post-riot-rebuild-L.A. spirit, Greg had successfully solicited substantial donations from wealthy Westside angels to provide funds for the Homeboy projects until they could be self-supporting.

Monday night the Homeboy Tortilla project is to be officially launched at the Seventy-fifth Anniversary party for the Grand Central Market—L.A.'s oldest market and the site where the Homeboy Tortilleria will be located. Wizard, Ghost, and Uno from Clarence plus Chango from Cuatro are on hand to present Homeboy T-shirts to Mayor Bradley and other political luminaries. Wizard is last to present and launches into a spontaneous stand-up routine.

"You know we aren't used to being in front of the light . . . unless there's a cop behind it!" he says this with flawless timing and the audience loves it.

However, later Monday night, there is another shooting. Someone from Cuatro shoots Player from TMC (again) and another kid from Clarence—Wizard's cousin and closest friend next to Ghost. Both injuries are serious but not fatal. Yet the shooting brings Clarence into the mix.

Since the Homeboy Tortilleria staff is a combination of Clarence and Cuatro guys, the shooting also throws the fate of the tortilleria into question. However, in an encouraging show of maturity, the tortilla staff members call an emergency meeting and agree that they have no quarrel with each other. They even vote to add another Cuatro homie in the next round of hiring.

"That's how G would want us to handle it," they say.

On Tuesday night, a community meeting is held in the church, with forty women and a couple of men in attendance. A walking schedule is quickly devised. After the meeting adjourns, the mothers march from one end of the projects to the other, announcing to the homies the beginning of the Love Walks.

The mothers are exhilarated by this new step in empowerment. "When Father Greg comes back he won't have to do it alone anymore," says Lupe Loera.

———

In early October, Greg has two evenly spaced breaks that he and his eleven Jesuit colleagues are accorded during their thirty days of silence. During the break, which is a half-day in length, the retreatant may read whatever mail has been piling up in his box and presumably write letters in return. The retreat is already having a positive effect on Greg, observably refreshing and inspiring him.

"In many ways my life has begun on this retreat," he writes to his fellow Jesuits. "All through it, Dolores Mission stands out as a parable of God's compassion bringing me to this radical personal tender love that I've never known in prayer before."

As usual, Greg's mailbox is crammed well past capacity with letters from the projects. Also in his box, Greg finds one unexpected piece of mail, a letter from Father Paul Belcher, the Provincial of the California Province of the Society of Jesus and Greg's immediate superior. (The Society of Jesus in America is divided into ten provinces, each administered by a Provincial together with a board of advisors called Consultors. After the Provincial, the next higher authority is the Superior General in Rome.)

The letter is pleasant in tone, and informs Greg that *he will not be returning to Dolores Mission—or to Los Angeles at all.* The reason given for this 180-degree reversal of direction is that Greg's presence in East Los Angeles might be undermining to the new pastoral team at Dolores Mission.

Greg reacts to the letter as if struck by lightning.

"If I'd ever been consulted . . ." he says, his voice faint with shock. "I just want a chance to be able to go where my heart is."

Greg seems completely at a loss. It is as if someone has suddenly arbitrarily told him he must divorce his wife and abandon his children. Mechanically he mouths the appropriate words. "I'm a good Jesuit," he says miserably. "And I would never deny the Provincial his ability to decide this. In any case I will be obedient. But . . . I just don't understand it . . . This is the most excruciating pain I've ever felt in my life."

Normally when a Jesuit is missioned to a new location or ministry, he goes through his own period of what is called *discernment* in which he attempts to determine what God wishes of him. He then shares his conclusions with his Provincial, whose job it is to *discern* for the "greater good," Jesuit jargon meaning the collective good of the Society of Jesus as a whole. The Provincial then makes the final decision.

Greg's case is unusual in that he was not consulted prior to the decision. Although he will be allowed to meet with Belcher to discuss the issue of his reassignment, the meeting will not take place until January. It may be assumed that Belcher hoped that Greg would "discern" in the course of his silent retreat that he, Belcher, was right in pulling the priest away from East L.A.

Such is not the case. When, on the day before Halloween, Greg emerges from silence, he is more irrevocably convinced than ever that he is called to return to the barrio.

"I've learned so much about what I did wrong." Greg says. "How I'd do it differently. And I understand that Tom and Pete have to deal with my ghost if I'm around. But let's *deal* with it! I'd even be willing to say, 'Please! Just give me a year!' This is where my heart is *so* called." For the first time within memory, Greg sounds almost helpless, pleading. "It's so humiliating," he says.

Greg makes much of the fact that never before, in his twenty years as a Jesuit, has his own process of discernment ever been so seemingly ignored.

Of course, Greg has never been famous before.

There are certain indiscretions that both the church and the Society of Jesus will tolerate of their priests, but perhaps fame is not one of them. Particularly if the fame is acquired by playing a bit outside the collective rules. To be a Jesuit is to give one's all for the collective. One may be a rebel, but only within the confines of certain acceptable parameters.

As if to prove the point, in a weird stroke of fate during the same week in which Greg gets his letter from his Jesuit Provincial, he also gets an "emergency" Federal Express. The Fed Ex is stamped as so urgent that Jesuits running the retreat bend the rules and give it to Greg before break day. The urgent communication turns out to be a letter from *McCall's* magazine informing Greg that he is to be featured in the November issue as one of the "Fifteen Greatest Men on Earth."

The letter sends Greg into a bout of rueful giddiness. "Well, if I'm one of the fifteen greatest men on earth," he says dourly, "then the earth is in some fucking bad shape!"

Greg decides not to share his bad news with anyone from the community, but deals with his emotions primarily by talking to the Jesuits in Detroit. Greg's fellow Jesuits, while sympathetic, counsel him to accept and be at peace with the Provincial's decision, good or bad.

"God writes straight with crooked lines," they say.

Greg hates the upbeat, fatalistic maxim.

———

Although Father Greg says nothing to anyone in the parish, a sense of unease and doubt about Greg's return begins to leach into community consciousness. This is in part due to the fact that seemingly overnight, the other Jesuits at Dolores Mission no longer talk about *when* Greg will return but *if* Greg will return—and even this is said in a tone that suggests they are preparing the parish for an unstated eventuality.

"Father Tom and Father Pete," says Pam, "sometimes I wonder if they really want Father Greg to come home."

One bright spot is a new Jesuit named Father Jerry Cowhig, who sits in what was once Greg's office. Father Jerry is a clean-cut, upbeat, earnest man who, more than the other priests, is making a concerted effort to extend himself to the gang members who, in turn, welcome the attention. But he is inexperienced, and, although caring, politically unsavvy. He tends mostly to spend time with the younger kids from TMC, thus infuriating the rest of the neighborhoods, particularly Cuatro.

Increasingly Dolores Mission is regarded as a TMC church, and no one seems to be doing much to disabuse the notion. Even the easiest link to Pico Gardens, the *Pandilla Mugrosa*—kids who without Greg are turning into Cuatro wannabes—have been all but banned from church grounds by Father Pete. The older PM'ers respond to the ouster by trashing Pete's office.

Even many of the TMC homies feel emotionally deserted by the Dolores Mission priests.

"They just don't care," says Drifter.

As fall turns to winter, shooting piles upon shooting, retaliation upon retaliation. Clarence is now not only pulled into the conflict, but there is a new homeboy calling the shots: Wizard. Whereas the brothers Clavo and Flavio led Clarence like Marine sergeants, Wizard is strategic. It is as if he is engaged in a game of realpolitik, barrio style, determined to bring once-fading CSL back as a potent force—and himself to a genuine, if dangerous, position of manhood.

Happy is spinning and confused in Greg's absence. He has decided he should be the peacemaker between all the Pico Aliso gangs and has taken to walking unarmed into bolas of enemy homies. These encounters usually end up provoking more than they reconcile.

When Rebel was arrested, Happy was hired at Tri-Star in his place. The job at first had a stabilizing effect, but now his punctuality has become sporadic. He has no car and so has to take the bus, where he says he keeps running into enemies. When finally the pressure becomes too great, he thanks the Tri-Star people profusely "for the chance you have given me"—and quits the job.

Ever the negotiator, Happy recommends someone as his successor: Shadow from TMC, who has just been released from the dope-selling charges. Despite the homie attrition rate, Tri-Star producer Wendy Finerman listens to Greg's long-distance pleading and generously agrees to hire one more gang member. Shadow is overjoyed when he learns he has been chosen for the position.

A week after Happy quits, Ridgway contrives to get Happy arrested.

"I'm not going to let what happened to Green Eyes happen to Happy," she says, after his hearing. "Without Father Greg around that's exactly where he's headed. He has no family, no one to help him, nowhere to go. He deserves better."

Father Greg has talked his superiors in Detroit into letting him spend the first two and a half months of his short-term ministry as assistant chaplain of Folsom Prison. At Folsom, Greg immediately takes to the inmates, finding nobility even in the most wretched of criminals. While he works at Folsom during the day, his nights are spent at a Jesuit community residence in Sacramento where he feels lonely and emotionally isolated, wondering if some of the senior Jesuits around him know more about his fate than he does. When the other Jesuits gather for their nightly before-dinner drink, Greg tends to go back to his room and answer letters from the 'hood.

The holiday months pass in a haze of longing. Homeboys, home-girls and mothers write Greg news of the parish, asking him if there is any way he can return early. The letters only increase Greg's distress.

At Dolores Mission the Jesuits begin to criticize Greg openly. They characterize his letters to the homies as a form of co-dependence, evidence of Greg's "unfreedom." There are myths floating around about Greg's spending, with numbers that inflate with each retelling.

At the same time, without Greg to raise money, the funds for the jobs programs are dwindling to the point of crisis. As the Jesuits struggle to bridge an ever-widening financial gap, they point illogically to Greg as the progenitor of the problem.

Ironically, concurrent with the Jesuits' growing criticism, in the larger L.A. community, Greg is being held up as heroic. He is invited to be part of a televised town hall meeting on urban violence organized by President Clinton's staff. (He declines.) When, at the turn of the year, the *Los Angeles Times* does a review of the significant events of 1992, Greg's exodus from Dolores Mission is listed prominently among them.

———

That the frail lifelines of Greg's letters and calls should be looked on as damaging has a tragic irony all its own. Of all the homies who are struggling for balance, the one who seems to be most in danger of falling into an abyss is Silent. First he has a quarrel with his boss at L.I.F.E. and loses his job. He and Joanna are fighting more and more. When I take him out to dinner, it is evident from our conversation that my maternal affection can only go so far. He needs a man—a father. I ask Father Tom to spend some time with him, say take him out for dinner. Silent is slipping, I say. There is a particular kind of desperateness in his voice, his face, that I have come to recognize as the last signs before something terrible happens.

"I'll try," responds Tom, bleakly. "But I'm really not cut out to be a father to these kids."

Rebel goes to trial in November. I have put in a call to Jerry Brown, with whom Rebel had gone on the campaign trip. Brown says he is so impressed with Rebel's potential that he would be willing to show up in court. During jury selection, the assistant D.A. asks every prospective juror if he or she will be swayed by the presence of the former governor of California.

At the trial itself, Rebel's attorney—Greg's old friend Jorge Gonzales—who has taken the case *pro bono*, endeavors to point out discrepancies in the police officers' testimony. At first the jurors are deadlocked. But the judge orders them to come to a decision, wishing to save the state the expense of another trial. They then vote to convict. Rebel is sentenced to seven years in California State Prison.

Rebel is philosophical. "Don't worry," he says, "it'll be all right. I don't like it, but I accept it. I'll get settled into the state system an' the time'll pass fast." He pauses to gather himself. "Being away from my daughter'll be the hardest."

Soon after Rebel is convicted, Wolf and Romeo beat their murder case and are back out on the street.

The first real casualty of Greg's absence occurs before Thanksgiving when Joanna calls Greg long distance in a panic to say that Silent has been arrested. There has been a shooting incident with the East L.A. Tiny Dukes. No one was hit, but Silent is one of those charged with shooting into an inhabited dwelling. Within twenty-four hours, the information changes. Another charge had been added, a 187—murder in the course of a robbery, which in the State of California carries a mandatory sentence of life without possibility of parole.

Greg is alarmed but believes the murder charge was erroneous and won't stick. "He's not a kid capable of awful things," he says. "He's the noble homie, the one who is most wedded to the code of honor that everyone else has abandoned."

By Christmas it is clear that, although everyone on the street knows Silent did not commit the murder (and who *did* commit it), the charge *has* stuck after all.

———

Father Greg is set to meet with his Provincial early in January. In the intervening months, the priest has grown hopeful that he can make a strong case for his return to L.A. The meeting takes place on January 8 in Los Gatos, a small town south of San Francisco. It does not go well. Greg presents his case. Belcher listens sympathetically, then says his return to Los Angeles is impossible.

Pam is the first person in the parish whom Greg calls. She dissolves into tears immediately. By the time she talks to me a few hours later, her grief has converted itself to fury. "Nobody asked us!" she says. "Why didn't they ask us what we needed? This is what God wants G to be doing. We all know that! Why don't this man, his boss, know that? Isn't he supposed to want what God wants?!"

Word spreads fast. After the initial shock, the community begins to mobilize.

In short order, petitions are circulated, demonstrations are organized. The homeboys of the four main neighborhoods decide to make a collective video message to send to Belcher. The *L.A. Times* and the local electronic media report on the ongoing conflict. Even Tom Brokaw does a piece on "NBC Nightly News." When Father Greg is asked for comment he will say only that he feels "unmistakably called" to work with gang members in East L.A., and that he "is first and foremost a Jesuit."

The Jesuits are not happy with the media attention. "It does make it much more difficult when he expresses his opinion as to his desire to come back," says Bob Fambrini, a Jesuit highly placed in the province, "when the desire of the Provincial and the desire of the province is that he be reassigned some other place. It *does* exacerbate the problem."

After a series of phone calls, Belcher agrees to meet with the community in February.

The official reasons given for Greg's removal seem to change from week to week. At first it is that the present pastoral team needs the room to establish their own programs, and that a pastor is rarely returned to his parish. But staff and community members are quick to point to various instances in which Jesuits have been left for twenty-year periods in the same posts. The next set of reasons is that the community has gotten too dependent on Father Greg.

When community members and media continue to press for reasons, some Jesuits hint darkly that Cardinal Mahony has had a hand in keeping Greg out of L.A. Mahony has never liked Greg since his earliest years at Dolores Mission when he was active in the sanctuary movement. And now that the Cardinal has launched his own multi-million-dollar, taxpayer-funded gang program, he likes Greg even less.

But Mahony had asked for Greg's removal six years before and the Jesuits declined to comply. So if Mahony is a factor, it is unlikely he is the determining reason.

"The other priests, they're just jealous," say the homies with characteristic candor, "'cause everybody loves G and everybody don't love them."

"The Jesuits typically marginalize all their visionary priests," is Leonardo's explanation. "They did it with the Berrigans. They did with . . ." and he names some other Jesuits who had stepped outside the corporate *linea*. "And they are doing it to Greg."

Serendipitously, a concerned friend sends Greg a popular book currently making the rounds in Jesuit reading circles, saying Greg might find it "interesting." The book by Ron Hansen, entitled *Mariette in Ecstasy*, is about a young girl who enters a New England convent around the turn of the century. The nuns of this convent are less devoted to charitable work than to seeking oneness with Christ through religious visions. Unlike the rest of her sisters, Mariette appears to be the real thing. She is having visions non-stop, stigmata, raptures—the whole nine yards. The book's plot hinges on the other nuns' reactions to finding in their midst a living example of the state that they have so long sought. By the end of the book Mariette has been driven out of the convent.

Greg reads the book but doesn't keep it. Instead, he purposely leaves it on an airplane seat when he next flies to Detroit. He does, however, copy down the book's last few lines, which he reads daily for a while:

. . . Christ reminds me, as he did in my greatest distress, that he loves me more, now that I am despised, than when I was so richly admired in the past.

And Christ still sends me roses. We try to be formed and held and kept by him, but instead he offers us freedom. And now when I try to know his will, his kindness floods me, his great love overwhelms me, and I hear him whisper, Surprise me.

At the end of January, just before his Folsom tenure is up, Greg sends a bus ticket to four of the TMC homies—Turtle, Dreamer, Youngster, and Blue—all best friends who have been dying to come and visit. (In past months, Dreamer has switched from Clarence to TMC.) Greg and the foursome drive to San Francisco and wander around Fisherman's Wharf, window-shopping and buying candy and postcards. Blue loiters at one window that looks into the office of a high-tech design firm, then whispers a private confession to Greg: He has a "crazy dream" of becoming an architect.

Back at the Jesuit residence, Greg stashes the homies in the downstairs guest room. He knocks on their door early in the morning. Getting no reply, he quietly opens the door and finds them still asleep, piled on each other in a tangle of legs and arms, like a brace of gangly puppies intertwined for warmth and security. He watches them silently, his eyes filling up with tears.

About two hundred mothers and homies fill the Dolores Mission cafeteria on an afternoon in February. It is the day Paul Belcher has set to meet with the Dolores Mission community. The place is once again loaded with both electronic and print media. Earlier in the week, Father Tom told the mothers that if word reached his ears that anyone had invited the press, he would personally call the meeting off. No problem, decided the mothers. They just wouldn't *tell* Tom. They would instruct the TV crews to park their vans out of sight around back and that would be that. When this plot was leaked to the Jesuits, Tom responded with additional threats, and the mothers became increasingly intractable. Even as the meeting is assembling, there is another round of, "The press can't come in!"—"Oh, yes they can!"—with Tom the loser.

There has been much discussion about the way to organize the meeting. Finally it is decided that selected community members will alternate as speakers with relevant supporters from outside the community—Jaime Corral, the head Juvenile Court Justice for Southern California; lead Housing officer Walter McKinney; L.A. City Council member Richard Alatorre; Mary Ridgway, of course. Even Mayor

Tom Bradley has sent his representative with a letter. Then the microphone will be opened up to comments from the floor. At that time the homies and anybody else who wants to can have their say.

The mothers are the real show. Some speaking in English, others in Spanish, they are brilliant, empowered, eloquent, stunning. They explain that although they have become much stronger under Greg's leadership, they still need him. "The patient isn't well yet," they say.

The outsiders also speak with great passion. McKinney from Housing Police tells how Greg inspired him to begin community-based policing. When Ridgway gets up to talk, she tears up halfway through and can barely continue. When the mike is opened up to the floor, Turtle and Joker are among those who speak with strength and clarity.

Finally, after ninety minutes of testimony, everyone sits down and waits for the Provincial's response, satisfied that the case has been made. After a pause, Belcher stands and walks stiffly to the microphone. He briefly compliments the community on their commitment, then mumbles something garbled about Greg and sits down.

People begin muttering wildly. "What'd he say? Did he say he'd decided? Did he say G was coming back? Did he say G *wasn't* coming back?"

Finally Lupe Loera cups her hands around her mouth and yells, "Father, we didn't understand what your decision was. Is Father Greg coming back or isn't he?"

Belcher gets up and steps once more up to the mike.

"The decision is that . . . my decision still stands. Father Greg won't be coming back any time in the near future."

"Why?" yell several of the mothers, unable to contain themselves.

"I'm not going to give you a reason," snaps Belcher.

It is at this point that the friendly tone in the room does an emotional 180. As the majority of the audience reels from Belcher's statement, Joker discovers that a second mike situated behind where Belcher is standing is still live. Suddenly Joker's voice booms through the speakers.

"Father, I don't think you understand what this means to us," Joker says, still polite but with force. "I'd be *dead* without Father Greg. A lot of youngsters out there are going to be dead without him. . . ."

Now the mothers are starting to shout comments from the floor. At the same time there are loud, ominous rumblings from the back of the room where most of the homies have, until now, perched quietly on benches and tables.

Joker, still in possession of the second mike, breaks into the vocal melee again to ask why it was that Belcher originally told Greg he would be coming back in June, ". . . and now you won't let him come back?!"

"I never told Father Greg that he was coming back," replies Belcher.

Yolanda Chavez, a former assistant to Mayor Bradley, who has been translating all the Spanish for the meeting and thus has a mike of her own, now leaps into the fray. "I beg your pardon, Father!" she says, her large eyes narrowing. "But I was at a meeting last year at which you told us that Father Greg would definitely be coming back here in some capacity!"

Belcher blinks angrily. "I don't recall saying anything like that."

Teresa, the normally soft-spoken woman who oversees the homeless shelter, bounces from her chair as if spring-loaded.

"I was at that meeting too!" she shouts.

From here things get progressively wilder. Uno, a CSL homie, gets the mike, then it is commandeered by a sobbing but articulate homegirl named Ophelia.

All at once, Joker grabs what had been Belcher's microphone at the center of the room, his mood gone from polite to enraged. With big *locs* covering his eyes, he turns to fix Belcher with a stun-gun stare, then spits out in low and menacing Spanish, words to the effect that the homies were going to burn the fucking place down, and the responsibility for the destruction would be on him, Belcher.

At this, Father Tom, who up until now has been sitting at the back of the room doing paperwork, awakes as if from a trance and hurtles himself forward to deliver a flying-tackle-cum-hug to Joker. Joker begins sobbing uncontrollably. Shadow, who up until this point has steadfastly refused to talk with TV cameras around, moves to Yolanda's mike and also begins sobbing while talk-shouting at Belcher.

"You don't understand!" Shadow gasps between sobs. "You *had* a father! You don't know what it's like to have a basehead for a mother and to live in the biggest rock house in Aliso village. Look at me! I don't want to be a gangster anymore! I don't want to be a gangster anymore! I'm dying inside! You don't understand what you're doing! We're dying! *We're dying!*"

At some point Tom tries to hug/tackle Shadow into submission, but Shadow shakes him angrily away. More homies and girls begin crying. Spanky pleads *basso profundo* from the back of the room. Belcher remains impassive.

All the while the TV cameras are rolling, collecting sound bites for the evening news.

"We begged him," says Lupe Loera, walking away in disgust, "and he turned his back on us."

"What the man's telling us," says Pam, crying furiously as she throws a motherly arm around Shadow, "is that church rules are more important than the lives of our children."

Into the chaos stride two police officers, who quietly ask Father Belcher to step outside. It seems that somebody has broken all the windows on Belcher's car and filled it with chunks of mud.

Although no one admits to anything, it quickly becomes evident that the culprits were Dreamer and Blue. Interestingly, Mary Ridgway happened outside just in time to see the two homies running away from the car and, for the one and only time in her career, Ridgway simply looked the other way.

"He's lucky they didn't burn it," she says.

———

On February first, Father Greg began the second leg of his Tertianship ministry on Islas Marias, a remote prison island twelve hours off the coast of Mazatlán, Mexico, reachable only by ferry. At Islas Marias—as at Folsom—Greg finds grace and meaning where most would perceive only despair, as he struggles to achieve at least a temporary peace with himself. In letters he writes movingly of working beside the *colonos*—the prisoners—grinding corn and sorghum to feed pigs and making bricks from mud, of watching new-hatched water beetles turn from translucent to mahogany on the ceiling of his mud-brick room. In another letter he tells of the time that he and five colonos fashioned contraband soup from four purloined vegetables and a couple of cans of tomato sauce.

"How clearly God was present in this moment," he writes, "in our laughter and in our glancing over our shoulder so as not to be caught with the stolen goods (prisoners are not allowed in the garden).

"I feel so deeply grateful for the depth of acceptance and *cariño* I feel from the *colonos*. These are the most forgotten, rejected, and maligned men in Mexico. Yet one would be hard pressed to find more noble or holy folk. . . . But here, as in Folsom, I feel like I can do this and do it reasonably well. But I am not called to do it. In E.L.A. I discovered what I am called and meant to do. It is such a gift and the denial of all this remains more painful than I often admit to myself."

The colonos, like the homies, give Father Greg a *nom de guerre*. They call him *Padre Malandrin—malandrin* meaning "baddest of the bad." Greg delights in the nickname. "I feel so loved by these folks, that I am daily consoled by this. But I operate at 75 percent of my gifts. I can do more. Work with gangs in E.L.A. utilized 100 percent of myself. This is hard to let go of, though it seems I must."

Because of the near impossibility of phoning the island, plus the infrequent mail delivery, Greg doesn't hear about the Belcher meeting until two weeks after the fact. When the mailboat finally comes in, he gets twenty-seven letters from the projects describing the meeting. Among them is a letter from Blue, who writes of the "depression" he feels:

> What got me so mad and not only me but all the homies is that the provincial doesn't want you to come back we talk to him and he said no. I felt so scanless "G" that me and Dreamer (don't get mad "G" we know we fucked up but at that time anger took over our minds) we broked his car windows and left it full of mud. I'm sorry "G" if you don't come back probably it's going to be our fault.

———

The thought that Father Greg will be taken from them for good is simply intolerable to the homies, and sends them into a state of vicious despair that is quickly converted into violence. As usual the violence is not directed toward the outside world, but toward each other. The impending war between TMC and Cuatro Flats, which has been heating up in fits and starts since Greg's departure, now becomes full-blown and deadly.

Gang warfare in this tightly bordered area of the barrio has always been tragic, but a war between TMC and Cuatro intensifies the tragedy logarithmically. Of all the neighborhoods, these are the two with the strongest ties to each other. In three cases, there are even sets of brothers split between the neighborhoods, among them Rebel and his brother Dino. These are also the two neighborhoods who have each most recently lost one of their number. Yet, like a wolf biting off its leg to get out of a trap, like abused children bashing their own foreheads bloody against walls, like suicidal boys willfully shattering their reflections, TMC and Cuatro begin to turn inexplicably and brutally against each other.

Shooting becomes nightly but soon bleeds into the daytime. By April there have been more than two dozen gunshot injuries. By May, no one feels that they can walk to the corner store in safety. Although the community mothers still continue the nightly Love Walks, the moms go inside at 10:00 P.M. at the latest. After that, the shooting starts.

"If only G was here!" is now the constant mantra chanted by homies on both sides. But Greg is back in Detroit and now barely feels he can call the projects since his calls inevitably upset the Jesuits.

I drive down to the barrio every weekend to walk the streets with Pam. We stay out after the others have gone in, sometimes 'til one and two in the morning. Together with Leonardo Vilchis, the community's lone male activist, we have formed an unlikely coalition of temporary Father Greg proxies to try to keep the two gangs from blowing each other to smithereens. But we are all at best a few small fingers trying to plug big holes in a badly leaking dike. And it is clear that, unless Greg returns, the deluge is coming.

————

On May 15, Casper from TMC has a dream. He is walking down a deserted beach when he sees one of his homeboys ahead of him running straight into the waves, waving his arms.

"Help! Help! They're going to leave me! They're going to leave me behind!" yells the homie whose face Casper cannot see.

Casper looks out to sea and sees an open boat, just beyond the surfline. It is filled with people whose faces look to him to be extraordinarily happy and peaceful. At the helm of the boat, Casper sees Jesus. He shouts to the boat to stop and wait. Then he swims with the unidentified homie out to the boat and helps him climb aboard.

Again the boat begins to pull away. Now Casper sees the homie's face. It is his friend Blue—his face now happy like the rest.

"What about me?" calls Casper to the retreating boat.

Jesus smiles the smile of heaven and shakes his head "no" in reply.

Turtle

I'm Victor Cervantes and I'm called Turtle cause I'm quick. A lot of times we're called the opposite of what we are. Like Midget is on the large side. I joined TMC because I had been hanging out with those same people since I was a kid. When I was jumped in I was the only one who wasn't in some gang or other. I was the last one. In the projects I would say 70 or 80 percent of the teenagers are in a gang. The people who are most into sports might not join.

I used to play sports. I was really into baseball. I was a good pitcher. I have seven trophies. The league where I was playing, you couldn't play after you were sixteen. If I could do it, I'd play sports even now. If I could play sports, I probably would not be in a gang.

I went to Dolores Mission Alternative after I got kicked out of Roosevelt High School because of gang banging. Somebody was always jumping me when I was at school, and one time I got mad and hit 'em back the next day. So I got kicked out. Dolores Mission Alternative was okay, but they don't have sports.

Getting jumped at school was scarier than being shot. Like one time, coming home from school, some guys from Rascals were chasing me with a gun. If I had not ran as fast as I did, they would have shot me. When they're chasing you you don't get scared 'cause you're just thinking about getting away. You get scared later.

If I would have one wish, I would wipe out everything from the past. I would wipe out being jumped into a gang. I would just want to be on my own with friends. I'd want friends who were just regular people, like people who go out to dancing and stuff.

But you can't wipe out the past. Even when I say I don't gang bang no more, I still have to fight. But I've been thinking, if I keep on telling them that I don't gang bang then pretty soon they'll have to believe me. The problem is, I keep hanging around with the homies. So maybe they won't believe me anyway.

When a full moon is out I stay in. 'Cause when a full moon is out, I get in trouble. I get picked up by the police, get shot at. Something. I think it's bad luck for me. I also try to stay at home when I'm feeling all crazy. I just stay home and watch TV and read books. I like to read the newspaper too. I read the Metro and the Sports and the View section.

People tell me I'm smart. The police and a lot of white people think gang members are animals. But I'd like people to know that a lot of us are smart. Midget, Wolf, Rebel, they're all smart. Midget tells a lot of jokes. Green Eyes was smart.

Dreamer is the one I spend the most time with. I hang around with him every day. He's a different person since he got out of jail. Before he wasn't into gang banging. Now he's more into it. And when I'm with him, I have to be behind him. Back him up. Sometimes that's a problem, because he wants to do some crazy stuff. I can't let him go by himself. If something happens to him, I'm going to feel responsible. Something already did happen to him. He's just real lucky. He doesn't care if he dies.

Dreamer needs a vacation. He either needs to go to jail or go on a real vacation, like to Mexico. If he doesn't, he's going to do something stupid. Dreamer is always there for me. When the other homies aren't around, he's there. He's a really good person. Maybe being locked up made him change. Or maybe it was his dad. Probably his dad. Because when my dad makes me feel like shit, that's when I go out in the street.

I know my dad loves me. He always told me, "Stay away from those gang members." But almost everybody's a gang member down here. The saddest thing that ever happened to me is that my dad won't talk to me no more. First we had an argument and he wouldn't talk to me. Then when I got my tack, he said he don't have a son no more. The funny thing is my dad has tattoos. My dad's in Mexico right now. But when he stays at my mom's, I have to stay at my sister's.

Before Dreamer, Shy Boy was my best friend. He was from Primera Flats, but we were always together at school. Then he got killed. Shy Boy shouldn't'a died. He shouldn't'a died. I wish I could trade places with him so it could be me instead. When I heard, I kept saying, "Not him! Not him!" He dressed like a gang banger, but he didn't bang. Me, I do stuff sometimes. But he never did. He shouldn't'a died. That's a thing I would change, if it could be me instead'a him.

The thing that makes somebody shoot is anger. See, you might say, "Why not beat 'em up instead?" But you can't. Like with East L.A., every time I run into one of them they've taken out a gun. So I have to run. If somebody shoots at you, you get mad and you shoot back. Some people shoot for fun, I know that. The same people go on the missions all the time. Those people have a lot of anger in them. Like me when I was mad at my parents. Or like after Green Eyes passed away. I would like to say I wouldn't ever pick up a gun again. But if I stay here in the projects I probably will. There's a gun wherever you go. We hide them in different places. Some in houses. Usually we have around three in each block. Only one or two people knows where the guns are. Then when we need them, they go get it. They won't let nobody know where they stashed it at. Whoever wants to be in charge can be in charge. I don't want to be in charge of any guns.

When I first got shot I thought I was going to die. I was hurt pretty bad. I thought of all the things I would miss in life. Dancing. Girls. Getting married, having kids. But I never thought of the homies. I wouldn't miss them. Only four would I miss: Dreamer, Blue, Youngster, and Pato. For a time, my mind was playing tricks on me or something. I just didn't care. You might say I was depressed. Maybe I was just low and feeling sorry for myself 'cause of my problems—especially after my mom spent that money.

When Green Eyes passed away I felt bad. He was different compared to other people. He had respect for everybody. He was cool. But he got killed because of gang banging. After he got killed I got in the state of mind again that I didn't care if I lived or not. I was in some kind of place where I didn't care about nothing. For a whole month straight I shot every day.

And then I stopped. It relieves the anger a little bit. It does. That's why a lot of people shoot. Or they start out wanting to prove something to the homies because they've just barely gotten in the neighborhood. Then they get used to it. You get in the habit. You keep on going back for more.

Green Eyes and me were close. Not like me and Dreamer, not that close. Blue, Dreamer, Youngster, Pato—we're really close. It would be the hardest if something happened to one of them. Whenever you see the homies you'll always see us in the same group.

Oso's family and my family were close too. We grew up together. My mother was the godmother to his brother. And his mom was my brother's godmother. We lived right next door to each other. We used to say we were cousins.

That thing that Father Greg said at the wake, about if you really loved Oso to listen to your conscience—that changed stuff for me. I think about it. Father Greg has done so much for me I couldn't even list it. Too much. I don't know if I deserved it or not.

Sometimes I think my blood runs too fast. I want to do all kinds of things at once. I don't know anybody else who wants to do four or five things at once. I want to do something for a few minutes and then go on and do something else. If I had a car, I could go to Dodger Stadium. I could go to Tijuana. I could go dancing. I'd go to the movies.

My favorite movie is *Ghost*. I liked the spirit, that man who died. Like I thought about it. I thought that could happen to me, to die like that, you never know. I can't decide where I would go if I would die right now, heaven or hell. Could be either one.

I did some bad things in my crazy period. There's a lot I would take back. If I could only take back one thing, I would take back this one time I shot a guy outside the projects. I know he got hurt. And I never knew what happened. Maybe he got hurt bad. Maybe he was lucky. I tried to forget about it. But I can't. I wish I could make up for it. I wish I knew a way. I guess since I did bad something bad's going to happen to me.

The truth is, I'm tired of banging. It's played out. Gang banging's played out for me. I'm bored with the homies. I'm bored with dressing like a gangster. I want to dress normal. I just want a normal life. I want to get away from the bad and go toward the good. I don't want to be down here in the projects no more. I want to go to Job Corps because when I come back I'll be different. I registered already but it takes a long time for them to call you. If I can just get away from here—get away from the projects, get away from the homies—I'll be different. I guarantee it. If I can just get away. That's the hard part. How do you find someplace else to go?

None of the crazy-ass wars would be happening if G was here. I just feel those other Jesuits on high don't want nobody helping gang members. Hardly nobody likes Mexican gang members. "Let them all kill each other off," that's what they say. We all know that.

I miss G so much. I feel like a different person without G. I feel lonely. I feel stuck.

Chapter 10

When you're long enough in the projects, you begin to play this game. It's called, "Which one could I stand to lose?" Greg plays it after a particularly touching telephone conversation with Wizard. "Wizard I couldn't stand to lose," he says. "I couldn't stand it." "Or Ghost," I add. "Or Ghost," he agrees. "Or Silent." "Or Rebel." Or Turtle, or Dreamer, or Blue, or . . . who? Which one can you stand to lose?

In the projects, there is always the inevitability that there will be another death. It is only a matter of when and whom. When things get crazy, you start mentally cataloguing the whereabouts of the favorite ones or the particularly vulnerable ones. Okay, this one's locked up, you think. So he'll be okay. That one's in Mexico visiting his grandmother. This one's been staying out of it, not banging. This mental cataloguing is akin to a hen frantically counting chicks when a hawk shadow passes overhead.

Blue wakes up on a Saturday morning in mid-May and decides, unaccountably, to change the plans he has with his girlfriend, Gabby. He has promised Gabby that they will go to the park today, but he wakes up with another idea in his head. He wants to go to the cemetery "to visit Green Eyes." He says he hasn't visited him in a long time. "You can do that another day," says Gabby, unhappy with his change of heart. "No, babe," says Blue, "I need to visit Green Eyes." They have a fight about it.

Then the weather intervenes. It starts to rain. It is an unseasonable rain, brought on by a tropical storm front moving in from the Pacific. Big drops rebound warm and steamy off the concrete in front of the azure-painted projects apartment building where Blue's mother lives. When Gabby and Blue walk out of the apartment, he looks up at the sky. "The sky is crying," he says. "What?" she says, startled by his words. He repeats it. "The sky is crying. See, babe," he says, looking skyward, then back at her with his sorrowful smile. "The clouds are sad and the sky is crying."

Gabby feels scared, but the feeling passes. Since the day is clearly inhospitable for any outdoor activity, the two stay inside Blue's mother's apartment laughing, talking, kissing, the strangeness of the morning disappeared.

Eventually the sun comes out and the day begins to heat up. Gabby and Blue walk over to Moon's store at the corner of Clarence and Third Streets, where they run into Freddy Silva, another one of the Termites, Blue's clique within TMC. The three of them buy ice creams and stand on the sidewalk in front of the store, licking the creamy sweetness like children.

Finally, Blue walks Gabby back to his mother's apartment. "I got something to do," he says. When she protests, he adds, "It's a surprise for you. I'll be back soon."

A half an hour later he reappears, as promised, a brand new pair of white Vans sneakers under his arm. Now that he is working steadily he wants to start getting her the things she needs, he says. Then he turns to leave again, telling her he is going to kick it for a while longer with some of the guys. "I'll go with you," offers Gabby. "No, babe, you stay home. I'll come and get you later." Gabby thinks this odd and argues. But Blue insists. Reluctantly, Gabby stays inside his mother's apartment.

Blue goes back to the church where he talks for a while with Freddy, Turtle, and some others who are hanging around in the rectory talking to the new priest, Father Jerry. When it is time for five o'clock mass, Blue and Freddy decide that they are going to go over to Moon's store again to cash Blue's paycheck and buy some soft drinks.

Gabby is asleep when Amelia, Blue's mother, hears the sound. At first Amelia isn't even sure it is shots. She waits and listens. No return fire. She wakes Gabby. "Where's Joseph?" she asks in Spanish. At the church, Gabby says. They wait together, listening for subsequent noises. It is a long time before they hear sirens. Gabby and Amelia race down the stairs from the third-floor apartment just in time to see a fire truck speeding down Clarence Street.

Gabby rushes ahead of Amelia, hurrying in the direction the fire truck has gone. Just as she reaches the street, she nearly collides with Turtle who is running straight for her, his face streaming with tears. Turtle grabs Gabby's shoulders.

"Something's happened!" he says. Then, although his mouth is still open and moving, fish-like, he makes only choking sounds instead of words, as if something is cutting off his wind from behind. Gabby breaks free of Turtle and begins to run.

The fire truck and the ambulance are parked at careless angles in the street near Moon's store and there is a crowd. The yellow police tape is already up.

At the center of the crowd Gabby sees two forms lying on the pavement, bloody but still moving. One is Freddy Silva. The other is Blue. Blue's father, a woeful, timid man whose naturally slight body has been made thinner by drugs, squats, limp and hapless, cradling his son's head and shoulders. Gabby falls forward to her knees and grabs hold of Blue's feet.

"Tell him that you love him! Tell him to hold on," someone whispers in her ear. Before she can do this, someone else pulls her upright and away from Blue as the paramedics move into her place.

The paramedics won't let Amelia and Gabby ride in the ambulance, so a friend drives them the two miles to USC County General Hospital. Inside the emergency room, Gabby tries to follow as five men in hospital coats push Blue's gurney full tilt down the hall toward surgery. From inside the swinging doors marked HOSPITAL STAFF ONLY Gabby can hear Blue's voice calling. First she hears him call, "Mom . . . ! Dad . . . !" A pause. Then, "Where's Gabby . . . ?" Gabby is scared because his voice sounds so weak and little. He calls her name again, but his voice is losing volume and timbre. "Gabby," he calls. "Help me . . ."

Then nothing. Gabby begins to cry because she cannot help him.

———

I don't hear the news until after midnight on Saturday night when I return home from the movies. When I check my answering machine, there are six messages from East L.A. Three are from Pam. Although the messages just say to call, when I hear the tone of her voice on the tape my heart sinks to my feet. I know the worst has happened.

"They shot Blue and little Freddy Silva in front of Moon's store," Pam says without preface when I call her back. "Blue died." Hysteria rises in her voice. "I'm all alone here," she says.

I know before she tells me that the shooters are from Cuatro Flats. "It was a drive-by," she says. "They used a basehead's truck and laid down in the back. I don't think those kids even saw it coming. Norma and my sister were there and Norma gave Blue CPR. Norma said he had this smile on his face like God was talking to him." She pauses. "It took the paramedics twenty-five minutes to come. Twenty-five fucking minutes."

Pam and I stay connected by phone for hours off and on, hanging up to make other calls, then calling back, each clinging to the other's voice out of fear of the silence of our own thoughts. Neither of us wants this death to become real.

There is no possible way to call Greg at this hour. Pam has already tried. The Jesuit residence in Detroit where he is once again living shuts off its phones at 6:00 P.M. on weekends. So we are on our own.

First there is the matter of the shooter. It is a ghastly fact that although we don't yet know the identity of the shooter, we *will* know. There are no secrets in the barrio. And when we hear the right name, it is a given that it will be a name that we know well, a kid that we care about.

"Who dies first?" We have both heard Greg say it to an out-of-control homie who was contemplating violence. "The one who gets the bullet or the one who pulls the trigger?" If we are to think in those terms, this night has already produced two deaths.

TMC will most assuredly retaliate. When Green Eyes was killed, the retaliation was swift and murderous. It will be worse now. Green Eyes was killed by a gang from across town. Blue was killed by those closest, likely by someone who he had known all his life. Pam wonders aloud what is happening even as we are speaking.

"At least I haven't heard any shots," she says.

Where is Turtle? Where is Dreamer? As Blue's best friends they are the most at risk. The fourth of their friendship quartet, Youngster, is with his mother in Guadalajara—safe, at least for the moment. I am frantic with the desire to somehow reach Turtle. Dreamer is not a talker, so a phone call cannot reel him in. He is too kinetic to respond to anything but physical presence when the situation has become this extreme. Besides, he will be out on the street now, feeling too desperate to go home and face his *pendejo* of a father.

But Turtle, like Wizard and Rebel, can sometimes be talked down. He might be on the street, but he is just as likely at the house of his girlfriend, Liliana. "My sister says she just passed by that house," says Pam. "All the lights are on. Call me back after you try him."

My son is staying at his father's tonight, and my desire to hug him or just to stare at his sleeping face is so sharp it starts to impede my breathing. I dial Liliana's number. It is exactly two-thirty when Turtle comes to the phone.

"They took my little Blue," he says. His voice is small. "They took my little dog." The latter is short for "role dog," the term of affection that in gang parlance means "best friend."

I make murmurs of comfort. "Can you stop yourself from wanting to do something crazy?" I ask him.

"No," he says.

"Well," I say then, "I understand you *want* to do something crazy, but can you stop yourself from actually *doing* something crazy?" There is a pause before he answers, "No," he says. "I got to do something." It is not a statement made in anger. It is a statement of fact. A recognition.

For the next forty-five minutes I talk without stopping. I search for words that will act as keys to unlock his anger just enough to prevent catastrophe. I know from watching Greg that sensible wisdom will have little or no effect here. Phrases like, "Hurting somebody else won't bring him back" or "You know that payback will only make things worse," will cause Turtle to agree with the logic and tell me he's got to do it anyway.

I try to say what Greg would say and feel frighteningly ill-equipped for the job. But I am Turtle's only option tonight, so I talk on and on to him of the pain. "This is unbearable," I say. "It is unbearable to lose somebody you love this much. I know that. I know how much you love Blue. So much. So much. And I know you want to do anything you can to make that pain not hurt so much. I know that. And if you go out and do harm to somebody the pain might actually almost go away for just a minute. But then it'll come back. And it'll be much, much worse. You know that what I'm telling you is the truth."

He is quiet as I talk, sometimes murmuring back a little here, crying a little there. But he listens. He is drinking the words so deeply I can almost hear the listening as a physical action. It is clear that Turtle longs to be talked away from the suicide cliff at which he presently stands. I try to spread the words over him like salve, like mother's kisses, like warm water washing away blood.

Finally, when there is nothing else to say, I ask him if he thinks he can sleep now. "Yeah," he says. "I think I can." A few moments later we ring off. I am also calmed enough to finally not be frightened of the silence. And, astonishingly, I am able to sleep myself. It is not my words to Turtle that have calmed me, or the lateness of the hour. I am calmed simply by the act of loving this boy. Loving another heals both the loved and the lover. Greg is right. Love is the answer. I say this to myself as I drift off into welcome unconsciousness. Love is the answer. For the moment, this is the only truth that matters.

The next morning, reality dawns early. Blue's freckled face has floated behind my eyes all night. It is still there in the morning when I shock to wakefulness.

The morning is taken up with gathering new information. It is unclear if TMC knows the identity of the shooter yet. I start calling the "big heads," anyone I can find. I want to assess how bad it is. I try for Shadow. Try for Wolf. I get one of the TMC girls. She tells me a Cuatro Flats homie was at the movies and she overheard him bragging, "We killed two Tamales last night."

"It's going to get crazy," she says.

It has already gotten crazy. Turtle got off the phone with me last night at 3:30 A.M. Just after 4:00 A.M., twenty members of TMC crept into Pico Gardens, all of them armed, some carrying Molotov cocktails. Four people were wounded. Three from Cuatro were shot, plus a girl from Primera Flats. At first I hear that every available TMC went. This turns out to be inaccurate. Everyone but Turtle went. He refused.

This last fact is both heartening and scary. Obviously the call to Turtle made the difference. But who will catch him the next time he is falling? And who will catch Dreamer? And Wolf and Romeo and all the rest?

I am just headed down to the projects when Father Greg finally returns my call.

"My heart is broken." That's all he says. Then we sit there quietly in each other's long-distance company.

This is the moment he has been dreading all the months he's been away, he says. And there is no way the Jesuits will let him return, even in this crisis, even for a few days. "Never," he says. "I couldn't even ask them."

He is, at least, ignoring the Jesuits' pressure about phone calls, and says he will call every kid he can find. "But there is only so much I can do on the phone," he says. "Being here is excruciating. Now I know how the homies feel when they're locked up. A kid I love has died, and I'm in prison."

Like an air traffic controller talking blind pilots to earth, he suggests strategies.

"Tonight will be the worst," he says. "If you can get through tonight, then it may ease off a bit until after the funeral. Although you still have to worry about Cuatro, chances are the TMC's won't want to risk getting arrested and missing the funeral." After the funeral, he says, expect anything.

I find Turtle and Dreamer at the car wash that is being held in the church parking lot to raise money for the burial. I suggest that we go to dinner, and they are both in my car almost before I can finish the sentence. We drive without talking—the music up loud—to a restaurant that I know is safe.

At the table I ask Dreamer if he and Turtle have talked to Blue's mother, Amelia. Turtle is the one who replies. "No," he says. Then he looks away. They both sit silently, fidgeting with their food. Finally Dreamer speaks. "See, it's like this," he says. "He's dead because of us. You know? She didn't cause him to die. We did. He's dead because of hanging around with us."

They're trying to get Youngster to come back from Guadalajara. "He and Blue grew up together," says Dreamer. "He needs to be here for the wake. If he isn't, he won't get to cry and let it out, you know. And then later he'll do something really crazy. That's how it is."

After dinner I am reluctant to let go of them. When we left the projects, the mood was edgy and escalating fast. I drop Turtle at his girlfriend's house after extracting a promise that he will stay inside. Dreamer is surprisingly willing to let me take him to his parents', who live ten minutes' driving time from the projects. This means he too will most likely stay off the street tonight.

By 9:00 P.M. the mood back in the projects has worsened. TMC's are gathering at "the Thai line," a former drug-selling location in a parking lot off Clarence Street, and now TMC's main on-street hang-out. They are unusually sober for a weekend night. And there are a lot of them—twenty-five or more. Older guys who haven't been seen in the projects in over a year are suddenly in evidence.

In the projects, the ambiance that precipitates violence is a thing so palpable it can nearly be touched—or heard as a sound. If it *was* a sound it would not be loud and angry, as you might suppose, but thin, shrill, high-pitched, a noise like a dog whistle that you feel traveling sharp and discomforting up your spine. That sound, if it was a sound, is there at the Thai line now and growing stronger.

The talk between the TMC homies is only about two things— Blue and battle strategy. The talk about Blue has an element of highly focused outrage that was absent from the shock that attended Green Eyes' death. After all was said and done, everyone knew that Green Eyes was dead because he had gone looking for it. But with Blue the shooting is regarded as unjust.

"He didn't deserve it," says Drifter.

"And it was a drive-by," says Crow, a usually wry-humored twenty-four-year-old with a Wolfman Jack beard. "Drive-by's are against the rules."

By "against the rules," Crow is referring to the no-drive-by dictum that had purportedly come down from the *pinta*—prison—after Christmas to all of *la raza* (literally "the race," but often used to denote Mexican gangs) from the EME—the Mexican Mafia. The question among outside observers had been *if* and *how* the EME intended to enforce this interesting new addition to standard unwritten gang code. But the EME is beside the point tonight. Tonight it is TMC who intends to do the enforcing.

Midget is normally TMC's jovial, witty voice of reason, but this night he is thin-lipped and tense. "All the homies are the same right now," he says. Then he glances off to the side, as if checking to see who is listening. "Now, we all have to have the same things in our mind." He pauses for a couple of beats. "The only thing anybody could do is put a cop car on that corner," he says, nodding toward Third and Clarence, "and leave it there all night." He says this casually, as if it is a joke. But it's not a joke. It's a suggestion.

By eleven the streets have grown quiet and breathless. The violent, soundless whine is now there, strong and pure. Pam and I are noticeably jumpy as we make our rounds in my car, startling at the noise of an apartment door slamming. We drive through Pico Gardens to her apartment in order to use the bathroom. No one—*no one*—is out. Not even the usual drug dealers at Fifth Street.

As we reemerge from Pam's apartment we see two figures, one short and one tall, scuttling rapidly across the parking lot. Both are wearing what is called "creeping gear," hooded sweatshirts with the hood pulled up so tight that all one can see is eyes.

The taller of the two creeping homies is clearly recognizable as Puma the shot caller for Cuatro. Puma and the second creeper, a younger homie named Tear Drop, are most likely headed over to the Thai line to blast at TMC.

Pam and I glance at each other, unsure what to do. We are in an awkward situation. We cannot, ourselves, drive to the Thai line to warn TMC because we will be seen and this will be interpreted as snitching.

Suddenly struck by an insane notion, I call out to Puma. He ignores me and keeps walking. I call again, yelling to him to come over to my car. He pauses, undecided. Then, correctly assessing that I am not going to give up, he lopes over to where I am standing. By this time I have popped open my car trunk and have pulled out a brightly wrapped gift, tied with a shiny ribbon on which yellow ducks have been printed.

From Greg I learned the practice of carrying a blank birthday card with me at all times, to be filled out as needed. I've often been stunned by the fact that mine will be the only physical acknowledgment a kid will get on his birthday. To this strategy I have recently added inexpensive baby gifts, since unfortunately homies seem to have babies almost as often as they have birthdays.

I hold the gift out to Puma, who looks at it as if I am holding a spider.

"I have something for your new baby," I say, grabbing one of his large hands and plopping the box in it. Nonplussed, he says nothing.

"I know this might seem like an odd time to give you a gift for your baby," I continue, "seeing as you're all dressed up to go creeping and everything." Puma stares at me. "But maybe it's the *best* time to give it to you. Because maybe now is the time you most need to remember that you have a wonderful new son. And that you're his only father. And that if something happens to you—if you get locked up, or killed—then this little boy will have no one." I pause for effect. "He deserves to have a father. Don't you think?" Puma blinks a couple of times. "Yeah," he mumbles, his eyes widening and narrowing alternately inside the sweatshirt hood. "Thanks," he says.

I give him a hug. "I have more faith in you than you know," I say, doing my best Father Greg imitation. With that I step back. After glancing again at me, he turns and trots away. On his way past Pam, Puma hands her the gift. "Hold this for me 'til morning," he says. Pam and I try not to look at each other, each stifling the kind of hysterical laughter that is grounded in fear.

When Puma is out of sight, we get in my car and race to the church. We decide to call the Jesuit residence for reinforcements.

In a few minutes, Leonardo pulls up with Tom in the car. Simultaneously, a kid walks right into the church parking lot all G'd up (gangster dressed) with a bandanna tied over his face, obviously packing a large gun. It is a Cuatro homie named Raccoon, looking for TMC's to shoot. This is a completely extraordinary event. The fact that a gang member would come on to the church grounds with the intent of killing someone is a staggering violation of the sanctified status the church has always possessed. When Greg was here such an act would have been completely beyond imagination.

Finding only us, Raccoon does an about-face and heads back to the street. Tom grabs at Raccoon but he barrels past, easily shrugging Tom away. Acting on panicky instinct I move after Raccoon, calling him by name. Leonardo yanks me back. "You can't say his name," he whispers. Leonardo is right. To identify him within possible earshot of his enemies is a serious breach. I could perhaps get away with it with Puma but not with Raccoon. The four of us hop into our respective cars and attempt to follow him, but Raccoon has long since melted into the darkness.

So Pam and I cruise. In the few minutes since we have left Pico Gardens, the moon has risen and all at once TMC territory has become a surreal landscape of menacing silhouettes. Creep-dressed homies are everywhere. Some stand as lookouts, still and watchful. Romeo is barely visible, pressing himself against a wall at the corner of one building. Another TMC crouches in the archway of Silent's grandmother's house. The rest are in motion, hunched over and furtive as they skitter from shadow to shadow.

We cruise cautiously across Fourth Street back into Pico Gardens. There, as if cued by some signal known only to the two enemy gangs, Cuatro has materialized in full force. Some Cuatros are dressed like Raccoon, with bandannas tied Western-style over their noses and mouths, dark knit ski caps yanked low over their foreheads. Others sport hooded sweatshirts like Puma's, the drawstring pursed tightly around their faces as if tied by a team of overanxious mothers protecting very tall toddlers from the cold.

Ragman from Cuatro is standing by himself at the intersection of Eagle and Clarence. As his disguise, he wears a woman's brunette bouffant wig that he has pulled, off-kilter and uncombed, too far down toward his eyes, which shine, affectless and glittery, reflecting the streetlight overhead. This sight is at once humorous and terrifying.

Pam laughs nervously, then stops with an abrupt intake of breath. "Girl," she says softly after she exhales, "I have never seen anything like this shit. Never."

We drive round and round through the insane landscape, hoping our presence will discourage the two guerrilla armies from firing.

Finally, well after midnight, several police black-and-whites screech into the projects. At last we can go home. I am so relieved I am close to tears. But if I start crying, I'm afraid I won't stop.

―――

With a homicide, the day of the funeral revolves around when the coroner releases the body to the mortuary. Evidently the past weekend was a busy time for murders in Los Angeles, so there is a backlog at the coroner's office. The funeral, originally set for Wednesday, has now been postponed until Thursday, leaving three more days to worry about. Neglecting other writing work, I find numerous flimsy excuses to drive down to check on Dreamer and Turtle. Each time I leave the projects, Turtle asks me when I am coming again.

Father Greg has written and mailed an opened letter to all the TMC homies. He has also wired six hundred dollars to Youngster's mother in Guadalajara so she and he can fly back to L.A. This is on the condition that he returns to Mexico the day after Blue is buried. When Greg talks to Youngster on the phone, he cries with terrible abandon.

Like the bodies of drowned sailors washing up to shore, the first names of those possibly responsible for Blue's death are now starting to surface. Since often the initial names are not the right ones, it is impossible to say if what we are hearing is actually true. Nonetheless, even from a distance Greg hears random talk among TMC's about blowing up the suspected shooter's house. "TMC could do it," he says grimly. "They have some good-sized explosives. Much bigger than cocktails." And Turtle is getting particularly pressured to take action, Greg says. It goes without saying that Turtle cannot withstand such pressure indefinitely.

Greg sounds very down. "It's torture not to be there," he says. "Torture." He says he has dug up the few pictures he has of Blue and propped them against the lamp on the desk in his bedroom. "When the Jesuits come in, I know they think it's peculiar. They don't understand why I feel like I'm being pummeled over and over again in the stomach."

Everybody's nerves are fraying badly. Pam calls late Wednesday night to tell me that Raccoon is furious at me for Sunday. "Talking shit" is the way she puts it. She says that her husband Bebee had to talk him down on my behalf. Things are better now, she says, but they were dicey.

"The big heads like Puma and Oscar trust you," she assures me, "but there're some little fools who don't know you as well." She pauses. "I don't want you to take this personal, but if you're going to go to the Thai line to see TMC, then maybe you can't come over to see Cuatro." She drops her voice. "It may even reflect bad on me."

I tell Pam that I can't possibly pick sides. "Not for you, not for anybody," I say. But when I get off the phone I am completely unnerved.

The following morning depression sets in. I call Greg for counsel but he's out. I consider calling some other friend, but I know that anyone else will only tell me to get the hell out of East L.A. That I don't live in the projects. That I'm a middle-aged, middle-class white woman writer who has gone way too far over the line.

Unexpectedly, Rebel calls from Wasco State prison, where he has just begun serving his sentence. I ask him if he's heard that his homies are planning to do houses. He is noncommittal. "They could." I ask him if anything can be done to stop it. "There's nothing you can do, Celeste," he says in his smooth voice. "You got to stay out of it. Let them do what they have to do. I don't want you to get hurt. The homies care for you, but bullets don't have no names. Somebody might not see you. Stay away from it. It's going to get real crazy. *Real* crazy. They're not going to let this go. I'm just glad I ain't out there, 'cause I'd be in the middle of it." He laughs lightly. "I guess God's got me in here for a reason." Right before he rings off he adds, as if as an afterthought, "Look. Don't worry about the houses. Leave that to me."

When Greg finally calls back, I tell him about the conversation with Pam. He takes a breath. "You can't get sucked into the taking-sides game. You have to always *aegere contra*," he says. "That's an Ignatian expression which means, 'to go against the grain,' you know, to get back on the bicycle after you've fallen off, to go into what you most fear." He takes another breath. "The most uncomfortable place for you to be right now is Cuatro. And that's exactly where you need to be. If you don't go back immediately, you'll never go back again."

The day of the funeral, the Hollenbeck Division of the LAPD has called a tactical alert. This is the same state of readiness that was put into place prior to the Rodney King verdicts, but on a more regionalized scale. Hollenbeck officers are working overtime, and additional officers have been pulled from Metro. There are sets of police snipers visible on the roofs of all the apartment buildings adjacent to the church. An LAPD helicopter circles constantly like an enormous blue wasp. The Pico Aliso projects are now officially an armed camp.

Although the funeral isn't until 7:00 P.M., the homies have already started to gather by five. Nearly everybody is wearing one of the requisite black sweatshirts. The letter from Greg has been distributed, and clumps of kids stand together reading it, their lips moving as they read.

A small, beautiful girl named Lupe is passing out black satin ribbon armbands that have "R.I.P. Blue" handpainted on them in white. She also has a paper bag full of tiny black satin bows with the same "R.I.P." inscription that people are safety-pinning to their clothes. Another girl holds a pile of photocopied commemorative leaflets that the homegirls had made up the day before.

As the mourners continue to gather, I deliberately take a quick walk over to Cuatro territory in Pico Gardens. I am about to take off my R.I.P. armband, but I change my mind and leave it on. There are very few Cuatro homies in evidence, but those I do see act distant and strange. Even the really young one, PM'ers Jaime and Tacho and Sal, all of whom have tumbled a hundred times in and out of my car like unruly puppies, seem strained and unfriendly.

I wonder how much of this is my imagination. Am I projecting a jittery weirdness of my own to which they are merely reacting? Or is Pam right? Have new lines been drawn? Has it suddenly become dangerous for me here and I'm too naive or stubborn or arrogant to believe it? For the first time in well over two years in the projects, I feel genuinely uneasy.

Back at the church, the pews are filling up fast. Half the homies make their way up to the balcony. The others crowd as close to the front as physical space will allow.

After the opening prayers, the choir files up to sing. There are only six of them. They nearly didn't come at all because the choir members were too scared. As usual, their first song is an emotional trigger. When the song begins, the TMC girls sitting near the front, dressed in black with blood-red lipstick, let go together in a flood of synchronized tears. A few bars later the crying becomes fuller, louder, more extravagant.

In every group of girls there are always a couple of screamers and fainters. These are inevitably not the ones closest to the dead boy. It is as if the latest death in the neighborhood gives permission for them to shriek with pain in a way they would like to do daily, if social mores would sanction it.

Today a young homegirl known as Silly Girl begins wailing midway through the choir's second song. "Why-i-i-i-y Blu-u-ue! Wh-y-y-i-i-i?!" She elongates the vowels to the furthest limits her breath will allow. A girl to my right collapses into my arms in heaving sobs. Janet—the girl who had been Blue's closest platonic girlfriend—looks straight ahead, her face running with tears.

The threesome of Turtle, Dreamer, and Youngster stand quietly, to the left of the coffin. Even inside the church, Dreamer wears the blackest of *locs* to cover his eyes. All three are exquisitely dignified, as if their grief is a dark, thick mantle draped invisibly across their collective shoulders, to be carried for Blue with straight-backed grace.

The new priest, Father Jerry, gives the homily. It is well-meaning, but the homies shift uncomfortably when he speaks. Then Turtle and Janet get up to read Father Greg's letter. Turtle starts reading first. "Dear Homies," he reads. "I write this with a love for you that is unchanging and forever." Turtle's reading is jerky and difficult. "How I wish I could be with you now . . ." Turtle's voice falters. He begins again. "I hold in my mind and in my broken heart, the vivid memory of Blue . . ." That's it for Turtle. Crying, he hands the letter to Janet.

Unsure of her own ability not to break down, Janet reads too quickly to the end of the letter, then rushes back to her seat.

Next Father Jerry nods to Blue's girlfriend Gabby, who walks to the podium at the left side of the altar and stands for a moment, a thin sheen of salt water making her face bright in the light. She is possessed by a grief so vivid it has lent her a kind of radiance.

"He loved every one of you." She says this slowly, looking from homie to homie, her gaze swimming, but steady. "He loved you. He cared about what happened to you. He would not want you to get crazy. He was there for you. And he was there for me. I need you there for me. I need you alive. Not dead in a little box like my Blue." Then she turns and steps down.

The room is completely silent for a long moment. If anything has invoked Father Greg's healing spirit tonight it is not his own letter or the other Jesuits, but this small girl, who for precious seconds has become Our Lady of Sorrows, her tears cleansing all assembled.

The spell is broken when the mortician startles back into action. He gestures to Father Jerry, who then dutifully jumps to prepare the coffin with prayer and incense. When Father Jerry is finished, the homies shuffle from their pews to form a line for viewing as the coffin is opened.

The sight is unsettling. Dead Blue doesn't look like live Blue. His freckles are muted by powder. His lips are swollen and strangely shaped. More than live Blue, he looks like dead Green Eyes and dead Oso, except for his hands. When Turtle gets to the casket, he strokes Blue's hands for several minutes. They are small, childish hands and unmistakably Blue's. These are the hands that held the broom as Blue swept Greg's office late at night, using clean-up as an excuse not to have to leave Greg's presence, hands I've seen a hundred times gripping the handlebars of a bike, usually with paint underneath the fingernails, evidence of the most recent tagging expedition.

Turtle strokes Blue's hands, then his cheek, then his hands again, over and over, as if soothing a sick child.

The homies leave the church single-file through the side door, then gather in the parking lot in expanding and contracting groups. Some recycle through the viewing line to see Blue again. Others squeeze into the rectory office to call Father Greg in Detroit. They take turns spewing short, teary monologues into the phone.

Turtle cannot leave the casket. Dreamer too stands up on the altar, directly behind the casket, a sentry of sorts. Occasionally he lists woozily in my direction, unconsciously drawing toward body contact, until I put my arm through his. Then he stands straight, guarding Blue for these last few possible minutes.

After a while, Dreamer pulls out the commemorative leaflet which he had stuffed folded into his pants pocket. He unfolds it and begins to turn the pages. On each page there are collaged prayers, poems, messages, and pictures, one a large photo that I had taken of Blue on his bike. Turtle has written three different prayers. Gabby, one.

The last page is a photocopied sheet that is not stapled to the rest of the funeral booklet. At the top of the page, a salutation is written in swirly script: "Blue Boy—From your loving homegirls." Then there is a waist-up photo of Blue standing in a white T-shirt, facing the camera, eyes sad as usual. His fingers are signing the letters: TMC. But in this photo, the effect of the hand gestures fails to be gangsterish. If you didn't know better, you might guess Blue was snapped in the act of making shadow animals on the wall for a younger child.

Below the picture is written the date of Blue's birth, 6/28/75, and of his death, 5/15/93. And then a poem, typed and personalized for this sheet by little Lupe, but originally written by some other anonymous girl to commemorate the death of some other anonymous homeboy:

I am not a metaphor or a symbol
This you hear is not the wind in the trees,
Nor a cat maimed in the street.
I am being maimed in the street.
It is I who weep, laugh, feel pain or joy.
Speak this because I exist.
This is my voice.
These words are my words.
My spirit speaks them.
My mind speaks them from above.
I am Blue.
It is my voice you hear
Near your ear.
Now I know I was in your heart from the start.

Dreamer stares wordlessly at the poem, his eyes enormous and stricken behind the *locs*.

Tomorrow Blue will be buried. After that all bets are off.

Joanna

My name is Joanna Escalante. I'm seventeen. I'm not in a gang, but I have a baby by a gang member, Silent, who is locked up right now for murder. Silent's birthday is May fifteenth, the same day as Blue passed away. I was hurt that Blue passed away but what hurt me even more was the people that I grew up with did it.

My mom lives in Pico Gardens and all the Cuatros were all the guys I grew up with, all my good friends. Now I'm living with a TMC. And Cuatro and TMC are in a war. It used to be that Silent could go back and forth between TMC and Cuatro and help squash things, 'cause he had a lot of respect. But after Father Greg left, it changed. Now, every time I go down to where my mom lives, the guys look at me and we don't talk. They never disrespect me. They never say anything bad to me. But I feel paranoid like maybe they hate me.

I'm not ashamed that I grew up in the projects. I know more about life than a lot of people. The hardest part of growing up in the projects is the violence. Like one time we were having a Valentine's party at the church and I was taking pictures and I ran out of film so I was walking to the store to get some more. I was standing at the light, pressing the button. And this car passes by, and shoots Sailor from Cuatro right in front of my eyes.

Scarier than that was when my dad was shot. Me and my best friend are walking in Pico. And we hear shots. And all of a sudden I see a homie running to me. He tells me my dad's been shot. At first I didn't believe him. I guess they were aiming for a gang member, but they got my dad instead.

He was shot in the side and it came out the other side. It really tore up his insides, his intestines and his lungs and his liver—everything. I ran over to where he was. He was dying on us, and calling for my mom.

At the hospital they thought for sure he was going to die, so they said the whole family should come. See, he was separated from my mom at the time. She had got a restraining order on him. And nobody in my family was talking to him. Myself and my mom were the only ones who would still be talking to him.

I have a really good relationship with my mom. She would do anything for us. All the girls around the projects near to us, all our friends—whenever they would run away from their own homes they would come to my mom's house. She would talk to them, help them to see that they were just going through a stage. I love my dad a lot too. He's a really good person. He would always fix things for our neighbors, like if their door was broken or something, he would fix it. But when my dad started drinking a lot and doing drugs that's when everything in our family fell apart.

My dad always drank all his life. About once a year my dad will drink all day, every day, for a month. He doesn't even eat. He just drinks until he's hospitalized. Then he'll get back on track for a while. Then he'll drink again. That's his routine. But drugs made it worse. Then he got all crazy a couple of times. And so Social Services told my mom they were going to take us away unless she helped to put my dad in jail. I was thirteen then, and it was bad.

At the same time we had my cousin Edgar and his little brother and sister living with us. His mother is my dad's sister. When Edgar's mom and dad got arrested they didn't tell anybody that they had three kids at home with nothing to eat. So nobody knew, until Edgar called my mom all sad and said he didn't have anything to eat, and he didn't have anything for the kids. So of course we took them to our house. We didn't even know where the parents were. The baby girl was two years old and she was really traumatized. She wouldn't let Edgar go out of the room. He was thirteen at the time. Edgar's been through a lot.

When my father got arrested, my sister and I started messing up. My older brother tried to play the dad role, but I wouldn't listen to him. During that time, sometimes my dad would get better, but then he'd get bad again and my mom would have to get another restraining order. He stole all the jewelry of most of the people in the family and sold it to buy drugs. He never stole any of my stuff. But he took the gold from my mom and my brothers, stuff that meant a lot to them. He even sold my brother's class ring.

One thing that hurted me a lot, is that some of the guys down here in the projects who're supposedly my friends, and who know he's my dad, they sell drugs to him. A lot of the guys knew what my dad was going through, and still they would slang to him. Some of the guys were respectful and would say, "No, I can't sell to you." But a lot of them did it. And that really hurt me a lot.

My dad's been sick as long as I've known him. I became a volunteer in the hospital, a Candy Striper, so I could be around him when he was in the hospital after he got shot. I was fourteen at the time and I was going to BRAVO, which is the medical magnet school for kids who want to be doctors and nurses. I got to work on his ward just to be with him because I knew he was lonely, and nobody was speaking to him again, except me and my mom.

I've wanted to be a doctor ever since I was little. I've known I was smart for a long time. When I was in the first grade I would go to second-grade classes. In the third grade, I would go with my sister Anna to her after-school magnet classes. She's always been an honors student too. She's two grades higher than me, but when we would go to these classes, the teachers would say to her, "Your little sister's as smart as you. Maybe even smarter." In the third grade they gave me an IQ test and I scored really high. So they helped my mom get me into one of those schools for highly gifted students.

In junior high I had to go back to regular school and that's when I started fucking up. I didn't fuck up in my classes. In my classes I would do good. When I was in seventh grade I was already in ninth-grade classes. But then we would get our report cards and we would all be comparing them at lunchtime. And everybody would be asking each other, "What'd you get? What'd you get?" Everybody'd have D's and F's and U's. And I would have A's. I never wanted to show mine, because I was embarrassed. I used to feel that the other girls were better than I was because they were getting F's. I don't know why. It seems dumb now. All the girls who were the popular ones would get bad grades.

So then I started messing around and getting suspended. Then I got kicked out of school for a while 'cause I was with another girl who had a knife in her purse. I didn't know anything about the knife but they thought I was a gang member because of who I hung around with, and 'cause of how I dressed.

See, the projects girls were always in the popular crowd. I wasn't really popular. My sister was. But I hung out with the popular girls. Not because they were popular, but because they were the ones I knew because I'd grown up with them.

After junior high I went to the medical magnet school. But then when I was fifteen, I got pregnant and I used that as an excuse to drop out. Silent had already de-virginized me once before he went to camp. Then when he came out, we were together this one time, he was drunk and I was half asleep. No protection was used and I got pregnant.

The reason girls don't use protection is because a lot of the guys will try to talk them out of it. And the girls want to make their guys happy. Then the girls don't get on the pill because you need your parents' consent and they don't want their moms to know that they're doing that stuff. So a lot of girls don't use anything.

It was a big, big shock for my mom when I got pregnant. My sister was also four months pregnant. When I got pregnant, Silent wanted me to move in with him and his grandmother. I wanted to please him so I did it. It was okay at first but then it started to get bad. Silent started hitting me and stuff. At first it was a joke but then it wasn't a joke anymore.

After a while I thought I'd ruined my life. Once I thought of killing myself even. Father Greg kind of saved my life. I had this terrible fight with Silent. He hit me and told me some really bad things. It's a blur in my mind because I've tried to forget about a lot of it. But anyway I was out in the projects running. I ran and I ran until I didn't know anywhere else to run. So I ran into Father Greg's office. And I started talking to him. I felt I was useless. That I was nothing. That everything was my fault. I blamed myself for everything bad. I didn't know what to do. I would have killed myself if he hadn't been there.

Father Greg was always there for me. He would not tell me to leave Silent. He would tell me that he loved Silent too. But he would tell me that I should tell him that I would leave him if he didn't change. Father Greg always told me I needed to draw, you know, lines. Boundaries.

I stayed with Silent 'cause I loved him. Inside him he's a really good person. He's a good person with everyone else but me. He would help old ladies or little kids. Anybody. The homies really respect him. I know he loves me but, I'll tell you the truth, he hasn't treated me with respect.

Now I'm moving out. I'm moving back to my mom's. The fact that he's in jail has nothing to do with it. I would have waited for him all my life. But I'm tired of the way we fight. And I'm tired of staying locked up in a house for two years. I'm young. I've been in this house since I was fifteen. I want to open some doors. I don't mean other guys. Other guys always try to talk to me but I always say no.

I've never gone out or done the things that other girls my age have done 'cause I've been living here. I never went to the mall with all my friends. I didn't go to parties or movies. And it isn't just the baby because a lot of my friends have babies but they still have their lives. I haven't had my life. I made my own choice, I know that. I wanted to make my man happy. So if he told me, "Don't do it," I didn't do it. I know it's hard for him now because he's in there and I'm out here. But that's not my fault.

One thing I do know. I know Silent is going to get out because he didn't do it. Everybody knows he didn't do the murder. Because everybody knows who *did* do it. Everybody knows.

I think things started going bad for Silent when his primo, Oso, got killed. He kept getting more and more depressed. It was hard for him. It hurted him more than anything. Then when Father Greg left, it's like he didn't want to do anything. He stopped working. He'd been a good worker. But then he started messing up at his job. He didn't want to talk to me. He was in his own little world.

I see my little brother going the direction of the gangs. He does it because it gives him more attention. The girls always like the gang members more. To girls, the gang members seem more exciting. The way they dress, the way they talk. It's like they have more glamour. It's hard to explain. But almost every girl will tell you the same thing, no matter who she is. It's crazy. Now when I hear these little girls talking the way I used to talk, I want to tell them how dumb it is. But you don't listen when you're that age.

With Silent it wasn't really that he was in a gang. It was that we could talk good. At the beginning we used to talk all night on the phone, hours and hours. We'd talk about everything, about our lives, about our families. And I liked him in a different way than anybody else.

The day that Oso died, he made me promise that I wouldn't ever leave Silent. He told me, "You got to understand my *primo*. He loves you." I remember because we were talking about that his birthday was coming up and Oso was going to stop drinking on his birthday. He said, to me, "Damn! I'm going to be twenty-one years old. I never thought I'd make it to twenty-one." And he didn't.

If Oso was alive, it never would have jumped off between TMC and Cuatro. He was always there when there was a fight, trying to solve the problem. He would've stopped it. After that only G could stop it. And G's gone.

I think the reason the Jesuits don't want him back is a political thing. They know he's a big help to our community, kind of like helping us grow up, get out of our problems. And I feel that they don't want him to help our community.

He helped my mom to get where she's at. Her whole life is changed because of him. My mom used to be the way I am with Silent. She would always be there for my dad no matter what. He would be loaded, drunk, and she would change him, shave him, put him to bed. Try to feed him. Take him to the hospital. One time my mom and I chased my dad all the way from White Memorial Hospital back to the projects in his bathrobe and he was running away from us the whole time. It was embarrassing. She would put up with so much. Now she's strong. She still lives with him but she doesn't take his shit. She goes to the community meetings. She's out there. She speaks out. Father Greg helped her do that. Now I'm starting to get strong too.

It's been scary when I was laying in my bed these past months, before Silent got locked up, and hearing the sounds of the war that's going on between Cuatro and TMC. Hearing all the shots. People running up and down the stairs to shoot from the roof. Shooting. Shooting. Shooting. All night long. Hearing the helicopter go over. Thinking, "Please let it pass by. Please let it pass by." And me inside, lying in my bed, knowing the father of my daughter was out there. And I couldn't go out and do anything because I didn't want to get shot myself. It makes you a little traumatized. I feel like I have a kind of shock inside me. I'll grow out of it eventually. But it's going to take a while.

Chapter 11

There is a psychological borderline one comes to when working in the projects beyond which lies a harsh land where one does not accept, but comprehends without judgment, acts that all the rest of civilized American society views as monstrous.

This is not the same crossing of borders that sometimes occurs in times of war, the dehumanization that permits atrocities. I think this border crossing is better described as an *ultra*-humanization, a staring deep into the heart of the species in which we all claim membership, to the place where both darkness and light coil together.

When I learn who killed Blue—the real name—I have no choice but to do what Greg has said one must do. I hold the two seemingly discrepant thoughts, side by side, one in each palm. In one hand, a kid whom I know and care very much about, a kid full of pain, yearning, possibility. In the other hand, the unendurable reality that this same kid has murdered a boy I had come to love.

At first it feels that if I hold the thoughts too close together they will spark a conflagration inside me. But in time I am able to bring them close enough to touch, and am disconcerted to find that one does not weigh more heavily in my heart than the other.

———

The burial is at nine. By the time I arrive at 8:00 A.M., the homies are already there and clearly have been there for some time, all wearing clean and well-ironed clothes.

Like last night, police are everywhere. Police snipers are again on the rooftops and a helicopter is circling. Some of the homies are in the church sitting with Blue's casket. Others mill out in front. Leonardo is there, as is Pam, and Ridgway. Father Jerry is the only Jesuit present.

Leonardo explains that Father Tom has gone to Santa Barbara for a retreat. And, on this day when the parish is in its most extreme crisis, Father Pete, the church's pastor, has decided to take his day off.

Just before the cars line up to head toward the cemetery, Ted Gabrielli shows up. Gabrielli, a Father Greg supporter, was transferred away from Dolores Mission a month ago and is attending the same retreat in Santa Barbara that Tom is attending. He has sneaked out to attend the burial, and is hoping to return before the retreat leaders miss him. His face is welcome. He knows the kids and is one more responsible adult.

At 8:45, the funeral cortege starts its motors. The fastest route to Resurrection Cemetery is up Gless Street, left on Fourth Street to the Santa Ana Freeway. But this would mean skirting the borders of Pico Gardens—Cuatro-land. Instead, the police escort leads the procession of cars on a roundabout route, down Gless and right on First Street. These precautions are not fanciful. Just as the procession of cars crawl in a line onto the freeway, another police contingent finds two Cuatro homies waiting near the Fourth Street freeway entrance with high-powered rifles.

At Resurrection, the service is brief and perfunctory, lacking Greg's sense of poetry. When it is over, the gang members wander off to elsewhere in the cemetery to visit various dead homies.

Wizard and other Clarence homies go to see Smoky and some others. Most of TMC goes to see Green Eyes. A stone plaque, paid for by the homeboys, has finally been placed on Green Eyes' grave. A photo of Green Eyes is etched into the stone. It is a good likeness. His hair is short, clean-cut, his expression optimistic. Above his name and the date of his birth and death, there is the message in graceful script: "I'm still here."

Turtle and Player clean the stone of dirt, wiping it to a shine with a bandanna. They have each brought a bouquet of flowers for Green Eyes, both supermarket-purchased "spring bouquets" in purples, whites, and yellows, with a single red gladiolus thrown in for height and color. There is an existing hole in the ground near the marker, but it is clogged and spits the bouquets back out. An elderly white man who has brought flowers for another grave nearby sees Player struggling and lends him a garden tool to clear the hole, and to dig a second one. Now the flowers can be made to stand upright. Turtle pats the earth around the bouquets for good measure, then stands.

The homies regard the stone and the flowers. "It looks *firme*," says Crow. Now attention is turned to a collection for Blue. "How much've we got already?" Player wants to know. All eyes turn to Turtle.

"Maybe eight hundred with the car washes and the food sale," he says. This money will barely cover the funeral. It leaves nothing for the stone. Crow starts a new collection.

"Only twenties or above," he says. Obediently, the homies fill Crow's hands with bills.

Outside the barrio, one rarely hears adolescents talk about the kind of funeral they want, unless perhaps it is a "cremation versus burial" discussion that is held in the abstract, discussed as one might discuss politics or philosophy. In the projects, kids talk about funerals the way suburban girls might deliberate kinds of weddings.

"I want to be buried in my red satin dress," Aurora, Angel's girlfriend, once announced to me. "And I want red lipstick and red nail polish. Everything red!" The most disquieting part of this conversation was not that Aurora had thought about it, but that she already had the dress and didn't expect it to be worn out.

So often, right before a death, the kid has expressed his or her wishes to one or two close friends. Oso had asked for mariachis and his song, "Someday We'll Be Together." The day before Blue was killed he remarked to Turtle that he didn't want people to cry at his funeral. "Give me a party, homes," he said. "I want everybody to be happy."

Now Turtle is determined to honor those wishes. The problem is where to hold the party. A clump of drinking TMC homies would provide a fish-in-a-barrel opportunity for anyone who would wish to take it. Finally it is decided that a barbecue will be held in the parking lot right across the street from the church.

Just before we leave the cemetery I take pictures of Turtle, Youngster, and Dreamer in front of Blue's casket. Homies always want pictures taken with the casket. This is a custom that at first seemed strange and morbid to my WASP perception. But now I have come to see the comfort in it. I have an edited video version of Green Eyes' funeral which was sent to me by the producers at *60 Minutes*. I would be embarrassed to admit how many times I've played it. I tell myself that I have played it only to evoke scenes and feelings for purposes of writing. But sometimes late at night, when my kid is asleep, I've played it. I fast forward to certain spots—the songs by the church choir, the moment just before Greg and the funeral director open the casket, when he swings the incense holder, its chain making a light clink-clink against the swinging brazier as he intones, "Incense is an ancient symbol. The smoke, as it rises, represents the best of our hopes." And I am comforted.

The rest of the day I rarely let the Turtle-Dreamer-Youngster threesome out of my sight. Although Turtle has organized the barbecue, it has turned drunken and unsupervised, and, surprisingly, he and the other two are eager to have an excuse to leave it.

Janet and Blue's twelve-year-old little brother, Beto, also pile into my car. I take them shopping for shoes to send to their friend Pato in camp, then to a Jack-in-the-Box to eat. The one near Dreamer's parents' house is deemed the safest.

Janet sits with me at one table while the guys are at a second table talking. Janet is a long-legged, loquacious seventeen-year-old who manages to play the role of smart, sensible sister to any number of homies from various neighborhoods. She was especially close to Blue and now spills out memories in a brightly colored stream. "He was going to apply to become a cop on Monday," she says. "He didn't want the homies to know. He was afraid they'd think it was dumb. Being a cop or an architect. Those were his two dreams. Most people don't know that."

After a while Dreamer gets up to follow a cute girl he has seen in the parking lot. Turtle and Youngster remain sitting across from each other staring into space without interaction. However, Turtle has reached across to Youngster and is lightly holding his hand in his own. It is a completely unselfconscious gesture. The way lovers might comfort each other without thinking, or the way a mother might comfort a son.

———

Back at the church, the atmosphere has grown frighteningly chaotic. TMC homies are drinking everywhere—in the parking lot, on the church steps. There are reports that a TMC homie was "taken to court," that is beaten up as a disciplinary action by his own homeboys. This in itself is not so alarming, but the fact that it took place right in front of the church is unbelievable.

Father Jerry's office—the office that once was Greg's—is open and filled with drunk homies making phone calls. Father Jerry is nowhere in sight and, by all accounts, has not been seen for some time. When the church phone rings, Nomad answers it, his words slurred and belligerent. In six years Greg never left homies alone in his office for more than a few moments. Drunk homies would be beyond imagination. What if someone should call? What if someone from Cuatro should call?

At around 3:00 P.M, an already intoxicated TMC homie chugs a full bottle of tequila and picks fights with everybody. It takes four homies plus Leonardo to keep him from wrecking the inside of the church.

Brother Ted had to go back to Santa Barbara right after the burial. No other Jesuits have appeared. There is only Leonardo, and Leonardo is not enough. Pam is in Pico Gardens with the Cuatros, where she is needed.

I make it my goal to get as many homies away from this place as I can. The church is no longer a sanctuary. There are no rules, no boundaries. No one is minding the store.

"How could they do this?!" asks Leonardo, meaning the Jesuits, as he races to quell yet another fight. "They don't want Greg back and yet they do *nothing* themselves."

By nightfall, I am a hen counting chickens. Wizard is safe. I have taken him home. Player and some others are safe; I saw them leave. However, I have lost the threesome. I drive worriedly through the projects, asking everyone if they have seen Turtle or Youngster or Dreamer. Finally, way at the back of the Thai line, I see a trio of familiar figures—all nearly the exact same height, all dressed in the same soft black. I speed my car in their direction and stop. Turtle sees me and signals the other two. They trot over to the car just as I get out, their expressions calm, almost peaceful. "We're going door to door collecting money for Blue's mom. For the stone," says Turtle. "We got over three hundred dollars," says Dreamer.

—

Sunday. It is not possible to go on like this. Pam is exhausted. Leonardo is exhausted. I am exhausted. Having wall-to-wall police has thus far prevented serious shooting. But the police will disappear after today. And then what?

"It cost a fortune to have the tactical alert called for the funeral and the burial," explains Ridgway, also exhausted. "Jack Forsman and Mike Marchello really stuck their necks out to get that to happen. We really owe them one." Of course, it was Ridgway who stuck *her* neck out to push Forsman and Marchello.

Today the Commite Pro Paz has a *carne asada*—a barbecue— planned with Cuatro. The idea was that the mothers would organize barbecues with each of the main four neighborhoods as an extension of the Love Walks. The barbecue dates were set before Blue's death, and the Cuatro barbecue is the first one on the schedule. Now some think that holding this barbecue is about as sensible as deciding to celebrate a citywide carnival in Honolulu on December 8, 1941, just because you happened to have it on the calendar.

The darkness in Pico Gardens is thick and black as tar. Maybe having the mothers outside cooking will bring back some sense of normalcy. Things cannot possibly get worse.

Father Greg has written an open letter to Cuatro, much like the one he wrote to TMC. He sent a letter to everyone whose address he had in his book, plus a packet of extras to Pam to distribute. Most of the homies received it yesterday.

The letter is written with Greg's usual political shrewdness, invoking the name of Oso, reminding the homies of the fact that Oso and Blue were friends. Maybe it will do some good.

I used to bring my son with me on the occasions when I would come to the projects on weekend days. He would play with the PM'ers. Now I never bring him. It is far too dangerous. I see the tension in Pam's face whenever her children stray too far from her apartment, even on sunny afternoons, even in the company of their father. No one would ever purposely hurt Star or little Bebee . . . or my kid, Will. But as the homies always say: bullets don't have names.

My East L.A. involvement is now wreaking havoc nearly everywhere else in my life. I've had a fight with one of my best friends because I've backpedaled on my agreement to help her with the school play, in which my son has a part. My mother walks out of the room whenever the subject of gangs enters the conversation. The producers of the movie I'm writing have straight-out asked me not to go down to the projects anymore. "With the stakes so high, how can I *not* go down?" I ask friends, family, colleagues—but most are no longer persuaded.

I have made a big Greek salad for the *carne asada*, plus a couple of baked chickens to take to Blue's family. I ask Turtle to ride with me in the car to run the food up to Amelia, Blue's mom. "Just drop me off at the church," he says when he returns. We are right at Third and Clarence when Rabbit from TMC runs up to the passenger side of the car. "Emergency! Emergency!" he yells. "A gang'a Cornflakes are at the church! Emergency!" Cornflakes is the pejorative term for Cuatro Flats.

Turtle opens the passenger door of the car and is out in a heartbeat.

"Damn it . . . !" I begin. But he is already running. He dodges through Liliana's house. I floor it to the church. I wonder if he is getting a gun.

At the church I try to make sense of what I see. Grim-faced TMC's are everywhere. Groups of them litter the parking lot. They are also stationed on the roof. Suddenly I notice a kid named Raymond Alvarez coming toward me with a wide grin that is inappropriate, out of context. "Hey! How're you doin'," he says as he comes with arms outstretched to give me a bear hug. I hug him and my mind struggles to process the incomprehensible fact that this is Raymond Alvarez, aka "Chango" from *Cuatro Flats*! He is the same Chango who used to work at the Tortilleria but who since this war has become a shooter. It is flat out impossible that he should be here with all these TMCs.

"Raymond!" I say stupidly. "It's good to see you." The whole scene has the unreality of viewing two unrelated pieces of film run side by side. Chango pulls away from the hug, still smiling strangely. He walks toward the passenger side of a car parked across the street from the church. Now that car comes into focus. Oscar is at the wheel, Poison and other Cuatro homies in the back. I walk with Chango over to the car and stare at Oscar. His expression is black and shimmery. "What're you doing here?" I ask, now genuinely alarmed.

"I came over to kill another one," says Oscar. I know it is a taunt, but the words feel like slaps.

Everything is perilous.

"We don't give a fuck about the church," Oscar continues, "or anybody in it. We don't give a fuck, y'understand? It's a fucking TMC church." Oscar's rage is so virulent it is as if his complexion itself grows darker as he speaks. Only his teeth shine white and angry. I ask him if he is going to the *carne asada*. "Yeah, we're going," says Poison. "I'll see you there," I say and turn my back and walk back to the church.

For the first time I see the rest of the situation: In the parking lot there are two more cars, revved up and ready to leave, both packed with Cuatro homies. Puma is at the wheel of the first one. I look around for other adults and at first see none. Then I notice Father Jerry sitting on the front steps of the church, staring out at the street with an expression that suggests a cherry bomb has just exploded right behind his eyes.

"What are you doing?!" I whisper urgently on my way past Jerry.

"I'm praying," he says.

Oh, great.

Feeling like a pacifist gazelle among panthers, I stride over to Puma's car and lean into the driver's side.

"I just talked to G. He gave me a message that's just for you." This is not strictly true, but invoking Greg is the best I can think up as I scramble for context. Is something about to happen? Or has something *already* happened?

"I'll tell you what he said at the *carne asada*." I try to imbue my words with as much weight and drama as possible, if for no other reason than to feel less frightened and out of control.

Next I grab an envelope out of my car and stalk in Wolf's direction. Wolf is standing in a bola of TMC's, and by sheer serendipity I have a letter for him from Greg. I use my mailman function as an excuse to ask what is going on.

"We just finished a meeting," says Wolf with his stone-calm smile. "With the *Carnales*."

The *Carnales*, aka the EME, aka the Mexican Mafia.

The story that spins out during the course of the rest of the afternoon and into the night outlines a dark miracle. Yesterday the EME called a secret meeting of all of the Boyle Heights gangs. Today the meeting took place. There has been talk since December that drive-by's are forbidden by the EME. Rumor has it that word has come down through the state system from Pelican Bay, the maximum-security prison where various highly placed members of the EME are being held.

It seems that the EME had planned to have meetings for some time. But Blue's drive-by death put push to shove. The main eastside neighborhoods were called together and the rules were laid down: No drive-by's. No shooting into houses. No shooting at anyone if they're with their lady or mother or family. One can still settle *pedo*— a quarrel. But it must be done within the rules. You walk up to an enemy. Hit'em up. Then if they claim their neighborhood back, you have the right to kill them. If they do not claim a neighborhood or say nothing you must walk away.

Some say the EME's motivation is noble, to stop *la raza* from killing *la raza*. Some say it is more practical in nature, that all these gang wars are bad for the drug business. Whatever the motivation, the murky star of the *Carnales* has sent down a beam of light to intervene when all seemed lost.

———

The violence doesn't stop immediately; rather, it shudders to a halt, with afterburns flaring up every hour or so. Yet, this replacement violence takes a curious form. A challenge will be called out by a member of one of the neighborhoods. "Let's go head up! C'mon. You an' me. One on one." Then a homie from the other side will stroll into the middle of the street to meet the challenger. Word of the impending fight spreads in seconds and suddenly everyone from both neighborhoods is running in the direction of the flash point.

All evening the police cruise—Housing and LAPD—and seem as confused as anybody by this new behavior. A few minutes after each new brawl starts, squad cars screech up, disgorging cops holding shotguns, at which point everyone backs off. But twenty minutes later it starts all over again. By dusk a few people, including Puma, have been arrested and released. Everybody is pretty well worn out.

As the light fades from the street, a group of twenty TMC's and Clarence have gathered across Fourth Street on the handball courts, a location that would have been suicidal only twelve hours before. Oddly, they are not hanging out drinking. They are having a barbecue of their own. Somebody has borrowed a round Weber-style grill, and there are hot dogs and burgers on the coals. It is a meager barbecue, not really enough food for all who have gathered. This seems not to matter. The barbecue appears to be a symbolic gesture. A small moment of average life—grilling dogs and burgers on an early summer evening in the public park—a right accorded any citizen of these United States, weather permitting.

"We can walk to the store now," says Turtle's girlfriend, Liliana, her face warmed by the red of the coals. "Just the way it used to be."

"We don't have to watch our backs," says Shooter from Clarence.

"See, let me tell you what this means," says Wolf. Of anyone, Wolf's expression is the most optimistic, the most vulnerable. "Today everything starts over. Today is the beginning. It's like yesterday I could have . . ." He searches for words. "I could have killed your mother and it wouldn't matter. Today we start all over. From the beginning."

Father Greg has said it so many times; in almost all cases the homies are searching for an excuse to stop, to turn back from the brink. Now, into the center of the most disastrous gang war this barrio has ever seen, a rescue rope has been tossed. Hands from all sides are grabbing for that rope.

As the days and weeks pass, what has come to be known as the "EME truce" still holds. The teeth behind the *Carnales'* intervention is based on a specific threat of force: Follow the rules, or your homies on the "inside" (that is in the jails and state prisons) will suffer. But unlike threats of force from the police, which too often only incite rebellion, the EME's threat has offered the gang members a reason to pull back without losing face, without sacrificing dignity. This is a crucial difference to adolescent boys of the barrio, for whom to be stripped of dignity is to be stripped of everything.

However, even the *Carnales'* peace will not last forever. The underlying causes of gang violence have not been altered. A window of opportunity has opened. Energy has been freed. But if that energy is not reorganized in the new direction, it will soon resume its original shape. The window will close unless someone comes along to seize the moment.

Someone like Greg.

Both the local press and the Pico Aliso community continue to lobby for Greg's return. Finally, in early June, one small ray of hope appears regarding the deadlock. Paul Belcher is scheduled to be replaced as Provincial by another Jesuit, a Father John Pravette. Pravette contacts Greg to schedule a meeting with the priest, himself, and Belcher. Greg doesn't know whether to be optimistic or not. Is he about to be formally reassigned away from Los Angeles? Or is there a chance Pravette would reverse Belcher's decision?

———

The day before he is to meet with his new boss, Greg reviews what he plans to say. He will point out once again that no valid reason has ever been given him for his non-return to East L.A., other than vague intimations of discomfort on the part of the current Jesuit team, and equally vague intimations of the disapproval on the part of the cardinal. He will again list the needs of the community. He will also again describe the results of his own soul-searching in terms of what he believes God calls him to do.

There is, of course, one obvious question: What if they won't ever let him go back to East Los Angeles? What then? Will he choose to serve what he believes God wants of him? Or will he choose the Society of Jesus? If it comes down to it, will he stay a Jesuit? Or will he leave?

Greg stops for a moment, imagining such a crossroads. "I would hope that my vocation is deep enough," he says. Then he quickly reconstitutes. "It is. I know it is." A long pause. "I became a Jesuit when I was eighteen years old. I've been a Jesuit longer than I *haven't* been a Jesuit . . . I don't know. It scares me when my mind goes down that road."

———

I am sitting in my kitchen, perched on my favorite rickety chair drinking coffee, my son already in school, when Greg calls with the news.

"They said they're going to send me back." The details, it seems, have to be worked out, but Greg talked with both the outgoing and incoming Provincial for over an hour and in the end they agreed to somehow "finesse" his return.

Relief blisters through me like too much over-hot liquid. In the middle of his telling I begin to cry. I am crying not only out of happiness that love and fairness has prevailed. The sharpest edge of the relief is personal. I am crying because I won't have to do it anymore. Pam and Leonardo and I can all take our wrong-sized fingers out of the holes in the dike, because the right person is finally coming.

When I get off the phone, I put my face in my hands and begin sobbing so hard I can't catch my breath. I never understood until this moment how much the last year has weighed on me. Not that I would have missed it for anything on this earth. The experience has changed me utterly, all for the good. And there is an exhilaration in feeling necessary, in believing one's particular presence can make the difference between life and death.

Now I will no longer be necessary. And, to be entirely honest, I'm crying about that too—I'm crying *because* I'm no longer necessary. But when all is said and done, it is not my talent, it is Greg's. It is not my life, it is Greg's.

Sometimes the distinction became blurred.

A Friday night in mid-June. For the first time in almost exactly a year, Father Greg is walking through the parish. Women and girls run out of apartment doors to greet him, the father/husband/war hero finally returning home. In theory he's doing the Love Walk with the Comite Pro Paz mothers, but the endless hugging delays him and he falls farther and farther behind the official walkers.

In Pico Gardens, the mood surrounding Greg is shocking, as if someone had sprinkled the projects with glitter and sunflowers. Puma is ridiculously giddy, shooting off little Mexican skyrockets one after the other, with the cheerful abandon of a nine-year-old. Oscar, the light back on inside him, acts as if another, much happier person has suddenly taken over his body.

"I had a great talk with G," he whispers.

As the Love Walk passes down Clarence Street toward Aliso, Amelia, Blue's mom, and his girlfriend Gabby join the walk. In Aliso Village, Greg falls still farther behind, waylaid by ever more *abrazos* and kisses. Gabby lingers behind too.

"Let's just stay and watch G," she says. "Look at him. He's so happy."

It's hard to quantify the talent Greg has with this neighborhood—and it is a talent. One might compare it to playing the piano. Most anybody who isn't tone deaf can learn to play the piano passably well if they are willing to put in the time and effort. And you might say that for a year now we've been hearing these guys, the current Jesuit team, play passably well. I've even learned how to play the piano and flatter myself that I have a slight bit of talent for it. But all the while we keep remembering this other guy who used to play for us who was really gifted at the piano.

Then, one day, the good piano player comes back. And we realize that even in our memory, we had not adequately understood the difference between passable and brilliant, between somebody who can hit all the right notes and someone who is *meant* to play. When the good piano player plays, it doesn't even sound like the same music.

That's how it is this day with Father Greg. He is God's own piano player in the barrio.

It took until January of 1994 before Greg was returned to East Los Angeles for real. Despite the new Provincial's promise to "finesse" his return, politics again prevailed and the Jesuits took to waffling about where to assign their most celebrated priest. A Jesuit investigative committee was appointed, whose job it was to interview all related parties at Dolores Mission—parishioners and Jesuits alike— then come back with a recommendation for Greg's future.

Infuriated by the church's seeming disregard for the needs of a city deep in a terrible gang crisis, a group of L.A. community leaders requested a hearing with the Jesuits. Those present included Mary Ridgway; Dr. Brian Johnston, head of Emergency for White Memorial Hospital; Walter McKinney, representing Housing Police; a representative from the District Attorney's office; Jamie Corral, head Juvenile Court Justice; and Pam McDuffie, among others.

Their message was simple: We need Father Greg back, and this issue is never going to go away.

"I hardly believe that Greg can walk on water like all of you are implying," sniffed Jesuit representative Father Mike Mandela in reply. "But if you want him back so much, then *you* provide him with a position, a budget, and financial oversight."

"I see," said Mary Ridgway after the meeting. "Father Greg is for sale."

Two such proposals were on the Provincial's desk within a week— one from White Memorial Hospital, the other from the Housing Authority.

The final blow in the battle to return Greg to East L.A. was struck by the mothers. In mid-November, a contingent of Comite Pro Paz mothers plus community girls Joanna and Janet scheduled a meeting with the new Provincial. At the meeting, the women were strong and politic. "We are carrying on the gang work on our own," they said, "but for the good of our community we need the guidance that Father Greg is best suited to give us. We have worked for more than a year with the other Jesuits and we are not getting what we need from them. We know our community's needs better than anyone else knows them. This is our church. We speak with one voice. We hope you will support us."

When Father Tom and Father Pete, who had insisted upon being present at the meeting, quarreled openly with the mothers' views, the women politely but firmly asked the two Jesuits to leave the room.

"This is not a Committee for Peace!" hissed Father Pete to the mothers on his way out the door. "This is a Committee for War!"

Attempting to cover all bases, the women had already taken the precaution of contacting Cardinal Mahony's office in order to back the publicity-conscious cardinal into going on record saying he would personally have ". . . no objection to Father Greg Boyle returning to Los Angeles"—thereby throwing the decision entirely in the lap of the Jesuits.

The Jesuits cracked. Offered a face-saving way out of what was ballooning into a P.R. nightmare, the Society of Jesus went for a combination of both the Housing and the White Memorial proposals, and informed Father Greg he would be allowed to resume a limited gang ministry in East L.A. as of January.

On January second, Greg set up a tiny storefront office on First Street, four blocks from the church, and immediately started lining up jobs for homeboys.

At first, Greg was not allowed to work directly with Dolores Mission. But when it was discovered that Father Tom's financial management had pushed the Dolores Mission's social programs to the brink of bankruptcy, Greg's skill as a money raiser suddenly became irresistibly attractive to Tom's replacement. Before long, Greg was officially running the Jobs for a Future programs—including the much publicized Homeboy Bakery, where Joker and others now work daily baking gourmet breads to be delivered all over the city.

Some things have not changed. Greg still works too hard. He eats junk food. He doesn't exercise. He is forever bewailing the state of his finances. Money still leaves his hands as fast or faster than the rate at which it enters them.

And yet he is different than before. His love is tougher. He no longer cruises the streets at all hours preventing shootouts. He puts the preponderance of his time and effort into getting kids jobs, getting them into school, getting them out of the projects.

"The real work is no longer being done at 3:00 A.M.," he says.

In the end, Father Greg Boyle did not make peace in the barrio. What he did instead was profoundly change the life of every gang member he came in contact with. The change didn't come en masse; rather, it took place on an individual basis, kid by kid, soul by soul. But although he could change them, in the end he really couldn't save them.

"I can walk you right up to the door of manhood," Greg has taken to saying to kids lately, "but I can't walk you through it. I thought I could, but I can't. You have to walk through that door by yourself."

Not all were able to find the strength to walk through the door—and sometimes the loss feels unbearable.

However, others have come to understand the thing that every son must understand of a father—if the son is to achieve true adulthood—and what every good parent must face with humility: *Greg's job was never to save them. It was to love them.* Yet it is precisely because of that love that gradually many of Father Greg's homeboys have finally become strong enough to save themselves.

Epilogue

As I said at the beginning, it has been eighteen years since I first drove to Pico Aliso to meet Father Greg Boyle, and fourteen years since I wrote the last page of the book you hold in your hands. In that time, Greg's small, self-run jobs program, Jobs for a Future, has grown into Homeboy Industries, the largest and arguably the most successful gang rehabilitation program in the world. It celebrates its twentieth anniversary this year.

Now it's not just the projects gangs who come to see Greg for help. Homeboy office records indicate that 8,000 homeboys and homegirls from nearly half the city's approximately 1,100 gangs walked through the Homeboy Industries doors last year. Some came looking for a job. Others wanted to get their tattoos removed. All were looking for a way out.

Yet nearly everyone who comes wants to see Greg. Despite the fact that Homeboy has an excellent and well-liked staff, he is still the father figure, the touchstone, the One Who Matters.

———

I assumed that once I had finished the project, my life would return to something resembling normal and I would go back to reporting subjects that were less, shall we say, *violent*. In retrospect, I see that to suppose I could easily walk away from Greg and the Pico Aliso community was ridiculous. After four years in which I spent several days a week in the projects, the homeboys and homegirls who had begun as interview subjects were now kids whose well-being mattered a great deal to me. Community women like Pam McDuffie were no longer merely sources; they were close friends. And there were other, more complicated ties. In 1992, when Joanna and Silent were planning the baptism of their daughter, Beatriz, then not yet a year old, they asked me to be her godmother. At first I was unsure what to say. This was not, after all, the sort of close relationship journalists are supposed to have with their subjects. Moreover, saying *yes* meant that I would have a lifelong commitment to a little girl who had a gang member for a father and a teenage mother whose emotional life was anything but stable. I said yes anyway. I have never regretted the decision, and there have been two other godchildren after Beatriz. Each has brought me a different kind of blessing.

And so it has gone. In ways both ordinary and profound, an increasing number of the lives I'd been chronicling for four years have become intricately interwoven with mine.

There were also professional reasons that yanked me repeatedly back to Boyle Heights. Underneath everything, I am a writer, a journalist. There is an old joke: *How can you tell a writer? He (or she) is the one taking notes at his mother's funeral.* It is not much of an exaggeration. Few of us with writing in our bones can resist the pull of a great human story. I was magnetized by the compelling stories I continued to see unfolding around me in L.A.'s poorest neighborhoods, so I continued to write columns and features for magazines and newspapers about the East L.A. homeboys and homegirls—and their brothers, sisters, parents, and friends—whose struggles seemed to provide insight into many of the most urgent problems facing urban America.

Hence, as the years passed, I was able to observe as the dozens of young men and women whom I'd initially met as teenagers grew up and moved into adulthood. As they got older, most attempted—with greater or lesser degrees of success—to fashion new lives for themselves and their families away from the street world that had claimed their youth.

Homeboys and homegirls typically join gangs in the hormonal rush of their early teens, when the need for love, identity, peer acceptance, and, in many cases, physical protection from other teenagers are the most desperate and intense. Statistically, we know that many kids at the fringe, if they don't get caught up in the criminal justice system, will linger only a year or two. But even among those who become entrenched, most are looking for a door out by their midtwenties. So it was with the gang members of Pico Aliso. As the 1990s drew to a close, the adolescents whom I'd seen come of age during L.A.'s most extreme and deadly gang years fought to leave the street behind in the hope of finding some form of normalcy and stability.

Suspecting I was witnessing something important, I began to record the patterns of change I was observing, reasoning that if Pico Aliso had been the perfect laboratory for the study of street gangs, it was also the world's richest context in which to examine both the elements required for a young man or woman to transcend the social and emotional damage of the gang experience, and the obstacles that stood in his or her way. The more I observed, the more convinced I became that the new story worth telling had little to do with why kids join gangs—a topic I'd already explored in the book you've just finished reading. It seemed now of more urgent importance to begin to deconstruct, through observation and analysis, what it took for a kid to successfully leave gang life behind. There are approximately 90,000 gang members at any given month in Los Angeles County, more than 750,000 nationwide. Was there any formula, I wondered, that could reasonably be applied to help those homeboys and homegirls to get out? Thus, what began as a four-year anecdotal narrative about Father Greg and his work with gangs has turned into an eighteen-year examination of what it actually takes for a homeboy or homegirl to step away from gang activity permanently.

Not all were able to succeed in freeing themselves from the undertows of their gang past. Several young men I knew were killed in gang-related shootings before they could make the break, a few even after it seemed they'd gotten out safely. Some of the homeboys you've met in this book are now locked up for a very long time. Still others morphed into their absent fathers and disappeared into drugs, alcohol, or some equivalent chasms of despair. Yet after nearly two decades of tracking the same kids from adolescence into adulthood, when I tally up what I've seen, I am surprised that there are more names on the positive side of the ledger than there are on the tragic side. To be exact, out of the thirty homeboys and a couple of homegirls who are most prominently featured in the book, six are dead (among them the three you know about—Green Eyes, Oso, and Blue). Four are in prison. Two are employed intermittently but struggle with drug addiction and depression. Three have jobs and have left gang life behind, but have yet to acquire real stability. Yet fifteen of the thirty have retooled their lives at the core.

For those who did make it out, none of the changes occurred overnight. The transformation inevitably came in fits and starts, four steps forward, three and a half back, and each person's battle had its own singular character. Success was easier to predict for certain kids. With others, the transformation seemed so impossibly unlikely that when it occurred, it looked like a magic trick, a miracle. Yet when I laid out as a collective whole all of the stories of those who were—and were not—able to transcend gang life, some patterns begin to emerge.

The Magic of Employment

According to the most recent count, today in America there are three million young adults between the ages of fourteen and twenty-four who are neither in school nor working. If we fail to either educate or employ those kids, should we be surprised when they find activities that are not to our liking? Recovering from gang life—and from everything I've seen and from what Greg says repeatedly, it *is* a process of recovery and rehabilitation—requires that the gang member be able to perceive a new life he or she might reasonably walk *toward*, as he or she walks away from the street. It isn't enough to hector a kid about how he must move out of the darkness. We must offer him or her some light in exchange. And, initially, the form of "light" mostly likely to inspire a former homeboy or homegirl to believe that change is possible is a job.

Wizard and Ghost mostly seemed to require a real opportunity at the right moment, plus liberal doses of encouragement. Wizard's break came ten years ago in the form of a job opening at a company that produced a TV show called *Babylon 5*. Father Greg got him the initial interview, but Wizard grabbed his moment of good fortune and ran with it. "I really wanted out," he told me. "I was ready. I just needed somebody to trust that I could do it and give me a door that I could walk through."

Since that time, Wizard has moved ahead steadily in the hyper-competitive professional world of episodic television. After *Babylon 5* folded, he went to work for Wolf Films, the company that produces the various *Law and Order* TV series, making his way up the corporate ladder. He was the postproduction supervisor for all of Wolf's primetime shows until a few years ago when he was made coproducer of one of the company's flagship *Law and Order* series.

"Producing and directing is what I'm hoping to do eventually," Wizard says. In addition to his day job, he is working on a film script about growing up in the projects, and he has a smart proposal for a reality show that he's been shopping around town. (I've promised not to reveal the name or the concept, but if a reality series with the word "homeboy" in the title pops up on your local TV schedule next year, Wizard is likely behind it.) He has also found stability in his personal life. He has been married to the same woman for more than a decade, and they have three kids together, whom he clearly adores. His two older kids live in Texas with their mother, Wizard's ex-girlfriend. After some quarrels in the early years, both parents have agreed that Wizard will stay very much involved with the kids' lives.

Wizard and I have talked frequently about how he made the leap from smart but troubled homeboy to devoted dad and aspiring producer. "Obviously, it takes some people caring about you," he said. "But unfortunately, when people are as messed up as Ghost and I were, the caring can't be short-term. That's why a lot of gang intervention doesn't work. Real caring requires commitment," he says. "And most people don't really want to commit that kind of time to a gang member. Fortunately for people like me, Father Greg and some of the people around him *were* really committed."

Of course, part of that commitment must come from the larger community in the form of employment. "Nothing Stops a Bullet Like a Job" is Greg's catchy motto for Homeboy Industries. And in the general sense it seemed to hold true. Over the years, I saw scores of instances in which a job gave a kid the strength to walk away from disaster.

Wizard told me that his own critical moment came in late February 1998, when he got a middle-of-the-night telephone call informing him that one of his closest friends, who had also been a Clarence Street Locos homeboy, had been beaten terribly in a gang-related incident and was now at White Memorial Hospital being kept nominally alive by machines. By then Wizard had been at *Babylon 5* for some time. But when the friend was taken off life support two days later, Wizard's grief and rage pulled him toward the old life with a frightening force. Fortunately, he chose the future, not the past. "Having that job made all the difference," Wizard said. "It meant I had somewhere else to go, with people who liked me and knew I was really worth something."

Ghost, Wizard's longtime best friend, got his start when Father Greg recommended him for a program called Streetlights, a nonprofit that trains at-risk young men and women to be production assistants, then tries to find them entry-level work with companies making feature films, television, and commercials. Ghost worked for more than a decade as a production assistant on films such as *The Nutty Professor*, *Liar, Liar*, *Big Fish*, and *The Princess Diaries*. In the last few years he's begun working as a second AD (assistant director) on a whole new string of projects such as the enormously popular *Bruce Almighty* and *Evan Almighty*, and the latest version of *The Fast and the Furious*. Five years ago, the film work allowed Ghost to buy a house. "At first it was scary to make the commitment," he said. "But now I'm Mr. Happy Homeowner. I mean, they know me by name at Home Depot!" He has also settled down with his longtime girlfriend, with whom he has a son, and is stepfather to her daughter. When we talk about the elements that have made his success possible, Ghost repeats the familiar mantra: "All I needed way back when was for someone to give me a chance to show what I could do."

Give a kid an opportunity. It seems like such a simple concept: we are supposed to be nation that believes in second chances. But in fact the majority of employers are extremely reluctant to hire former gang members, especially if they have run afoul of the law. Five years ago, Turtle was recruited for a great new job with a major oil and gas company. (He had already been working in the oil and gas industry for the past several years.) The new company courted Turtle strenuously, but then, a few days after a job offer was made and accepted, a background check revealed that Turtle had a 1996 misdemeanor conviction on his record. The personnel office got a bad case of cold feet. It took a stack of letters and phone calls from people like me, Father Greg, and probation officer Mary Ridgway to calm these corporate jitters. Now, mind you, we're talking about an eight-year-old, nonviolent, non-drug-related *misdemeanor* here. If a former homeboy has a *felony* on his record, it gets about a thousand times harder.

Puma, Cuatro Flats's surly former shot-caller, is an interesting case in point. It took Puma several years to find his way out of the anger of his gang years, a process that included a stint in prison. But upon his release, Puma seemed to have acquired a clarity and sense of direction that nothing could derail. Fast forward: Puma is now happily married to his longtime girlfriend, with three kids who appear to be the light of his life, and a job he loves working for a large multinational car company. "I'm part of the emissions lab team," he says. "We're the last stop in the production line. It's a really great job."

In a lot of ways, Puma says, it's his past that indirectly gave him the strength to succeed. "I know what I've been through, what I've done, but I got out of it," he says. "The way I feel, if I could make the changes I've made, I can do *anything*."

There is, however, a small twist to Puma's story. Although his corporate bosses are crazy about him, they know nothing of his prison past. If they did, would they ever have hired him? "Probably not," he says. Yet, they *didn't* know, and they *did* hire him. As with Turtle, they recruited him from another company because his performance there was outstanding.

"Serving time in prison is the most stigmatizing thing there is in terms of getting a job," says Joan Petersilia, professor of criminology and consultant to the U.S. Department of Justice. "Nationally, 65 percent of employers say they won't hire someone with a criminal record. Most landlords say they won't rent to someone with a record. And if they've committed a drug crime, they can never again get public assistance or live in public housing. The barriers are incredible."[1]

When Is a Job Like a Family?

The two areas of work in which the Pico Aliso homeboys have most often found success are entry-level jobs in the entertainment business and apprenticeship positions in the building-trade unions. This may be due, in part, to the fact that tattoos and other evidences of a checkered past are more easily tolerated on a movie set or a construction crew than elsewhere. But I suspect there are also deeper reasons. Unlike a job unloading boxes in a warehouse, even the lowest entry-level position in TV, film, or radio doesn't seem like a dead-end to a smart, industrious homeboy. If he lands a minimum-wage job in the entertainment business, he can legitimately allow himself to dream bigger dreams. This is similarly true of a job in one of the trade unions, which has discernable benchmarks that, if met, allow a man or woman to move up the ladder of responsibility and salary to a satisfying and profitable lifelong career.

Then, too, both professions allow one to feel a sense of discernable accomplishment. Homeboys who've spent a lifetime believing that they have only a negative effect on their community tell me that they love coming home at the end of each day satisfyingly tired but knowing that so many feet of pipe have been laid or so much drywall is now in place. "You feel like you've, you know, done something that matters," said a former East L.A. Dukes gangster who has been working on the East L.A. extension of L.A.'s metro system. The same is true in the entertainment business where, at the end of the day, video footage has been shot that will eventually become a TV episode, a movie, or a commercial. No matter how lowly their position, the former homeboy or homegirl can feel they had a part in it.

It also helps that a job in either production or union construction means that a worker is part of a team—in other words, a surrogate family. If a gang is a harmful form of family replacement, a production or union job is its positive analogue.

Perhaps for all of these reasons, Romeo and Midget each thrived in staff jobs with Power 106, L.A.'s monster hip-hop radio station:

Romeo is now a "board operator" in charge of coordinating music and commercials on late-night shows; Midget worked his way up the ladder in advertising sales and programming before leaving the station for a new and promising job. "You know me, I wasn't exactly a very trusting person," said Midget. "But the people at Power were nice, right from the beginning, giving me a real opportunity to learn. And I'm still learning daily. Honestly, what could be better than that?"

The Landscape of Change

Why one person succeeds and another doesn't has been a topic of research and philosophical argument for centuries. For most of the past twenty years, social scientists primarily measured *risk factors* to predict whether an individual was likely to overcome a bad past. More recently, however, researchers have discovered that, in determining the probability of recovery for any population—abused children, drug addicts, parolees, or gang members—it's far more effective to examine *protective* factors. This glass-half-full approach to recovery and recidivism is known as "resilience" research or "resiliency" theory.

"In simplest terms," said Nan Henderson, author of *Resiliency In Action: Practical Ideas for Overcoming Risks and Building Strengths in Youth, Families and Communities,* "there are six basic human needs, which are also the main factors that build resiliency: caring and support; high expectation for success; opportunities for meaningful participation; positive bonds; clear and consistent boundaries; and good life skills. If people don't get these needs met in a pro-social way, they'll get them in an anti-social way—like in a gang. For a kid to find the strength to move out of the gang, these needs have to be met in a healthy way."

Dr. Edith H. Grotberg, psychologist and lecturer at George Washington University School of Public Health and internationally known for her research on resilience, puts it another way. "People need to be taught to assess the bumps in the road and know how to deal with them," she says. "A few years ago, the government started putting money into research in this area, because they finally realized that *resiliency* is something we can teach. And when it isn't learned either in the family or elsewhere, it requires that the larger community step in. Otherwise we've got trouble."

In basic terms, resilience theory suggests that a successful life is best achieved by *adding* to the good, protective, and generative elements in a person's existence instead of only attempting to *subtract* the negative or risky elements. In other words, if you want to help someone heal and get ahead, don't spend all your efforts trying to control the downside; emphasize the positive, and the negative may dissipate of its own accord. Unfortunately, most public policy still clings unproductively to the idea of trying to eliminate risk. This strategy is evident in American prisons, which, since the mid-1980s, have been designed to punish rather than rehabilitate. A similar pattern exists in the nation's probation and parole programs, in which overburdened parole officers can offer little concrete help to those on their enormous caseloads and so are mostly forced to monitor for mistakes. The result is a shockingly high U.S. recidivism rate: 70 percent of all those paroled are expected to be locked up again within three years. In California, two-thirds of the men and women who reenter prison have not committed new crimes but are returned for a technical violation of parole.

Although Greg arrived at his methods through instinct and experience rather than research, the tenets of resilience theory are nearly identical to the principles that the priest has practiced for a long time, at first on his own, now on a larger scale with Homeboy Industries. Yet even his thinking on the subject has evolved. "I used to say that the *caring adult who pays attention* is the most important factor to help a kid succeed," he says. "But I've now come to believe that the necessary context for that attention is community—meaning a place that reminds you of your goodness and your talent each day. That's what I think we do here at Homeboy. We provide a place of 'no-matter-what-ness,' a place of unconditional love. Ideally it's not just a person who offers that, it's a community of feeling and connection and kinship that becomes a touchstone that you can return to when you hit life's inevitable difficulties. It's community that helps a kid discover the truth of who he is, in order that he can inhabit that truth. That's the kid who will be able to withstand the obstacles life throws at him and be okay."

Dr. Jorja Leap, adjunct professor of social welfare at UCLA's School of Public Affairs and advisor on gangs and youth violence for the National Institute of Justice and for L.A. Sheriff Lee Baca, puts it in more clinical terms. "One of the most important factors in gang recovery is the opportunity for community involvement and attachment," Leap says. "That's something that Homeboy Industries provides better than any other program I've seen."

Tracking the Girls

When I began my research into gang life, like most journalists and academics, I mainly focused on the guys in and around the gang world since they were the ones whose actions were wreaking so much havoc. It was only after I finished writing *G-Dog and the Homeboys* that I turned my attention to the girls. While a certain small percentage of the girls caught up in the gang milieu were officially "courted in" to the gangs, and others functioned like a women's auxiliary, most were never gang members themselves. They were the girlfriends, the ones who had babies by homeboys, and, in too many cases, were batted around by the same young men who swore they'd never behave like their fathers but did. These girls were the ones left to care for the babies when the homeboys got arrested. On weekends, it was the girls who waited in line for three or four hours at the L.A. County Men's Central Jail to see their respective guys for the fifteen-minute visit the county allowed. Then, if their guy got killed or convicted or simply disappeared, it was the girls who bit the bullet and raised the kids alone.

Watching such young women as they grow up is like watching a high-wire act in which getting across the wire to safety often seems all but impossible. Astonishingly, as with the homeboys, more of them made it than not.

Joanna is an example. She was, if you remember, a teenage mother who dropped out of school when she got pregnant. Her own father was a gentle man but strung out on drugs. Her boyfriend, Silent, loved her, but also hit her. When Silent was accused of murder, Joanna did her best to visit him and otherwise support him emotionally—meanwhile taking care of their daughter, who was by then a toddler.

In any other milieu, Joanna would have been a standout. Like Wizard and Ghost, she is loaded with natural gifts—talent, intelligence, a winning personality, plus honest-to-goodness, heart-stopping beauty. Yet in the first years after her daughter Beatriz was born, she was barely treading water.

After Silent was convicted, Joanna eventually got herself a part-time job working at the Homeboy Tortilleria, one of Father Greg's earliest Homeboy ventures. When she and Silent finally split, Joanna hooked up with another former homeboy, a guy from Cuatro Flats named Luis Royo. Joanna and Luis married and have three kids, including Beatriz, whom Luis has informally adopted. Luis makes a good living driving trucks for United Rentals, while Joanna has built an impressive career as a production coordinator for big, national TV commercials. (If you watch television at all, you've seen spots featuring her work for companies like Budweiser, AOL, Chevrolet Silverado, and Mercedes Benz.)

They bought a home together a few years ago, but last year, like many American couples, they got a divorce. Yet I have watched them both struggle to ensure that their kids' well-being comes first. Two weeks ago, Luis and Joanna threw a Sweet Sixteen party for Beatriz, now a lovely, bright young woman with detailed plans for college and an interest in becoming an actress. As I snapped photos of my goddaughter—first hugging her mother and then leaning affectionately against her beaming, teary stepfather, Luis—I realized that this girl with the good grades, the fresh-faced friends, the loving parents, and the shiny future was at that moment almost exactly the age that her mother was on the day I drove Joanna to the hospital—gasping from labor pains—to deliver her daughter.

So what got once-suicidal Joanna from there to here? Like Wizard, she says that an offer of employment with real potential brought with it an essential shift in self-perception. "When I got my very first job in production," she says, "it showed me that a whole other life was possible. Before that, I honestly didn't know. I didn't have the experience of going past the boundaries I grew up with. Now when I go back to the projects and I see some of the guys and women my age still stuck in the same old life, I want to scream at them: 'Look, you have two arms, and two legs. Get up and do something!' But I also realize, if you don't have the opportunity and the support, you don't really know there's a whole other world out there. Father Greg, and my mom, and people like that told me I could go for it. Otherwise, even if you get a little look at another kind of life, you don't have any way of believing that you can be a part of that world."

To emphasize the point, Joanna tells a story about another young projects woman whom we both know. I'll call her Stella. Not too long ago, Joanna hired Stella to work as an assistant on one of her commercial shoots. Stella was shy at first, but she ultimately did fine, says Joanna. "Then when it was over, she went home and had what you might call a nervous breakdown. She's okay now. But seeing that big world that she'd missed all her life, that she couldn't believe would really accept her . . . it completely freaked her out."

This turns out to be a common pattern. A young man or woman would find their initial plunge into the mainstream so shockingly foreign that, in the beginning, they'd often fall apart or find some way to fail—just to relieve the pressure. When a rare employer was able to recognize the meltdown for what it was and move into a mentoring role, most kids seemed to eventually right themselves and find their stride.

"People elsewhere in our society really don't understand what a lot of our kids face," says civil rights attorney Connie Rice. "Unless they've been through it, most people honestly don't get it."

Though a remarkable number of homeboys managed to cross that psychological Rubicon, it often took them a while. Oscar from Cuatro, and Wolf, Drifter, and Joker from TMC, once stubbornly and dangerously stuck in the gang ethos, are all four responsible working-men who delight in talking about their kids. Thumper from Cuatro (the guy with the scarily bullet-parted hair) has also long been a working family man. Champ from Cuatro was decidedly wobbly when he first got out of prison a few years ago, but is now working at the recently reopened Homeboy Bakery and has just thrown a *quinceañera* for his daughter. The Twin, once one of the primary troublemakers for the East L.A. Dukes, now mans the reception desk at the Homeboy Industries office with a calm, almost Zen-like presence, and helps gangsters from all over the city—many of them once his enemies—to find employment. (His future goal, he told me the other day, is to go back to school and become a counselor.) Largo, the enormous gangster who briefly stepped into the leadership breach for

Cuatro after Oso's death, is now a gentle and devoted family man making twenty bucks an hour plus overtime putting in various construction-union jobs for the City of Los Angeles. Several years ago he began studying to become a Christian pastor. "It's my real calling," Largo says.

The Wounds of Family

On numerous occasions Spanky revealed to Father Greg and to me the ways his mother had been abusive during his childhood, yet the conversation always discomforted him. As a consequence, I didn't learn the real extent of the abuse until long after the book was published. The memories were too painful, too humiliating, so he kept them hidden even from those who care about him. As it turns out, Spanky's mom didn't just whack him with belts and electrical cords. When she was angriest, she burned his skin with cigarettes or, in a homegrown version of "waterboarding," held his head in the toilet and flushed it repeatedly until he was on the verge of drowning. During the worst of the physical abuse, the mother would scream that the little boy was just like his father, whose face his must have resembled.

Spanky's situation is emblematic of the homeboys for whom the prior wounds of life are so deep, the sense of self so damaged, that some more elementary kind of psychological healing has to be addressed before any consistent forward progress can be made. Cisco, Happy, and Shadow also all came from extravagantly dysfunctional families where abuse and/or neglect were big factors. For them and others like them, depression has been a lurking presence, like a malevolent dragon waiting in the weeds as they painstakingly made their way down the road to success and well-being.

As I mentioned earlier, close to one-third of the kids living in America's most violent urban neighborhoods have posttraumatic stress disorder—nearly twice the rate reported for troops returning from war zones in Iraq. In 2000 officials from the Los Angeles Unified School District wanted to know if the students in their urban schools were suffering from PTSD at the rate that the national research suggested, so they collaborated with the RAND Corporation and with researchers at UCLA Health Services to produce a study. Of one thousand students randomly selected, 90 percent had been victims of or witnesses to community violence and between 27 and 34 percent were suffering from PTSD.[2] In 2004 the researchers completed a more extensive study, this time using forty-eight thousand middle school kids. The results were every bit as bad.[3]

Experts say that in kids, PTSD can resemble attention deficit disorder. Adolescents with PTSD will have trouble concentrating and will appear emotionally withdrawn. They can become depressed, angry, distrustful, fearful, and alienated, and they may feel betrayed. Many do not feel they have a future or believe they will reach adulthood. "This is especially common among adolescents who are chronically exposed to community violence," i.e., gang members and those living in gang areas.[4]

If a third of L.A.'s inner-city school kids have PTSD, what does that say about dropout former gangsters like Spanky, who has been severely abused, seen friends shot in front of him, shot at people, and been shot and badly wounded himself?

Amazingly, Spanky grew up to be man with a great sense of humor and an enormous heart. Yet there were also some colossal emotional scars that seemed always to get in the way of anything he tried to build for himself. He would do very well on a job for months or a year, then a bout of despair would make it difficult for him to get out of bed for days. After a particularly paralyzing period a few years ago, Father Greg and some others at Homeboy Industries persuaded Spanky to be evaluated by doctors at UCLA's Neuropsychiatric Institute. The NPI doctors quickly diagnosed Spanky as suffering from a significant case of clinical depression.

In the first months after he got the news, Spanky found the diagnosis a revelation. "I always thought there was something really wrong with me," he says, "like I was weak or something. So I was scared to tell people how I was really feeling. Now I guess you could say I've been depressed all my life. But, the way I look at it, is now that I know what it is, I can do something about it. That really freed up my mind like you couldn't believe. I feel like the biggest rocks in the world have been taken off my back."

Yet the emotional reprieve was short-lived. For a while Spanky saw a therapist who was donating hours to Homeboy, but he stopped after a few months and, without any kind of treatment, the depression returned. At times Spanky battled it; other times he self-medicated. Soon he was back to the pattern of getting but not keeping jobs. "I love the guy," said Wizard, "and Ghost even got him a job on a movie. But then he started showing up late, which you can't do on a set. So Ghost had to let him go. I remember when we were kids and he lived at our house for a while because he couldn't stay with his mother. Even then he never wanted to admit how bad things were."

Mental health is the unacknowledged elephant in the living room in the world of gang intervention. First the trauma of an abusive or neglectful family withers a kid's hopes and aspirations. (In addition to the garden-variety abuse, we have begun to see evidence that a significant percentage of male gang members were also sexually abused as children.) Then posttraumatic stress produced by life on the street increases the damage exponentially. Yet, once again, there is very little in the way of public policy that seems to recognize and address these facts at all.

As a culture, we have finally come to acknowledge the psychological harm suffered by military men and women who return from combat. But we are blind when it comes to understanding that the very same harm has come to adolescents growing up in America's urban war zones. It is as though we believe gang membership or even proximity to gangs has rendered these young of the streets unworthy of our consideration.

To see the effect of the one-two punch of childhood neglect and exposure to street violence, one need look no further than Turtle. Smart, outgoing Turtle is doing extremely well now. Yet when I spoke with him on the phone while I was working on this new edition of the book, he again reminded me that his future was once nearly extinguished by demons from his past. The crisis occurred in the mid-1990s, around six months after Greg's return, when Turtle decided that the only way to escape the magnetic pull of the street was to leave Pico Aliso altogether. He moved with his girlfriend, Liliana, to a California desert community near the Salton Sea. For a while, the strategy worked fine. He and Liliana both found jobs, and though their financial situation was tenuous, they appeared to be making their way slowly toward a cautious stability. But the psychological wounds of Turtle's gang years turned out to be much harder to shake than gang life itself. He began having regular nightmares. Even in his waking hours, a vicious malaise over the deaths of Blue, Green Eyes, and others crept over him like a malign fog. Soon he was drinking, and he and Liliana started fighting. Eventually Turtle began to talk about killing himself. Finally, one afternoon when Liliana was back in Los Angeles visiting her mother, he left chilling "Good-bye, I'm sorry," messages for all those he was close to—including me and Father Greg. The situation was made even more frightening by the fact that those of us who might have had a shot at wrenching him back from the brink were 125 miles away by car—too far to get there in time if Turtle really made a suicide attempt.

Unsure how else to proceed, Greg and I called the local police and asked them to pick Turtle up. But when the officers arrived at his apartment, an articulate Turtle assured the cops he would never dream of hurting himself. An hour or so later, he called Greg from a pay phone and, sobbing wildly, told the priest he was so, so sorry, but he was truly going to kill himself this time, and there was nothing anybody could do about it.

For nearly an hour, Father Greg used every trick he knew to keep Turtle on the phone while, on another line, I tried to persuade a police dispatch operator that, no matter what Turtle might say to a new team of officers, if they didn't transport him—by force if necessary—to the nearest hospital on a seventy-two-hour psych hold, a wonderful young man would be dead by morning. At first the police were reluctant, figuring that we were overreacting. Finally, the woman dispatcher took my pleading seriously, pushed her cards and her job to the center of the table, and made the cops take Turtle to the hospital.

At the time, he was outraged. But multiple times in the last decade Turtle told Greg and me individually that the hospitalization saved his life. It was also a turning point, he said—in part because, unlike Spanky and Happy, Turtle got a modicum of professional help in facing his demons.

Now he and Liliana are married with three children. (Their eldest, a girl, has just turned fourteen.) The couple has purchased their first house, a small but pretty ranch-style home with a big backyard pool for the kids. Four years ago, Turtle told me that his next career goal was to move up the professional ladder into management at the multinational oil and gas company where he works. Now as a fleet manager he oversees forty-three drivers. "It's my job to make sure that all my guys are happy," he said, "that their morale is good, that they get where they're going safely. I love it! And I seem to be pretty good at it."

Once insecure about his ability to succeed in a corporate world, he has grown confident that he will continue to ascend into higher management. Yet Turtle also strives for balance, and makes sure to allocate time to be around his kids. "You know, to go to their games and things. My dad didn't get to do none of that stuff. But it keeps me young."

"Life is great," he told me. "Once you get out of the little world of the projects and see what life is really about, it's awesome. But you have to get out of the gang world. You have to leave. Otherwise, you can just go to the store and get caught up in something, because the street life don't ever let you go."

A few years ago Turtle was visiting Liliana's family in East L.A. and decided to drive over to Resurrection Cemetery to visit Blue. "While I was there I saw so many people—you know, Green Eyes, Oso, and . . ." He named off a string of homeboys buried at Resurrection. I asked him if the cemetery depressed him. "No," he answered slowly. "It was good for me. Because I know if I didn't get the help that I did, I'd be there. I wouldn't be locked up. I'd be dead. I don't think that. I know it."

Turtle's close friend, Youngster, was blown around by similar emotional hurricanes and feels that a strong dose of religion helped to heal the old griefs that otherwise might have killed him. Ten years ago, Youngster married Turtle's wife's sister, Linda Lee, but they have since divorced. Now he works as a long-distance truck driver while he tries to save money to start his own trucking company.

"Father Greg helped me make the break from the neighborhood," he says. Yet it was his involvement with a local Christian church that provided him with an embracing community of support. "And counseling," he says. "They do counseling at my church, and that really helps me when I start to feel . . . you know . . . bad. I see so many people that I grew up with who needed something like that, you know? They needed a lot more help, but never got it."

Cisco is one who fell into this category. He probably stopped gang banging first of any of the homeboys I'd gotten to know. Drinking was Cisco's primary challenge. Abused as a child, shot seven times as a teenager, most of his best friends dead, Cisco was a gentle, humorous man beset by ghosts. He silenced them as his father before him had silenced whatever bad angels had plagued him and made him beat his wife and kids. Drinking killed Cisco's dad. And like his dad, Cisco was in and out of various forms of employment. When Cisco was sober, he was a skillful worker and very well liked on the job. But as the years passed, the sober periods were fewer and fewer. Finally, in the fall of 2003, Cisco was found in the street, dead of a drug and alcohol overdose.

With some homeboys, the wounds don't result in physical death, but seem to trigger cycles of defeat that, uninterrupted, continue to repeat. Player appears to have the personality, intelligence, wit, and good looks to succeed. But his drug-addict mother, incarcerated and drug-addicted father, and abusive foster mother left him with a lousy sense of self. Player tends to do fine for a while, then to lose heart and self-destruct. The implosion usually involves drugs. As a result, he's been cycling through the revolving prison door on minor charges for the past fifteen years. A few months ago, he was sentenced to another four years in prison for charges stemming from a stash of drugs belonging to a housemate. (It hardly needs to be said that it is unwise for a man with drug crimes on his record to share living quarters with a drug dealer, small-time or otherwise.) Player's girlfriend, a likeable woman with her own problem past, told me that she will give him one more chance, but that's the end of it. "My kids love him," she told me, "and he swears he'll do whatever it takes not to lose me, that he'll stop doing drugs . . ." She paused. "Leaving him would be hard for me," she said. "But I'll do it."

Happy is another for whom the wounds of family, or of a *lack* of family, seemed persistently to be his undoing. Once Mary Ridgway's favorite, Happy has been on and off drugs, in and out of prison, since 1995. Each time he'd come out he'd call me loaded with hope and good intentions. Six months or eight months later I'd get collect calls from a new correctional institution.

As I write this, Happy is out again and working at Homeboy. He looks good and seems sadder, wiser, and, in a subtle way, stronger than before. He told me that this time he'll stay out and not violate his parole, not start chipping away at crystal meth, not fail—for reasons he can never adequately explain—to report to his parole officer. He has developed some impressive skills as a tattoo artist, which is how, he said, he would like to make his living. "I'm working to develop a style that's my own, that you can recognize," he said. "Some people say I'm there, but I know I've got a long way to go." Eventually Happy wants a tattoo shop of his own.

When I asked what he thinks will keep him from getting locked up again, he paused for a long time. "I'm tired," he said. "I'm fed up. I don't want to keep going to jail. I'm tired of disappointing people, disappointing myself. I want a future."

Four steps forward, three and a half back. Both Greg and I are cautiously hopeful that the bright, handsome, charming, undeniably wounded Happy will hold on to his potential this time. In the gang recovery business, you take progress whenever and however you find it.

Bad Judgment, Bad Luck, and Bad Law

Sometimes the difference between the desperate kid who makes it out of a violent childhood to a thriving, happy adulthood and the one who doesn't is luck, plain and simple. When it comes to former gang members, often the luck—good or bad—has to do with the law.

Dreamer's bad luck came in the form of an immigration statute. He was brought to the United States by his parents when he was four years old, and although he was born in Mexico, he never thought of himself as anything else but American. As the years passed, Dreamer and his parents did manage to become legal U.S. residents.

At nineteen, Dreamer was arrested for a gang-related felony. (A gun was fired. No one was hit or hurt.) As is usually the case, his public defender advised him to take a deal, and Dreamer complied. He was sentenced to five years. His attorney assured him there would be no adverse immigration consequences.

Dreamer served his sentence without complaint and was, by all accounts, a model prisoner. He read more books than he'd ever read during his years in school and got whatever job training the facility offered. As his release day approached in late 1998, he made plans to begin his life over far away from the projects and the world of gangs. His mother, dad, and sister had relocated to Tulsa, Oklahoma, and told him that they'd help him start clean. Despite his dad's previous rejection and verbal abuse the man seemed to be making a genuine gesture, and Dreamer gratefully accepted the offer. But when his release date finally arrived, Dreamer was told that the law had changed while he was locked up. In 1996, a statute known as the Illegal Immigration Reform and Immigrant Responsibility Act was passed by Congress. One of its provisions dictated that if a noncitizen immigrant committed a crime, even if a permanent legal resident, he or she was to be tossed out of the country. So under the new law, Dreamer's felony conviction retroactively earned him an automatic one-way deportation ticket to Mexico.

Dreamer knew no one at all in Mexico except some distant relatives who had zero interest in helping him. Undone at the prospect, Dreamer attempted to appeal his case. For months, he pored over law books, then attempted to represent himself in court. Although the judge complimented him warmly on his presentation, he also said there was little he could do and ordered Dreamer deported. He was deposited just across the Arizona-Mexico border without benefit of even the $200 gate money accorded every other prisoner released from incarceration in the state of California.

For a month, Dreamer got by the best he could until his mother wired him the money for a bus ticket. He swam the Rio Grande at Reynosa to McAllen, Texas, then took a Greyhound to Tulsa.

The next three years were the happiest of Dreamer's life. In short order, he found good work as a carpenter, fell in love, had a kid, and had a second on the way. Dreamer was making plans to get married and baptize his two babies when a freak contact with law enforcement brought him to the attention of the INS. Once again, Dreamer was deported.

Miserable away from his children, Dreamer eventually made the crossing again, this time through the Arizona desert. Back in Tulsa, he thrived as a father and worker, gradually building up a house-framing business with his legal resident brother. But the worry about being discovered ate away at him. (If he was caught for being in the United States after deportation, he could have faced a prison sentence of between five and twenty years.) "It's the little things that get to you," he said. "Like my son loves softball, and I do too, and they asked me to coach his Little League team." But coaching Little League required that the coach show some sort of valid identification, like a driver's license, which Dreamer didn't have. "So I had to turn them down," he said.

Dreamer talked to immigration attorneys in the hope of somehow remedying his legal situation, but everyone told him they could do nothing. Eventually the worry-born stress made Dreamer physically ill and he decided there was no rational choice but to leave for Mexico where he would try to earn enough money to eventually bring his family to live with him. When we last spoke, he was living on subsistence wages as a part-time taxi driver in Monterey and grieving for his absent family. "My kids need a dad," he said miserably. "I hope sometime soon they'll have one."

Silent's bad luck was also legal in nature. In his case, it was a public defender who didn't give a damn. In July 1994 Silent was tried for a murder that he did not commit. (I can say this with certainty because I know who *did* it. Everyone in the projects does.)

Although several people could definitively place him elsewhere on the night of the crime, Silent's uninterested public defender never called a single alibi witness. Worse, the public defender failed to deliver closing arguments. After the DA rested his case, so did the lawyer, without an additional word in Silent's defense. And so, the same week that O. J. Simpson assembled his multimillion-dollar legal team, Silent was convicted of first-degree murder and sentenced to life without possibility of parole in a level 4, maximum-security prison, where he has remained for the past fifteen years.

Rebel's situation was a combination of bad judgment *and* bad luck. After he was convicted of two counts of assault with a deadly weapon, Rebel served four and a half years in the California State Prison at Norco. In March of 1996 he was paroled at age twenty-five with $200 in his pocket, no material assets, and no job prospects. What he did have was an eight-year-old daughter whom he adored and a ferocious determination to yank himself from the wreckage of his history to become a good father and a good man.

For a time, it appeared he had done exactly that. In his first months out, Rebel landed an entry-level job in the movie business, then, over the next few years, worked so diligently that he attracted the attention of some influential Hollywood veterans. By the fall of 1998 he'd set a goal of becoming a cameraman, gained a famous cinematographer as a mentor, and put in nearly enough hours as an assistant to qualify for Local 600, the cinematographers guild. This meant a big bump in earnings and a considerable boost up the professional ladder. Rebel moved into his own apartment, began taking courses in cinematography, and went to court to gain joint custody of his daughter. At the end of December 2000 Rebel was an extraordinary success story by any standard.

Then on March 31, 2001, after a big argument with his girlfriend, Rebel went to a downtown nightclub with a friend, a fight broke out, and Rebel and the friend decided to leave. Outside, a group of the fighters were still looking for trouble. They jumped Rebel and his companion, smashing a bottle over Rebel's head, cutting him severely. Bleeding and outnumbered, Rebel panicked and, using the younger friend's gun, applied lethal force of his own in the form of seven bullets. By night's end a man lay bleeding to death on the pavement. A week later, police came looking for Rebel with a murder warrant.

Five witnesses, including the dead man's companions, described Rebel's actions as a deadly overreaction—meaning he would likely face a manslaughter conviction. But a sixth witness, a local basehead, described an entirely different scene in which Rebel deliberately plotted to kill the victim. An ambitious prosecutor based her case around witness number six and pushed for murder. Although the prosecution had access to all the witness statements, the jury did not. Thus on February 27, 2004, Rebel was convicted of first-degree murder. He is now serving a 126-year sentence at Pelican Bay State Prison. With the help of small donations from his still-supportive movie business friends, he is paying a jailhouse lawyer—another inmate with some legal skills—to help him file an appeal before his time to do so runs out in the summer of 2008.

"I'll play that night [in the nightclub] over and over in my mind until the day I die," Rebel told me the phone during one of his once-a-month collect calls. "Seeing what I could have done, what I should have done. But I can't change it. So I try to be optimistic that one day I might get a chance to get out and make up for the things I can't take back. I accept responsibility. Nobody did what I did but me. But I believe I'm a good man. I try to be. I see so many things I've done wrong. But I think my heart is more open now."

As the days and years pass, Rebel grabs for any opportunity to improve himself, although at a high-security facility like Pelican Bay State Prison the chances are few and far between. Since he arrived in 2004, he has put in numerous job requests asking to do any kind of work the facility might offer. "I told 'em I'd do anything they got," he said. He was always turned down. But the last time Rebel called, he told me a job had finally come through. "I'm cutting hair!" he said. "And I'm good at it!" Such victories are small, but Rebel holds to them tightly. "Look, I know where I am. This is prison. It is what it is. But I'm trying to make the best of it. What else can I do?"

The Physics of Change

If there's one thing I've learned in the past nearly two decades, it is to never, ever give up on a kid. Multiple times I've run into a homeboy or homegirl whom I've not seen in a while and had all but written off only to find that they have somehow managed to take hold of a deeper, truer part of themselves and have morphed into respectable working men and soccer dads. When, at my request, they explain the specifics of their individual psychological journeys from gangster to suburban dad (or mom), they never fail to stun me with their courage. Redemption may not be easy, but it is possible—probable even.

In 1994, when I finished *G-Dog and the Homeboys*, some of my friends asked me why I continued to go down to Pico Aliso. "It's so depressing," they said.

"I go there for the hope," I told them. What I meant was, I go there because young men and women like Wizard . . . Turtle . . . Joanna . . . Largo . . . The Twin . . . Puma . . . demonstrate to me over and over that there's so much more hope in the world than the nightly news and our own pessimism would have us believe.

I've also learned from my years of observation, that hope, unlike despair, doesn't grow in isolation—unless it's foolish hope. For hope to come to fruition, it requires active and ferocious participation, not only in your own life, but in the lives of those around you. As Greg puts it, we have to act as if we belong to each other. This is, by the way, a practical dictum, not a romantic one. For a social structure to work, be it a family, a community, a town, a tribe, a county, a state, a nation, everybody has to show up and get busy.

The opportunities for involvement are infinite and varied. Mentor somebody. Give a homeboy or an ex-felon a job. Teach a class at the local juvenile hall. Tell your senators and legislators that we need less money for incarceration, and more money for job programs, counseling, improved urban schools, and community-based diversion and reentry programs that kick in when kids break the law. Explain that our prisons must become adult education centers and mental health clinics, not merely temples of punishment. Gang strategies should be chosen, not because of political pressure, but because they are "evidence-based," in other words, because they've been tested and proven to work. Remind lawmakers that all the money for programs need not come out of pocket. Give tax breaks to companies that hire felons or at-risk youth. Reduce tuition for college students who sign up for a year's mentoring work after graduation. All hands on deck. We can no longer afford to talk about what *those* kids are doing, *those* guys, *those* irresponsible girls having babies. These are our kids, our sons, our daughters. We're all in this together.

This is not to say that the task is always a cheery one. In the years since I finished the original G-Dog manuscript, I've been to a lot of funerals. My son, Will, who is now grown, once asked how I coped with the deaths of so many kids. "And how does Father Greg stand it?" he asked me. "He's been to a lot more funerals than you have. Does he ever get used to it?" The answer is: no. You don't get used to the deaths of the young. If you try to wall yourself off from that brand of grief, you do so at your soul's peril. So how does one cope? Frankly, there is a cost. Scarring occurs. How could it be otherwise?

But here's the truth: during my time in Pico Aliso, the miracles have always far outweighed the sorrow—even on those days when the sorrow was considerable. When I am around Greg and the homeboys and homegirls whose lives I've been lucky enough to enter over the years, the dark has always, *always* been outweighed by light.

The tally isn't even close.

By the way, there's one more thing you ought to know. In early 2003 Greg Boyle was diagnosed with chronic lymphocytic leukemia. That same year, he went through a months-long course of intensive chemotherapy. The disease is presently in remission. But unlike other forms of leukemia, CLL never entirely goes away. It is a progressive disease for which there is no cure—at least not yet. If Greg comes out of remission, the doctors will treat the disease more aggressively. With luck he could live successfully with CLL for many decades. Yet this is the same disease that killed *60 Minutes* correspondent Ed Bradley.

When word got out that Greg had cancer, the news hit with hurricane-like effect. For days, gang members—both former and current—streamed in and out of the Homeboy building, frantic at the thought that this man who had always been there for them, who had faced down bullets for them when necessary, was now confronting a form of mortality that they felt powerless to combat. "I'll do anything to help," said Rebel every time he called from jail. "Anything at all."

It was Spanky who sat down in Greg's office with the most specific offer. "I got a gang a' things that you could have if you need 'em," he said gravely. "You know, lungs . . . a heart . . ."

It has been more than five years since Greg's initial diagnosis and the early panic has been replaced by a drumbeat of watchfulness. Homeboys nag Greg about eating well, getting enough exercise, getting enough sleep. Frances Aguilar, a former homegirl who served for a time as Greg's assistant, secretly badgered all visitors who met with the priest to wash their hands before shaking his. The hypervigilance has waned a little now that Greg appears to be so healthy. But the worry never entirely disappears. And it begets a question: if something *did* happen, who could possibly replace Greg Boyle?

The first and the truest answer is this: No one. Greg is irreplaceable.

There is, however, a second answer that is also true: Homeboy Industries is now strong enough that the many bright people who work in and around it can certainly keep its various programs running. Yet, is an office full of functioning programs enough? What about the soul of the place? Who other than Father Greg Boyle can embody that mysterious and fragile quality?

This is where a third answer to the question comes into play. In the past year or so, Greg has developed an A-team of public speakers, former gang members who have each wrestled their way out of agonizing pasts and gained the skill, heart, and charisma to bring the house down whenever they address audiences. Joseph Holguin, one of the gang member/poets I mentioned earlier, is among them. "See, Father Greg loved me, until I could love myself," Joseph told me recently. "He believed in me until I could believe in myself. He did that for a lot of us. And now it's our job to do that for other people. Now it's our job to carry it on however we can."

Homeboys like Turtle have their own version of the concept. "Now that I'm a manager," he said when we talked last, "there are some nice perks. For example, we're allowed to donate five hundred bucks every eight months to a charitable organization. Naturally, I give my five hundred to Homeboy. And I started getting some of the other managers to donate with me too, so last October we were able to give Father Greg four thousand dollars. My goal when the next donation time rolls around is to push that four thousand number a lot higher."

That's great, I told him. You're really giving back. I'm so proud of you.

"No, but see, it's more than that," said Turtle. "You know what I'm going to do when I retire in thirty years from now? I'm going to dedicate my time to Homeboy Industries. I mean it. I've already talked to Liliana about it, and she's totally down for the idea. And here's the thing, Celeste. I know now that I can make a difference for kids who're like I was. Back in the day, I couldn't have imagined I could be where I am now. I couldn't have imagined it. But I've learned that I have strengths. I have talents. And I'm not the only one. I think there are a lot of us who, when the time is right, will come back and make a difference. So, yeah. No matter what happens, we're Father Greg's legacy. We're his children. His work goes on in us. For real."

Notes

1. Joan Petersilia, *When Prisoners Come Home* (New York: Oxford University Press, 2003).

2. Jill Tucker, "Study Finds Emotional Trauma Can Alter Size of a Child's Brain" (*San Francisco Chronicle*, August 26, 2007).

3. The National Child Traumatic Stress Network (Los Angeles: March 2005).

4. The National Center for PTSD, United States Department of Veteran's Affairs.

Photograph: ©Kelly Fremon

About the Author

Celeste Fremon is an award-winning freelance journalist specializing in gangs, law enforcement, criminal justice, and education policy. She is a Pereira Visiting Writer at UC Irvine, a senior fellow for Social Justice/New Media at the USC Annenberg Institute for Justice and Journalism, and the creator and editor of WitnessLA.com.